D0934739

WITHDRAWN

ELIZABETH BOWEN

A Study of the Short Fiction

Also available in Twayne's Studies in Short Fiction Series

Twayne's Studies in Short Fiction

Gordon Weaver, General Editor
Oklahoma State University

ELIZABETH BOWEN
Photo by Angus McBean

ELIZABETH BOWEN

A Study of the Short Fiction

Phyllis Lassner
University of Michigan

TWAYNE PUBLISHERS • NEW YORK
Maxwell Macmillan Canada • Toronto
Maxwell Macmillan International • New York Oxford Singapore Sydney

Twayne's Studies in Short Fiction Series, No. 27

Copyright © 1991 by G. K. Hall & Co.

Twayne Publishers
Macmillan Publishing Company
866 Third Avenue
New York, NY 10022

Maxwell Macmillan Canada, Inc.
1200 Eglinton Avenue East
Suite 200
Don Mills, Ontario M3C 3N1

Macmillan Publishing Company is part of the Maxwell Communication Group of Companies.

Library of Congress Cataloging-in-Publication Data

Lassner, Phyllis.
  Elizabeth Bowen : a study of the short fiction/Phyllis Lassner.
  p. cm. — (Twayne's studies in short fiction: no. 27)
  Includes bibliographical references and index.
  ISBN 0–8057–8336–9
  1. Bowen, Elizabeth, 1899–1973—Criticism and interpretation.
  2. Short story. I. Title. II. Series.
  PR6003.06757Z674   1991
  823'.912—dc20   91-2202
                                                                                    CIP

Copyediting supervised by Barbara Sutton.
Book production and design by Janet Z. Reynolds.
Typeset by Compset, Inc., Beverly, Massachusetts.

10 9 8 7 6 5 4 3 2 1

To Jake, Liz, Jason, and Mary,
stalwart listeners
to stories about Elizabeth Bowen.

Contents

Contents

Preface

Although Elizabeth Bowen's reputation as a major writer is now firmly in place, little critical attention has been paid to her short fiction.[1] Her stories of World War II, celebrated as among the best of that period, are widely anthologized but are not read in the context of her short fiction oeuvre, which consists of 79 collected and 14 uncollected stories.[2] Readers of her novels never fail to refer to her stories, but the latter are usually read as glosses on the longer works. This study seeks to explore Bowen's short fiction as a separate artistic achievement, related to her other work in its themes and concerns but relying on a vision, method, and effect that she sharply distinguished from the novels: "The art of the short story permits a break at what in the novel would be the crux of the plot: the short story, free from the *longeurs* of the novel, is also exempt from the novel's conclusiveness—too often forced and false: it may thus more nearly than the novel approach aesthetic and moral truth. It can, while remaining rightly prosaic and circumstantial, give scene, action, event, character a poetic new actuality. It must have had, to the writer, moments of unfamiliarity, where it imposed itself."[3]

In all their range and breadth of subject and technique, Bowen's short fiction can be read as a whole. Within the comedies, ghost stories, elegies of loss, and tales of terror runs a thread that merges her sense of "aesthetic and moral truth" as a vision of history interpreted by fictional design. The "break" in the plot, the poetic image, the stories that are "flashes"—these add up to what she called "questions posed" about the relationship between past and present.[4] This relationship takes many forms in the stories: between parent and child, between the characters' cultural heritage and their individual destinies, and between the unresolved fears and anxieties of ancestors and their residual effects on young heirs.

Because of the overarching thematic concern I see in all Bowen's stories, I have arranged them into five modes instead of addressing them chronologically: "The Ghostly Origins of Female Character," "Comedies of Sex and Manners," "Children's 'Disconcerting Questions,'" "Comedies of Sex and Terror," and "Elegies of Loss and Dispossession." I conclude with a discussion of three masterworks. While there are many stories I could have chosen for this last section, "The Disinherited," "Summer Night," and "The Happy Autumn Fields" each combine the features of the five modes. This is not to say that Bowen had but one story to tell. Her investigation into the boundaries between past and present and fiction and history poses literary, social, ideological, and epistemological questions that in turn encourage multilayered perspectives on her work. Her stories are filled with ambiguity, ambivalence, and contradiction; her interweaving of comedy, terror, elegy, and conundrum makes her thematic concerns even more complex.

"The Ghostly Origins of Female Character" explores the costs of failing to recognize the persistence of the past. In stories like "The Back Drawing-Room" and "Foothold," ghostly women carry the grief that originates in lost and oppressive homes into the present by haunting new occupants. In their efforts to remake the past by restoring old houses or elegant customs, the living women become ghostlike figures themselves, haunted by a desire for human connectedness but oppressed by the constraints of a past endlessly replayed.

Bowen's "Comedies of Sex and Manners" are distinguished by an exuberance easily associated with the adolescent energy she often called "farouche." Savage in their scorn of traditional manners and morals, these stories tear through the social and literary conventions and moral dilemmas that shaped the stories she greatly admired. Bowen's stories recall the drawing-room comedies of Henry James and Chekhov but also parody them, a strategy that serves her purpose of reviewing the concerns and conclusions of earlier masters in order to clarify her own. In the stories originally published in 1923 and 1926 in *Encounters* and *Ann Lee's*, Bowen responds to all the finely wrought complexities of her predecessors' moral and social critiques. In a voice she later criticized as too harsh and mocking,[5] her stories expose the earlier writers' judgments, showing how they were tainted by the very values and assumptions they were condemning. If Bowen's stories often seem ambivalent toward those very writers and traditions she acknowledged as influences, they also question the values on which her own imperatives and insights are founded.

"Children's 'Disconcerting Questions'"[6] traces the insecurities of Bowen's characters to betrayals originating in parents' vulnerability to their own social and historic circumstances. Always empathetic to the insatiable demands of children for unconditional nurture and stability, Bowen used her own childhood tragedies as the source of her understanding. Her father's illness when she was 7 and her mother's death when she was 13 gave her the personal grounds to claim the world as unknowable. In her stories, when children lose or fear losing a parent, they have no capacity to imagine themselves as anything but guilty and responsible for their loss; at the same time, they are enraged at the parent, whom they feel holds the key to their fate. In turn, these stories depict parents clinging to traditional authoritative roles as a safeguard against the fragility of the worlds they uphold.

The stories I call "Comedies of Sex and Terror" enact the violent emotions hinted at in Bowen's "Comedies of Sex and Manners." The ghosts in these stories do not weep; they inspire suicide, murder, and betrayal, each of which is the result of rage against their own feelings of betrayal. The drawing rooms in these stories are ripped apart by the release of suppressed desires for sexual possession and self-expression. In several of these stories, such as "Making Arrangements," "The Cat Jumps," and "Dead Mabelle," the battle of the sexes illuminates women's struggle for autonomy within social and economic codes that both constrain them and provide security. If Bowen shows men to be the upholders of these codes, she also makes it clear they are damaged by them.

Bowen's "Elegies of Loss and Dispossession" strip away the imaginative props of ghosts and comedy to expose the stark and startling effects of losing one's sense of place and human connectedness. The characters' impulses in many of these stories are to deny historical change in order to insulate themselves from recognizing that their worlds of privilege cannot be saved because they are already in ruin. Obsessed with stability, characters from "The Tommy Crans" to those who live in "Attractive Modern Houses" hold themselves hostage to myths of order and tradition embodied by family homes. These stories demystify all romantic visions as fundamentally entrapping, whether such vision is the creative imagination of the artist or that of the soldier who found his sense of being and purpose in the war.

"The Disinherited," "Summer Night," and "The Happy Autumn Fields," in weaving together the concerns and modes examined in the other five chapters, meld Bowen's vision of history and character with her critiques of traditional social codes that are both oppressive and saving graces. In each of these stories at least two different plots and sets of characters intersect so that each one becomes a commentary on the other. Past and present, history in the making, and the reconstructing of history as fiction each provide internal and external views of characters who feel lost in their own time and place. Combining so many of Bowen's concerns, these three stories question how history and character create and clarify each other but also leave these matters open to further questioning.

Part 2 presents selections from Bowen's nonfiction in which she considers the art of the short story as well as those elements in her background which profoundly influenced her. Some excerpts, such as her preface to *The Demon Lover*, are well known and widely anthologized, while other selections appear here for the first time since their original publication. Notes from a lecture delivered at Wellesley College are reprinted here for the first time. I hope this combination provides the necessary link in the interrelationship between the writer and the reader.

Part 3 consists of an overview of the various critical responses to Bowen's short stories, as well as two reviews of her collected stories. Because only certain of her stories have been studied, the existing body of criticism provides no view of her work as a whole. On the other hand, William Trevor and Eudora Welty offer comprehensive and incisive commentary on Bowen's full range of stories. Perhaps because they too are masters of the art, and because Trevor is Irish himself and Welty knew Bowen and studied her work, they are in the best position to offer the most useful insights into her stories.

Although there are many collections of stories by Elizabeth Bowen, most are currently unavailable and their contents overlap. Accordingly, I have chosen as my primary source *The Collected Stories*, a volume that contains all previously collected stories and is currently in print.

Notes

1. Two book-length studies, *The English Short Story: 1880—1945*, ed. Joseph M. Flora (Boston: G. K. Hall, 1985), and *The English Short Story: 1945–1980*, ed. Dennis Vannatta (Boston: G. K. Hall), 1985, fail to mention Bowen. W. J. McCormack, in his review of Bowen's *Collected Stories*, argues that the reason she "has never been fully assimilated to the canon of modern English literature" is that her models are more Irish and European than English ("Mask and Mood," *New Statesman* 103 [3 February 1981]: 19).

2. Typical is Walter Allen's study *The Short Story in English* (Oxford: Oxford University Press, 1981), which observes that Bowen's short stories span

her 50-year career but, aside from one early work, discusses only her World War II stories.

3. Review of *The Faber Book of Modern Short Stories*, in *Collected Impressions* (New York: Knopf, 1950), 43.

4. Preface to *Ann Lee's and Other Stories*, in *Afterthought* (London: Longmans Green, 1952), 93–94.

5. Preface to *Encounters*, in *The Mulberry Tree: Writings of Elizabeth Bowen*, ed. Hermione Lee (New York: Harcourt Brace Jovanovich, 1986), 120–21.

6. In an essay titled "The Art of Reserve or the Art of Respecting Boundaries" (*Vogue*, 1 April 1952), Bowen observed, "One can but respect those who are straightforward truly—the child with its naive, disconcerting questions, the simple-spoken, primitive country person. Nothing asked in innocence can offend, and nothing stated in innocence is unseemly" (117).

Acknowledgments

The 1950 studio portrait of Elizabeth Bowen by Angus McBean is reprinted by permission of George Weidenfeld & Nicolson Limited.

Excerpts from *The Collected Stories of Elizabeth Bowen*. Copyright © by Curtis Brown Ltd., literary executors of the estate of Elizabeth Bowen. Reprinted by permission of Alfred A. Knopf Inc. and Jonathan Cape Limited.

From *Bowen's Court*, by Elizabeth Bowen. Copyright 1942, © 1964 and renewed 1970 by Elizabeth Bowen. Reprinted by permission of Alfred A. Knopf Inc. and Virago Press.

From *The Mulberry Tree*, by Elizabeth Bowen, edited by Hermione Lee. © 1986 by Curtis Brown Ltd., literary executors of the estate of Elizabeth Bowen. Reprinted by permission of Virago Press and Harcourt Brace Jovanovich, Inc.

From "The Experience of Writing," notes from a lecture delivered by Elizabeth Bowen at Wellesley College on 20 March 1950. Copyright © by Curtis Brown Ltd., literary executors of the estate of Elizabeth Bowen. Reprinted by permission of the Henry W. and Albert A. Berg Collection, the New York Public Library, Astor, Lenox, and Tilden Foundations.

"The Short Story in England," excerpts from the Preface to *The Faber Book of Modern Short Stories*, "D. H. Lawrence," "Gorki's Stories," the Preface to *Ann Lee's*, the Preface to *The Second Ghost Book*, "Sources of Influence," "I Died of Love," "Just Imagine," and "The Forgotten Art of Living," by Elizabeth Bowen, reprinted by permission of Curtis Brown Ltd., literary executors of the estate of Elizabeth Bowen.

"Seventy-nine Stories to Read Again," by Eudora Welty. Reprinted by permission of the author and the *New York Times*. © 1981.

"Between Holyhead and Dun Laoghaire," by William Trevor. Reprinted by permission of the author and Times Newspapers Limited. © 1981.

I would like to thank Liz Fowler for her unwavering enthusiasm and great good sense in guiding this book through its different aspects and stages.

Part 1

THE SHORT FICTION

Introduction

The past that forms the central concerns of Elizabeth Bowen's stories is her own Anglo-Irish history. Her readers have consistently pointed to the horrors of Ireland's endless civil strife as the inspiration for Bowen's tales of terror and to her dual identity as the source of her insights into two cultures. Howard Moss describes this relationship succinctly: "Bowen is essentially the product of a divided culture, a divided family, and a divided nation, and no one is better on the demon relationships of opposing—but mutual—interests that tie servants and masters, the innocent and the worldly, the loving and the unlovable together. Irish in England and English in Ireland, she grasped early the colonial mentality from both sides, and saw how, in the end, it was a mirror image of the most exploitative relationship of all: that of the adult and the child."[1]

After acknowledging the significance of Bowen's background, most readers go on to interpret her works as psychological studies that universalize the terror of modern alienation.[2] The oppositions Moss points to are indeed psychological, and Bowen herself speaks of creatively transforming intensely felt individual experience: She describes her collection of stories *Encounters* as a "ring of emotion . . . which, in fact, was transposed biography."[3] As this reading of her short fiction will show, however, Bowen's idea of psychological experience is never ahistorical. Instead, it consists of a personal and cultural history shaped by social, economic, and political forces internalized as the individual's sense of self.

As imagined in Bowen's work, this individual experience cannot be universalized except as it represents the varying responses of men and women participating in a continuum of a specific historic past that resonates in the present. Thus, even her most powerful portrayals of the psychological pain parents and children inflict on each other also depict conflicts between the needs of an adult upper-middle-class Anglo-Irish or English world to maintain order through traditional values and those of the young to assert their own priorities and identity by rebelling against the genteel old order. In stories from "Coming Home" to "Sun-

3

day Afternoon," young girls in Anglo-Irish "big houses" or in town-houses reminiscent of the one in which Bowen grew up in Dublin defy conventions of decorum and stability in "flashes" of unbridled aggression. From many perspectives, her short stories dramatize the way in which consciousness shapes history. They show characters refashioning the past according to what their deepest wishes and fears will accommodate. This is a process of fictionalizing the past, of understanding it by reimagining it:

> We must not shy at the fact that we cull the past from fiction rather than history . . . and so, falsify. Raw history, in its implications, is unnerving; and even so, it only chronicles the survivors. . . . If the greater part of the past had not been, mercifully, forgotten, the effect upon our modern sensibility would be unbearable: it would not be only injustice and bloodshed that we should have to remember but the dismay, the apathy, the brutalising humiliations of people for whom there was no break. . . . [T]he past is veiled from us by our illusion—our own illusion. It is that which we seek. It is not the past but the idea of the past which draws us.[4]

In Bowen's stories, the past is alive in the memories, relationships, wishes, and fears of her characters. The economic and social trials of the past haunt the present in the shape of ghostly sensations and presences and as new relationships, wishes, and fears replay old ones. The past imprints itself on the present in the form of manners and morals that translate history's "brutalizing humiliations" and "injustice" into the conventional relationships of family and domestic life. When a second world war intensifies the horrors of the first, when marriage replays the oppressive obligations of family traditions, or when young people are pushed into circumstances that repeat the losses of their elders, the past is experienced as a need to protect oneself from feeling the prevailing effects of a brutal history. Only when Bowen's characters give up their protective shields and allow their feelings to merge with those issuing from the past are they able to recognize the ways in which their present constraints are part of a cultural heritage whose values they perpetuate. When they deny the continuing power of this heritage, they are doomed to perpetuate its constraints. Denial for Bowen's characters becomes a self-destructive strategy that only deepens their tie to the past as it turns into obsession.

Most frequently, this obsession takes the form of houses that, in their hold over the characters, are agents of personal and cultural history. Embodying family and domestic traditions as well as an unbroken tie to the past, Bowen's houses become her stories' controlling "poetic image." As Bowen said of Chekhov, such an "emotional landscape . . . let[s] in what might appear inchoate or nebulous . . . that involuntary sub-life of the spirit."[5] In stories like "Foothold," "The Back Drawing-Room," and "In the Square," this "sub-life" is contained in an ineluctable bond between characters and their houses. In all of Bowen's work, fiction and nonfiction alike, houses are haunted by the wishes and fears its original owners invested in them. Bowen's Court, the model for this idea, inspired her to write, "I know of no house (no house that has not changed hands) in which, while the present seems to be there forever, the past is not pervadingly felt."[6] The ghosts of the past are "let in" by its present owners, who perpetuate the anxiety that its "intense, centripetal life" may not validate their own (*BC*, 20). Incorporating the economic and social designs of the past, Bowen's houses represent codes of privilege that their occupants take as promises to fulfill the sense of purpose, order, and stability they crave.

All the houses in Bowen's work, however, betray such promises as empty and destructive. Sometimes it is a weeping woman, as in "The Back Drawing-Room," who signifies promises turned into loss and dispossession. In "In the Square" a woman loses her sense of self as her London home loses its aura of exclusive privilege when it is invaded by army personnel during the Blitz. Occasionally, haunted houses are the vehicle for satirizing melodramatic and romanticized visions of the past, as in "The Cat Jumps" and "The Disinherited." Whether they are depicted satirically or elegiacally, haunted houses represent the ground on which traditional values of class and gender are questioned and sometimes threatened by social and political change. Bowen's ghost stories, unlike the conventional stories, are always part of the history that connects past with present; they never constitute simply an isolated narrative incident.

Bowen's inheritance of an Anglo-Irish big house gave her the historical data on which to base her vision of an incalculable tie between people and the history and traditions their homes represent. She described "life in the big house" as "saturated with character: this is, I suppose, the element of the spell. The indefinite ghosts of the past, of the dead who lived here and pursued this same routine of life in these walls add something, a sort of order, a reason for living, to every minute and hour. This is the order, the form of life, the tradition to which big house people still sacrifice much."[7] No matter what her setting—English country house, London townhouse, suburban housing estate, or Irish castle—Bowen's subject is the simultaneous quest for and denial of the history that bound England and Anglo-Ireland together and produced traditions and codes of conduct that prevail into the modern times of her stories.

In this volume I explore Bowen's short fiction as a response to her dual heritage and to the turbulent and unresolved history of Ireland. In this way, her stories, in all their variety and breadth of technique and subject, can be read as a coherent, creative transformation of the history that chronicles the lives of not only "the survivors" but also the lost. This is the violent history that began in Ireland 200 years before Bowen's birth and whose aftershocks she felt and imagined through two world wars in the England she made her home. Thus, stories set in times of war or economic depression derive their plots, imagery, and characters not only from the contemporary reality Bowen saw and experienced but also from her interpretation of her Anglo-Irish history. It is my contention that Bowen's stories "cull the past from fiction" through characters who find themselves trapped in the social and economic circumstances of a past that makes itself felt even as it seems unknowable to them. Too terrible to bear, the historic past is often replaced by fantasies of a romantic or mythic past, "illusions" that revise history but become self-defeating obsessions.

Although Bowen is critical of those who would escape the past, she acknowledges the impossibility of ever fully knowing or understanding it. This stance influences her method, for her stories can be seen as enacting what John Bayley calls "the investigative anecdote, an event used as the occasion for opinion and enquiry," but unlike the novel, in which "there is no mystery, and there *is* an answer," the stories are defined by "something withheld and mysterious."[8] Bayley feels that short stories convey a special kind of relationship between writer and reader, one in which "it is more important that [the writer] should be telling us—sharing with us—something of significance, than that we should grasp—that there should be any possibility of us grasping—exactly what this is. The writer's secret—what it may mean to him [or her]—has itself become the justification of the tale, its subject the reader's sense of fascination and curiosity" (Bayley, 39).

The secret Bowen shares with us originates in her own ambivalence about her cultural history that she will never fully resolve. Her stories conduct an inquiry into this ambivalence from every conceivable angle and invite our participation as readers at every turn, but we are left with the sense, as Bayley observes, that "the short story always tries either to avoid an ending, or to suggest there is none" (Bayley, 39). In Bowen's work, the combination of ambivalence and uncertainty about the past produces isolated and unexplained comic moments and sensations of terror that seem endless. Together, the comic and the horrific reflect her characters' dangerous and absurd desire to know and yet deny their responsibility in the history and traditions they perpetuate. Calling such close attention to her own history, she indicts herself as well.

The last and only female heir to an Anglo-Irish country estate, Bowen felt both sustained and burdened by it. Images of its stark beauty and intense social and family life sustained her as reminders of continuity and stability in times of war and personal loss. But its upkeep became oppressive when she could no longer afford it. Understanding the dangers of romanticizing the "big house," she interrogates her ancestors' roles in the violent conquest of Ireland and holds them fully responsible for their exploitation of the land and people. In her family chronicle, *Bowen's Court*, she reflects:

> The stretches of the past I have had to cover have been, on the whole, painful: my family got their position and drew their power from a situation that shows an inherent wrong. . . . The Bowens' relation to history was an unconscious one. I can only suggest a compulsion they did not know of by . . . interleaving the family story with passages from the history of Ireland. My family, though notably "unhistoric," had their part in a drama outside themselves. Their assertions, their compliances, their refusals as men and women went, year by year, generation by generation, to give history direction, as well as colour and stuff. Each of the family, in their different manners, were more than their time's products; they were its agents. (*BC*, 453–52)

Bowen's sense of how people unconsciously give "history" direction combines her political and literary consciousnesses. From Proust and Chekhov she learned the technique of reconstructing a whole society through emblematic social conventions that shape the consciousnesses of those who thrive and those who are entrapped in them. She shows how past and present merge in a single consciousness as the product of both self-protective memory and a past that cannot be escaped. As an instrument that both recognizes and denies the past, Bowen sees "memory . . . as Proust has it, so oblique and selective . . . through a subjective haze."[9]

The immediacy of this subjectivity in many of Bowen's early stories is modeled on Henry James's drawing-room moral dramas.[10] Caught in the trap of needs that defy social convention and codes of conduct, characters in "The Confidante," "Requiscat," and other stories barely recognize their own complicity in failed rebellions. But Bowen moves away from James as she situates this entrapment in female characters who are sometimes also capable of engineering their own escape. Because she is most often viewed as "a conservative with an aristocratic temperament" and as "hostile" to feminism, Bowen's sympathy for women's plights is usually ignored.[11] But from the very beginning of her career through her last stories, women are exemplars of social and economic oppression as well as harbingers of alternative strategies for survival. Although Bowen claimed that she read Katherine Mansfield only after having composed her own first stories, parallels in their attitudes toward women's situations point to a canny understanding of how women come to participate in their own entrapment. Like Mansfield, Bowen uses the natural world to convey the unnaturalness in fatefully assigning nurturing and caretaker roles of domestic and family life to women.

This contrast between the author's empathy for the character's fate and the narrative design that ensures it also resembles D. H. Lawrence's expressionistic stories. In her rendering of a "ring of emotion," Bowen creates what Joseph M. Flora has referred to in Lawrence as "psychological energy and intensity" that derive from the author's relationship to character.[12] This quality is an involvement with character that "may represent a thought or a feeling so fleeting or so subliminal that the character has no clear awareness of it and could not himself give it articulation" (Flora, 47–48). Unlike James Joyce and Virginia Woolf, with their distanced involvement with character, Bowen is simultaneously inside and outside the character. The capacity of her characters to recognize danger and imagine alternatives is embedded in compressed but elaborate patterns, in abstract and opaque dialogue, and in the elusive sensations and ghostly presences that haunt her houses and the characters themselves. Bowen's review of D. H. Lawrence's stories reveals her affinity with his fusion of social and psychological concerns: "We who read him young are now called upon to live out the day Lawrence foresaw. First the war; now the new raw personal social consciousness, with its lifting of the protective veil between individuals. . . . We want the form of naturalism, with at the same time a kind of internal burning—in Lawrence, every bush burns."[13]

Because Bowen wrote 10 novels in which she had more than ample opportunity to explore what she called "rational behaviour and social portraiture," we are left with the question of why she found it necessary to subject her creative concerns to the "tensing-up" of short stories.[14] She herself answered this question in the preface she wrote to a collection of her own stories: "The short story, as I see it to be, allows for what is crazy about humanity: obstinacies, inordinate heroisms, immortal longings" (*MT*, 130).

The Ghostly Origins
of Female Character

> Ghosts have grown up. Far behind lie their clanking and moan-
> ing days; they have laid aside their original bag of tricks—
> bleeding hands, luminous skulls. . . . Their manifestations
> are, like their personalities, oblique and subtle, perfectly cal-
> culated to get the modern person under the skin. . . . Ghosts
> exploit the horror latent behind reality. [15]

Bowen's ghost stories are marked by the influence of Anglo-Irish
writers like Sheridan LeFanu and Maria Edgeworth, who used the
myths and history of the Protestant Ascendancy to explore the oppressive hold it maintained over its heirs. [16] In the work of these earlier
writers, haunting presences provide a psychological and historic link to
a turbulent past whose unresolved conflicts continually erupt in violence. Similarly, Bowen accounts for her use of ghosts as a way of representing this violent and enigmatic past in her chronicle of her
ancestral history, *Bowen's Court*. She reports the transformation of this
literary and cultural heritage into a creative fictional vision: "A scene
burned itself into me, a building magnetized me, a mood or season of
Nature's penetrated me, history suddenly appeared to me in some tiny
act or a face had begun to haunt me before I glanced at it" (*MT*, 129).

Ghosts are neither tricks nor figments of the imagination in Bowen's
stories. Experienced as inexplicable presences, as sounds or changes
in the atmosphere of a house, or as disembodied voices, they are the
conduit to a past that reaches out as though asking to be reexperienced
but that cannot even be understood by the haunted characters. This
past is, of course, the continuous residue of human history, for no matter what their form, Bowen's ghosts project very human feelings. [17] Terrifying because they conjure up the worst fears of the haunted, ghosts
thus imply that even if they could be explained, the explanation would
be too terrible to bear.

Of the didactic role played by her mysterious presences, Bowen wrote, "The past . . . discharges its load of feeling into the anaesthe-tized and bewildered present. It is the 'I' that is sought—and retrieved, at the cost of no little pain. And the ghosts . . . what part do they play? They are the certainties. . . . [T]hey fill the vacuum for the uncertain 'I.'"[18]

Ghosts of "the Air Which Knew Them"

"The Back Drawing-Room" is a framed tale that begins as a satire on the vagaries of pretentious, intellectualized talk about "fitness to sur-vive" and "the visibility or . . . perceptibility of thought-forms."[19] But then a "little man," clearly an outsider to the Sunday soiree, tells an Irish ghost story that provides a corrective, showing that the group has no concept by which to explain an enigma (200). The little man de-scribes wandering into an unlocked Anglo-Irish house for shelter. No one comes, but a door at the back of the hall suddenly opens to reveal a woman standing there. He then follows her into a drawing room, where he finds her crying and looking as if she were "drowning" (208). More disturbed than distressed, he escapes, learning later that the house was burned two years earlier in the 1920–21 "Troubles" of Irish civil war.

The ghost of the weeping woman taunts the discussion group. She represents a history destined to remain unknowable to them as long as they deny her suffering. Moreover, in its emotional power, her tale attacks the group's hollow rationalizations. As the little man talks, he is constantly interrupted by their second-guessing, but the abstractions and literary allusions they deploy to dismiss the tale's effect only render it more elusive. The listeners offer metaphysical speculations about the existence of the soul, or "a sense of immanence . . . something com-ing up from the earth, down from the skies," but the ghost is a palpable and unavoidable presence (205). It represents not a psychic puzzle but an experience in which the little man's empathy is the only key to understanding. No literary or philosophical frame of reference can ex-plain the stubborn presence of a woman in the home she cannot save.

Historic realities doomed the Anglo-Irish and their self-proclaimed right to rule, which they called the Ascendancy. They simply failed to invest politically and economically in the welfare of the land and peo-ple they conquered. And yet we cannot understand Ireland without feeling the Ascendancy's powerful, indeed almost-supranatural tie to houses that the Anglo-Irish built in order to create a sense of purpose and identity for themselves. Bowen sees the woman's ghostly presence as expressing those "obsessions [which] stay in the air which knew them, as a corpse stays nailed down under a floor" (*A*, 103). The little man is thus told by his Irish cousin's wife that the women of the big house are still alive, and yet "how can one feel they're alive? How can they be, any more than plants one's pulled up? They've nothing to grow in, or hold on to" (210). These women have no life without their houses, and Bowen's stories preserve them only in their intense sense of loss. Thus loss is personified, embodied in the ghost of an inconsolable woman who represents a past that can never be undone.

Transmitting that sense of loss to the little man who has no stake in these houses but is rather the conduit of their tales is a cry to involve the outside world. Without him, the ghost's story remains self-enclosed, like a dirge mourning the ever-narrowing circle of a self-centered society. Although the ghost's story pokes fun at the romantic vision of the soiree's hostess, Mrs. Henneker, it also verifies that there is much to cry about in Ireland: "'Ireland,' said Mrs. Henneker, 'unforgettably and almost terribly afflicted me. The contact was so intimate as to be almost intolerable. Those gulls about the piers of Kingstown, crying, crying: they are an overture to Ireland. One lives in a dream there, a dream oppressed and shifting, such as one dreams in a house with trees about it, on a sultry night'" (203). Crying is both the medium and the message, suggesting an experience of loss so profound that there is no recovery.

Deeply attached to her own ancestral home, Bowen understood the elation and anxiety of feeling so rooted and responsible for an Anglo-Irish estate whose purpose was for her always questionable. The anxiety of a haunting past and an uncertain tomorrow sets the atmosphere of "Foothold," a story whose setting is never identified. Nevertheless, the obsession of its women with their home clearly suggests the venue is Anglo-Ireland. Nominally, the story is concerned with whether a ghostly woman haunts the Georgian house that Janet and Gerard have painstakingly restored. By the end of the story, we have our answer: Janet has established a secret relationship with the ghost, Clara.

The story works around two opposed experiences of knowing and understanding. Gerard and the friend who visits for the weekend, Thomas, are skeptical, even dismissive of the ghost. Even at the end, when they overhear Janet address Clara by name, Gerard still denies the ghost's reality and his wife's acceptance of her. If the men live and explore knowledge on a different plane than Janet, it is because for them home is a safe, comfortable retreat from an unstable world, a retreat guaranteed by the domestic presence of knowable, predictable women. The conventions of married life produce a kind of decorum in which all things have an easily recognizable place and purpose. What becomes intolerable for Thomas and Gerard is that Janet, through her relationship with Clara, reveals a "hypothetical faculty being used to exhaustion," that is, an acutely private emotional and intellectual experience that is drawing her away from them and possibly destabilizing her (305).

This faculty, which turns out to be Janet's identification with Clara and the house, forms a triangular arrangement threatening the men's domestic model of stability. As Thomas reflects on the changes he senses in Janet, he is repelled by the possibility that a "peevish dead woman" might have succeeded with Janet "where we've failed. . . . [H]ow much less humiliating for [us] both it would have been if she'd taken a lover" (305).[20] The men are humiliated because Janet's communion with Clara reflects an intimacy that transcends male desire and subverts male hegemony. This "disruptive" relationship undermines Janet's imperative to be "civilized . . . maternal and sensual" (305) and destabilizes the domestic harmony.

What exhausts Janet and drives her to seek the experience is the same phenomenon that makes Clara a haunting presence: the house. The pleasure Janet takes in restoring the late-Georgian structure is subsumed by the sense that it has a life of its own. That life overwhelms both her and Clara: "I do feel the house has grown since we've been in it. The rooms seem to take so much longer to get across" (299). It is as though this place that promises identity and purpose overwhelms any sense of self women have outside of being housewife and mother. Janet tries to explain to Thomas that she "lives two states of life . . . run [ning] parallel" (301). Although Thomas adds, "never meeting," he assumes she is referring to a separation between Gerard and their children (302). He cannot see that one plane of experience is reserved for herself and the other is where she fulfills her domestic duties. It is on this first plane where she meets Clara. Joined together by a house that threatens to engulf them, the women experience their communion in a "sickening loneliness" neither can bear without the other (313).

Ghostly presence in this story testifies to the limitations of a female domestic life that offers no outlet for self-expression other than decorating and managing the family home. Like the ghostly women of the Anglo-Irish big house in Bowen's novel *The Heat of the Day*, women without other outlets are silenced. Ironically, in their very silence they rebel against an ongoing tradition of domestic oppression. Wherever they appear in Bowen's fiction, the silent enduring presence of women past and present forms a female community that violates the stability of home life.

In three other stories, one of which has an identified Irish setting, houses are haunting presences to the men who own or visit them and to the women who are tied to domestic space. In "Her Table Spread" and "Human Habitation" the women characters are so isolated in their homes that one appears deranged and the others live in a state of persistent fear and anxiety. The men who visit have designs on ownership, both of the property and, by implication, of the women who live there, designs that provide the source of the women's anxiety. In "The Shadowy Third" a house conveys ominous signs linking the fortunes of two women. As a pregnant young woman settles into her husband Martin's home, her future becomes determined by the shadowy fate of his first wife. Pussy's every move, whether the choice of a new cupboard or the use of an old thimble case, begins to replicate that of the first wife, whose disappearance under somewhat uncertain circumstances casts doubt on the suggestion that she died in childbirth. Feeling both that she can make the house hers and that it still belongs to her predecessor, Pussy expresses concerns to her husband that obliquely link the two women's destinies: "I was thinking it would be so terrible not to be happy. I was trying to imagine what I'd feel like if you didn't care" (82). Pussy, the pet second wife, finds communion with the unknown woman her husband thinks of as "Her" (81). Like the ghost Clara and the wife Janet in "Foothold," these two women are bound to a house in which their fates are determined and yet kept hidden from them. The house, in turn, becomes an instrument of the wives' self-expression, absorbing and emitting the women's unsatisfied questions. Thus Martin feels "as though those windows were watching him; their gaze was hostile, full of comment and criticism" (80).

Here too the house inscribes an anxious tale of women losing their individuality and being subsumed by a relentless cycle of domestic life and male domination. Because family homes cannot exist without women, their absence is felt as an indelible presence, emanating from the very structure that consumed them. As in "Her Table Spread," an Irish story, "The Shadowy Third," makes clear that women become ghosts as a result of being sacrificed to the life and purpose of a house. Whether Martin is responsible for his first wife's death is less important than the pervasive sense emitted by his own home that, however much the women change the curtains and move the furniture, the basic forms of domestic life are designed by him for the purpose of providing order and stability. In their own desire for stability and purpose, the women in these ghost stories comply with a domestic ideology that celebrates their needed presence but leaves them no means to create a reality of their own. Indeed, part of what makes the women—both living and dead—ghostlike is that they lose their individuality as they keep duplicating each other, timeless presences in a timeless environment.

At one level "Her Table Spread" is a romantic comedy, its wacky juxtapositions recalling British and American film comedies of the thirties. Its Irish setting, however, turns romance into a scathing critique of the values that sacrifice men and women to the ongoing rituals of the Ascendancy's inglorious past. To be sure, there are no actual ghosts in this story, but the Anglo-Irish past lives on in the haunted consciousness of Valeria Cuffe, heiress to an Irish castle. Valeria's attention is divided between her stultifying aristocratic heritage and the equally ghostly but exciting presence of a naval destroyer anchored in the estuary leading to her demesne.[21]

"At twenty-five, of statuesque development, still detained in childhood," Valeria roams her estate clearly in need of rescue from an Anglo-Irish heritage that is haunting her present and is likely to stall her future (418). But instead of a prince to liberate her, there is only Mr. Alban, whose "attitude to women was negative" and who plays the piano badly (418). With these two as the stars of a romance, the prospect of restoring order and vitality to the castle produces only farce. In Bowen's version of the sleeping beauty, the man assigned to woo Valeria is too unimaginative and enervated to appreciate or rescue the princess from her historical bind. The vision of Valeria dancing around the piano on which Mr. Alban plays his loud but inept waltz signals the story's shift from his perspective to hers and from romance to elegy. While dancing, she imagines inviting the personnel from the destroyer to her ornately ceremonial wedding.[22] Her delightfully immodest vision suggests that, against all expectations, she may take charge of her own life, thus shifting this comedy from the conventional ground of the rescuing hero to a flight of fancy in which the heroine rescues herself.

But it is the image of the destroyer that sets the historic and political

15

context of the story. The intrusion of a modern leviathan recalls the violent past that created Valeria's ancestral domain, for no matter how remote and insulated her castle might appear, it cannot escape the encroachment of political events. Ireland, for Bowen, is never neutral, despite its pronouncements to the contrary. Just as the landed families of the Ascendancy denied their responsibility in the civil wars of the 1920s, so they remain inured to the global conflict of World War II.[23] Bowen's story shows how such indifference shapes the consciousness of a woman and renders the men it touches inert.

As the living ghost of her country's past, irrational as its history, Valeria haunts the lonely estate, waving her lantern at the destroyer, which ignores her. The violent past that her people take pride in as heroic literally burns itself out. Having survived the Irish Troubles, Valeria's castle is nonetheless a ruin. Like Bowen's own ancestral home, which survived Irish civil war intact, these houses seem fated to end as they began—a wish-fulfillment fantasy of power and purpose. Of Bowen's Court, the writer wrote, "If the Anglo-Irish live on and for a myth, for that myth they constantly shed their blood" (*BC*, 436). In "Her Table Spread" Anglo-Ireland is already drained of its lifeblood.

Ghosts of a "Devouring Darkness"

A story Bowen wrote immediately after World War II resembles "Her Table Spread" in several ways while adding a further historical gloss. "The Good Earl" concerns the obsession of an extraordinarily wealthy aristocrat to improve his corner of Anglo-Ireland. Making up for the abuses of his dissolute forebears, he improves the farms of his reluctant tenants but, sacrificing the well-being of his daughter and other dependents, then squanders his energy and resources to build a hotel on the shore of his estate. To celebrate this monument to his noblesse, he plans a steamboat ride up the estuary for his guests. But like the destroyer in "Her Table Spread," the steamer signifies a nightmare. It becomes a hearse, bringing the earl's body home and hence serving as a sign of the destructive solipsism of the Anglo-Irish Ascendancy.

The dangerous consequences of myths of power and historic purpose underlie the ghostly presence in "Human Habitation." Even more than in the other ghost stories, the unknowable history here is located in a no-man's-land between the worlds of women and men.[24] Structurally, the story delineates the world of men as an unconquerable landscape, the world of women as a carefully ordered domestic space, with each area threatening the other. Lost in the rain-swept English countryside, two men, Jefferies and Jameson, are rescued by the hospitality of a young wife waiting for her husband to return. In contrast to the emptiness outside, her home is a "dazzling glory" (154). But emanating from the warmth of the house is also a feeling of dread, a fear of profound loss and dispossession.

The immediate cause of concern is that the woman's husband may have fallen into one of the canals that ring the area. But as the visitors relax and Jameson comfortably assumes the role of orator-instructor, the story develops another disturbance. Having made himself at home, Jameson paints a picture of "that new Earth which was to be a new Heaven for them which he, Jameson, and others were to be swift to bring about. He intimated that *they* even might participate in its creation" (157). The shape of this paradise is the family home, whose "rooms that were little guarded squares of light walled in carefully against the hungry darkness, the ultimately all-devouring darkness[,] . . . was the stage of every drama" (157). This "New Jerusalem" turns out to be a place where women are "the soul of hospitality," keeping the home fires burning for the men, whose plan, like that of the good earl, fulfills an ultimately destructive myth of creation and order: "Jameson . . . beamed; his lips, slimy with excitement," uncannily articulate the very design that imprisons women in "a great perfect machine . . . roar[ing] round in an ecstasy" (157, 154, 157). Like other myths of creation, this one eroticizes male power while harnessing women to run its machinery.[25]

As "The Good Earl" shows, translating such a creation myth into a utopian plan is dangerous. By ignoring history it may revive and perpetuate the brutal consequences of rounds of violent ecstasy from the past. The consequences of Jameson's plan are reflected in the threatening and unknown landscape no domestic order can offset. As the men leave the house for "the cave of darkness beyond the threshold" and the woman is anxiously bound to her home, the natural world is shown to reflect the anxieties of the hearth (159). Domestic space cannot be a haven from a violent and confused history if women lace their hospitality with their fears of isolation and loss.

Bowen's method in this and other stories of an anxious and unmanageable history incorporates a satiric edge. Jefferies's reflections cut through the smugness of Jameson's bombastic oration, and by implication, question the horrors of the unknown with a kind of cynical rationalism that doesn't supply answers but helps to allay the story's prescient malaise. When the unknown is a function of moral or emotional confusion, satire and horror are embedded in each other.

In "The Working Party" horror and satire intensify and yet deflate each other as Mrs. Fisk's terror of the inert cowherd on her backstairs overwhelms her zealous game of one-upmanship with the ladies at her working/tea party. The narrator's gently satiric observations of the working party merge with an ominous vision as Mrs. Fisk's responses to the cowherd and her guests begin to fuse. As her efforts to be the most elegant hostess escalate to near hysteria, Mrs. Fisk's callous treatment of her maid and disgust at the cowherd are shown to be less a function of her snobbery than a sign of her entrapment in domestic space.[26] On the one hand, the narrator prompts us to scoff at Mrs. Fisk's "terror of dropping the urn" because it suggests social pretension; on the other hand, this scene of domestic purpose and order shows us that Mrs. Fisk is more victim than villain (295).

At the end of the story, when Mrs. Fisk runs out of the house and away from the man on the stairs, her disgust turns to pure fear. In images that are both comic and horrific—"tottering on her high heels" across fields that are "uncomforting, the very colour of silence"— Bowen once again shows how the anxieties of domestic life are intertwined with the equally threatening unknown world outside (296). The cowherd, dead or sick and barely alive, has brought the unknowable outside inside; his "earthy and sour" smell suggests death and decay without any hope that nature is inherently regenerative or can be tidied up by domestic order (296). As the expansive, unknowable world outside and the constricted, ordered one inside impinge on each other, they create a disturbing imbalance in each. It is as though the "great perfect machine" designed to build the "New Jerusalem' is flawed by its very purpose, that is, to separate the two worlds and tame them, for domestic order is threatened not only by the "cold shadow" of nature's silence but by the self-defeating myth that promised order in the first place. In this sense, the cowherd is only a more graphic image of the enervation plaguing so many of the men in these stories. A ghost of a living death, he appears defeated by his work outdoors and by domestic order. Although bustling with movement, the women in this story are shown to be useless if not used up, like the cowherd, because the only outlet for their creative and social energies is a kind of piecework. The quilting party thus becomes a metaphor for women's fragmented and elusive sense of purpose, which can only culminate in a grim, life-denying competition for lustrous tea tables and urns.

The ghosts of "Human Habitation" and "The Working Party" haunt the easement between houses and the unfathomable terrain outside. But ironically, the horror derives from a lack of boundaries between the two domains, a lack resulting in characters like Mrs. Fisk and the women in "Human Habitation" feeling the threat of one in the other: "With the dread of her home behind her [Mrs. Fisk] fled up the empty valley" (296). That a ghostly presence also emerges in the gaps between what people say and feel is nowhere more apparent than in the conventions governing relations among women. Mrs. Fisk runs away from her home because she is about to suffocate. Her fear of the cowherd is mirrored in being stifled by the conventions of women playing at work. As she dances around the tea table, waiting for compliments on her linen and service, her energy turns to anger as her individuality is subsumed by team competition, the result of which is a fear that, individually, she does not exist.

"The Hazy Queerness" of Female Character

In "The Secession," "Ann Lee's," "Recent Photograph," "A Queer Heart," and "The Inherited Clock," terror and ghostly presence emerge as signs of women's struggle against an assigned identity. "The Secession" concerns the "meticulously accurate" Miss Selby's long-awaited visit to Rome, heightened by the tense relationship she sets up between the gentleman friend whose marriage proposal she has put off and a "perfectly civilized" new woman friend (167,165). Miss Selby feels safe only when passion is repressed. Denied other outlets, her passion and energy are expressed as rage. When Miss Selby faces the consequences of her displaced passions, she disappears, but her violent emotion haunts her rival, Miss Phelps, and would-be lover, Mr. Carr, in her absence. The story builds to this climax through several contrasts. The tidy proprieties of the Pension Hebe are set against a backdrop of the ruins of pagan Rome, while Miss Selby's "strong intellectual appetites" vie with Miss Phelps's capacity to come "quickly and frothily to the boil" (161). And yet not all is what it seems, for as Miss Selby's friend Mr. Carr notices, "behind the gaudy silk she was like some palpitating wild thing, a bird half-seen," but one whose emotion "left him numb" (163). A mood of intense jealousy and misgiving is created by the unacknowledged emotional signals transmitted among Miss Selby, Miss Phelps, and Mr. Carr. The brush of one shoulder on another, ambiguous pronouns, references to the Roman landscape—all convey repressed emotion about to burst in the spaces between feeling and failed expression.

Unrecognized by Mr. Carr and Miss Phelps, the seething, unsettled character of Miss Selby remains an unknowable ghost. When she disappears, all that is left of her are the terrible words her friends read in her diary: "I wonder . . . why I have not pushed [Miss Phelps] through the window. It was so much in my mind to do this, and I see now it could have been done more easily than I thought" (169). Passion expressed as rage is the final threat preventing Mr. Carr and Miss Phelps from yielding to their growing attraction. Miss Selby's presence is thus an indelible scar on a world clinging to decorum for stability. Like the haunting ruins of ancient Rome, she represents energy that cannot be understood from the restrained perspective of her friends' civilization. On a visit to Hadrian's Villa, Miss Phelps observes that "the very air of Rome" makes one feel "intensified," but Mr. Carr reminds her that these are Miss Selby's words and do "not even make sense" (166). It is as though a woman's intensity is like the best-forgotten excesses of ancient Rome. They are both made to be mysterious by a language of interpretation that works as a distancing device. Thus Mr. Carr shies away from the feeling both women represent, while Miss Phelps declares the Roman Philosopher's Hall to be "beautiful . . . suggestive" (167). Like this relic of an unknowable history, Miss Selby triumphs over discretion. Her sense of herself remains hers alone, perplexing and haunting.

In her preface to the collection in which these stories first appeared, Bowen acknowledges that "the fate of the missing woman in 'The Secession' is not hinted at" (*A*, 94). Neither is the true nature of Ann Lee, the title character of a story written in the same period. Ann Lee's is the name of a hat shop, hidden away "in one of the dimmer and more silent streets" of London (103). Its owner remains unknowable, living "mysteriously" behind an "impenetrable" facade (103). That Bowen names the story for the hat shop warns us that though we may be intrigued and even disturbed by the owner, we will know only her art. Like Ann Lee's two customers and her male visitor, we are chilled by something far more ominous than the engulfing London fog, but whatever it is remains indefinable, even indescribable.

Bowen's method of repeating certain key details creates a portentous atmosphere out of the mundane. "Ann Lee's" has no ghosts, but its central character is so ineffable as to be ghostly, despite her clearly detailed presence. Part of what makes Ann Lee so mysterious is her classlessness. With the shop "not far from Sloan Street" but not easy to find, with her reputation of being "practically a lady [but] a queer creature," her clients can't "place her" (103–4). One minute a "priestess," another like "the mother—Niobe, Rachel," she invites speculation about her character and yet puts us off (108). The two customers' concern about money, the issue that also seems to connect Ann Lee and her male visitor, only heightens the sense of a more threatening relationship. The shop owner's inscrutability focuses attention on the problem of even knowing how to know, as money turns out to be a canard as the two women customers and the male intruder scrutinize one another in their futile efforts to figure out Ann Lee. Ann Lee's power over her customers seems prosaic; it expresses itself as the "feeling . . . that if Ann Lee had wished, Lulu would have had that other hat, and then another and another" (110).[27] But as Lulu and Letty leave the shop and the male visitor passes them by, we and "they [know] how terrible it had been—terrible" (111).

The unidentified distress of the man coincides with the indefinable character of Ann Lee. Breaking all her appointments with him, Ann Lee also shatters the expectation that she can be pinned down by any conventional categories of female character. Hiding her creative process behind her shop curtain, she implies that she cannot be understood as the sum of her place in society, her appearance, and her work. Bowen wrote about this story's unresolved conclusion in the preface to the collection *Ann Lee's*: "I cannot consider those trick endings; more, it seemed to me that from true predicaments there *is* no way out" (*A*, 94). The true predicament in the story is to define "the hazy queerness" Bowen felt about female character (*A*, 92). What is haunted about Ann Lee's is the secret space behind the curtain into which its owner disappears and then returns carrying her wares. Similarly, in the story "I Died of Love" the dressmaker's domain is the central location but is a "mystery factory."[28] We are never invited into this space. Its mystery points to the way a woman's character is hidden behind the social positions that shape her. Bound up with the proprieties on which the dressmaker's livelihood depends, "her humanity" disappears like "a whole cargo lost [:] . . . in its timelessness the establishment had no story" except the futile quest to discover it ("Died," 132, 130).

"Recent Photograph" concerns just such a futile quest. Hot on the trail of a story about a man who has murdered his wife, a newspaper reporter accepts the first explanation he is given. But his scoop is undermined by his attraction to a young woman, Verbena, who offers a different version. The real mystery in this story is to determine the character of the murdered wife and that of the young woman storyteller, for despite Verbena's questions, which point to the complexity and ambiguity of the wife's character and her own, the reporter understands women only though his stereotypical view.

In "A Queer Heart," written many years later, Bowen is still concerned with the ghostly origins of female character, but here she splits her inquiry into two mystifying women, sisters who reflect aspects of but cannot understand each other. Now in their sixties, they compete for the affection and loyalty of Hilda's daughter, Lucille. The central question the story poses is whether Lucille will turn out to be more like her mother or her aunt, and what that tells us about the development of female character.

Trapped in jealous resemblance, the sisters are stalled in their development. By temperament, Hilda Cadman is lively, sensuous, and easygoing, but since the death of her husband, who had kept Rosa's "chill wind" at bay, the widow and her daughter have lived in a "state of cheerless meekness" (558, 556). Rosa, by contrast, is "joyless" and considers marriage "low" (558). Increasingly, Lucille becomes more like her aunt than her mother. What revelation there is about the origins of these women's characters is available in the form of psychological motivation; their differences are ascribed to sibling rivalry going back to early childhood. At the end, when Rosa calls Hilda to her bedside, it is to reveal the source of her bitterness: One Christmas, craving the beautiful blond angel crowning the tree, she watched helplessly as the younger Hilda enchanted everyone with her singing and was rewarded with the doll. Hilda now realizes that Rosa's vengeance is to win back the doll in the form of Lucille.

The story is too neatly packaged in its psychological and literary symmetry, but it leaves the question of female character intriguingly open. The sisters' revelations come not only too late but too little. Like Hilda, we understand their differences but not the force of Rosa's vindictiveness. The narrative design, however, provides a clue in connecting the sisters' characters to marriage and the family. Despite Hilda's recollections of marital bliss, the story questions the institution of marriage. The domain designed to protect and support women, Mr. Cadman's "rumbustious fortification," is shattered with his death, leaving his widow defenseless against her sister's assault (558). It is only when the two women have no husband or father to deflect attention from their conflict that the illusory nature of domestic order and security becomes apparent. Rosa's actions mark a rebellion against the traditional family as she claims her birthright through the sister's child, who is becoming her replica. The likeness is presented both satirically and with horror. Like a ventriloquist's dummy, Lucille mouths Rosa's words, parodying them but also parroting them in a way that suggests the insidious power of the repressed as ghostly presence.

In an even later story, Bowen takes up the impact that inherited family order and the violence it conceals have on the formation of female character. Set during World War II, "The Inherited Clock" concerns Clara's amnesia about a childhood incident involving her, her cousin Paul, and a clock that she inherits but Paul wanted. Forgetting the incident is Clara's effort to ignore the way she relinquishes responsibility for her life. As her life ticks away with no change in sight, the ticking of the clock becomes horrible to her, a ghostly reminder of a past that augured much but delivered little.

For as long as she can remember, Clara has known about her cousin Rosanna's will and has hitched her prospects to its promise of "immense change. Not unreasonably, she expected everything to go better. She perceived that her nature was of the kind that is only able to flower in clement air" (630). But the cheery promises resonating from the past into her future are accompanied by a darker fatefulness: "Was it impossible that the past should be able to injure the future irreparably?" (631). Clara's goal is to wait; inertia defines her character. The story thus presents her life as a time bomb waiting to go off, set to the ticking of her inherited clock, but is anticlimactic: The clock continues to tick, Clara continues to wait, and thus fulfillment is thwarted.

Living as though there are no boundaries between past and present, obsessed with time and inheritance, Clara is doomed to replay the past. When Paul insists she put her finger in the clockworks, just as he forced her to do when they were children, the pain releases the meaning of her life's pattern: a relentless return of repressed desire, frustration, and rage. By insisting that Clara and Paul wait for their inheritance, Aunt Rosanna manipulates them into replaying her own frustrated wait for her uncle's money. But her plot also enacts her revenge against the uncle and her own frustrated passions. Clara's shock at repeating the childhood incident both removes and replaces boundaries between her memory, her consciousness, and the time that defines her life. Clara's finger stops the clockworks and ends her wait as the ticking stops. She must now face the implications of her suspended life and decide whether she can purge herself of the unresolved past and end a relationship with a married man that is doomed to noncommitment and endlessly frustrated waiting.

With its embedded tale of a woman's betrayed love avenged by shaping a younger woman's life, "The Inherited Clock" recalls Dickens's *Great Expectations*. Even the title resonates with literary memory. In Bowen's story the ghost is not so much a dead relic of the past as a presence haunting the relationships between women as they are shaped by an oppressive history. The story of female characters waiting for their predetermined fates to unfold seems interminable and intractable. From Dickens's Estella through Henry James's Catherine Slope, Bowen inherits the legacy of creating female characters who have no outlets to express passion. This legacy itself becomes a ghost haunting the creative imagination. While this literary history may be entirely knowable, its powerful effect on a writer's ability to question it and to imagine alternative plots for female character remains open-ended.

Whether they are felt as a kind of disembodied anguish or terror or whether they materialize as human beings, Bowen's ghostly women dramatize the dead end of substituting self-aggrandizing myths for a confrontation with the losses of a brutal past. Those who are the haunted in these stories still cling to myths of self-importance and domestic order. Martin in "The Shadowy Third," the visitors in "Human Habitation," Mr. Carr in "The Seccession," and Mrs. Fisk in "The Working Party" act as though repeating the past is a corrective to its violence. Thus Martin marries a replica of his first wife and is disturbed when her attempts at refurnishing fail to revise the fate built into domestic order. Only when characters empathize with the dispossessed is there a possibility for change. Both the "little man," who tells the tale of the inconsolable woman in "The Back Drawing-Room," and Janet, who forms a bond with the ghost in "Foothold," represent a kind of recognition that is a first step toward reassessing the ideologies based on a desire for order. Their emotional response to haunting presences subverts order by embracing the irrational, destabilized experience offered by unrestrained feeling. In communion with past suffering, they encourage the presence of ghosts and open up the carefully ordered— even claustrophobic—home to a range of understanding that will allow the past and its women to become knowable.

Comedies of Sex and Manners

Bowen's comedies of sex and manners depict the moment of uncertainty when upper-middle-class codes of conduct are challenged. Ranging widely from staid Edwardian homes to a world Blitzed into disarray by a second world war, these stories dramatize the exuberance and anxiety that accompany social upheaval in any age. Whatever their time and place, they often re-create the carefully ordered drawing rooms Henry James and Anton Chekhov used to portray stable worlds threatened by change. Bowen's self-conscious use of this technique shows how the despair paralyzing an earlier age lingers until it is overcome by personal unrest or political chaos. Her women and men are shaken out of their complacency and torpor and left to face each other, no longer able to hide behind traditional social and moral codes. The comedy arises when the characters' shock gives way to recognition that henceforth everything is changed, and the world filled with open-ended possibilities, but there are no instructions on which to rely.

Bowen accomplishes her comic revolution by developing a narrative point of view that initially seems Jamesian in its detachment but, like Chekhov's comedies, is actually a highly charged commentary. Bowen presents a delicately balanced view of the sexual dances concealed by the world of manners but at the same time exposes her characters' repressed desires and assesses them as absurd. The balance is achieved by juxtaposing the cryptic dialogue characterizing Jamesian reserve with images of intense feeling, even violence.

Inconclusive and Ironic Distances

Bowen uses the inconclusive nature of the short story to suggest that female characters are indeterminate as they search for self-definition in a world that is not only highly conventional but also mutable.[29] "The Confidante" takes one of Bowen's favorite themes—betrayal—and converts it to comedy through the partial revelations of a female character. Penelope, who serves as interlocutor and confidante to the reticent lovers Maurice and Veronica, manipulates their inability to face their own feelings. In a drawing room fashioned by discretion, Penelope breaks through the veneer of "allusions, insinuations, and *double entendres*," the language with which the lovers conduct their liaisons (30). Dispensing with the propriety that keeps Veronica engaged to marry a man she does not love, Penelope "left a gap she knew to be unbridgeable for [Maurice and Veronica]. They were face to face with the hideous simplicity of life" (39). By asserting her own desires, Penelope openly acknowledges the lovers' "secret preoccupation" with each other, which heretofore had been "perceptible" only between the cracks of their polite apologies and through the narrator's ironic, often-caustic commentary (35). But Penelope's revelations neither legitimize the lovers' behavior nor reveal what lies hidden behind "the hideous simplicity of life." She lets them know only that Veronica's exquisite manners and dutiful protestations conceal a narcissism that keeps her fiancé and lover dangling at the center of an unnecessarily painful quadrangle. The secret Bowen shares with us is that Penelope is only too happy to comfort Veronica's betrayed fiancé and leave the lovers to "gasp in [the] inclement air" now that they are left alone with each other (39).

Bowen's story reveals a crack much wider than the one Henry James intended in his geometric arrangement of two deceiving and self-deceived couples in *The Golden Bowl*. Compressing a similar arrangement into a short story and making one of the women both interlocutor and agent provocateur serve to upset several Jamesian applecarts, for Penelope's wise and wily ways result not in social ostracism and emotional isolation, as they would in James, but in a reordering of the sexual landscape. Her point of view emerges as a remodeling of James's Maggie Verver and Charlotte Stant; Penelope rearranges their primary qualities to fit her rebellious character. Like Maggie Verver, Penelope first decodes and then manipulates the manners of the drawing room to expose the sexual repression that inevitably leads to betrayal. She does so, moreover, while finessing center stage away from the femme fatale. But as an "other woman," she also parodies Jamesian moral delicacies and then triumphantly transforms them into farce. The reason Veronica and Maurice are "dazzled by a flash of comprehension" at the end of "The Confidante" is that this new woman has "upset their bowl"—or, we could say, James's golden bowl—and in so doing has revealed that the crack has widened enough to let a new woman through to assert her own moral and sexual authority (39).

Penelope's sly rebellion reveals that Veronica's insidious behavior derives from a tradition of moral drama that traps women in the world of manners designed to protect them.[30] Like James's Charlotte Stant, Veronica is defeated by upholding the very system that conditions her to think she must marry for property and convenience.[31] The end, however, is ambiguous. The way is cleared for Veronica to have Maurice, but because of the couple's reticence we really don't know if that is what they wanted, and, of course, she has lost the man on whom she depended for order and security. When the story ends, Veronica, Maurice, and the reader are dazzled by Penelope's coup but puzzled by the remaining mysteries and the story's self-reflecting ironies.

Despite allusions to James, Bowen's work is not derivative; instead, it explores the tension between the moral irresolution of his plots and the social changes she observed in her lifetime. The result is female characters capable of reshaping those plots. In "The Confidante" Bowen asks us to consider the degree of Penelope's self-consciousness and the effect of reworking a traditional plot on the fate of female characters. Were Penelope not to intervene, she would most likely become a conventional spinster and all the characters would bask in the misery of moral and emotional uncertainty.[32] Her machinations subvert that ending, however, and leave the characters in an even more open ending than James, for one, will allow.

It is this area of the unknown that provides a sense of mystery in all Bowen stories that John Bayley describes as central to the way the short story form resembles a poem but is so unlike the novel: "The fulfillment in inconclusiveness . . . is a speciality of the short story method" (23). Character, in this sense, "remains incomplete, seen in terms of hints and suggestions" (Bayley, 38). In Bowen's use of this method, Penelope represents author and character on the brink of discovery, for her plots shake the foundations of propriety and leave them unreconstructed.

The narrative method just described is evident in Bowen's early story "Breakfast," in which the perspective resembles that of a comic strip. Like the father and reluctant lovers in Chekhov's "The Proposal," these characters are drawn without gradations. Their "profiles . . . in silhouette" or "three-quarter faces" nevertheless sharply etch a comic war between the sexes (15). Nervous sexual energy is transmitted in the tension between the "silence of suspended munching" and the rapid-fire dialogue between the women at the boarding-house table and the blushing bachelor Mr. Rossiter (15).[33] In high spirits, Bowen's provocative narrator leaves us to sort out "the coffee and the bacon and the hostility and the christian forbearance [that] blew out before them into the chilly hall" (20).

This kind of summing up, which leaves the characters swathed in shadow despite the strong material details, is a hallmark of Bowen's short story form. As William Trevor points out, "[Bowen] was well aware that the short story is the art of the glimpse, that in craftily withholding information it tells as little as it dares."[34] Our glimpse of that final eruption in "The Breakfast" is accompanied by a comic shock that results from including an unexpected emotion—"hostility"—in a dance of sexual manners and "christian forbearance." This narrative move erases any expectation we might have of affectionate camaraderie among the teasing boarders.

But the narrator offers no explanation. Instead, readers are left to ponder the sense of mystery that informs all Bowen's work but is intensified in the compressed form of her short stories. Within the shadowy presence of the group there is always an onlooker, an embodiment of otherness. The group is bound together by something this outsider can never know, and this aspect creates the sense of mystery. Sometimes, as in "Breakfast," the outsider is the narrator, the one who may upset the status quo with a withering glance but who lacks the authority of the traditional omniscient narrator. He or she stands for those of us outside the story, trying to know what those on the inside know. The mystery we are left with derives from the nature of the connections made in the story: the discordant emotional interchanges between characters or between the narrator and the characters; the clash between the atmosphere established through descriptive language and the characters' actions; and, finally, the complicated interaction between our responses as readers and all the aforementioned elements.

In an uncollected 1931 story, "Flavia," the sense of mystery and ambiguity results from a split in the central character that makes her both an onlooker and an object under scrutiny. Flavia is the pen name of Caroline, who writes to Bernard after being attracted to the persona in his letter to the *Athaenaeum*. Bernard meets Caroline at a mutual friend's, and when they marry, he has not yet discovered that the dark and sophisticated Flavia and the fair, "nice and modest" Caroline are one and the same.[35]

Soon enough, Caroline's unpretentious intelligence drives Bernard to resume his correspondence with Flavia. The story's tension builds less from Caroline's deception of Bernard than from Bernard's self-deception and its effect on Caroline's character, for while she despairs the loss of his love, she knows her real character is trapped within his fantasy of Flavia. At the end, Caroline reveals Flavia's identity, only to face her husband's disbelief. Retreating on the heels of total rejection, she threatens to divorce him if he does not forgive her. In effect, she begs forgiveness for being herself and thus dissolves into his fantasy of Flavia, the woman she could become if given the chance.

Although Bernard is painted with a broad comic stroke, Caroline's triumph is not so funny. Her world offers no opportunities for her to combine both sides of her character and be a wife. It is clear that Bernard is attracted to Flavia because she remains unreal, untested, and unmarriageable, whereas he is drawn to Caroline only because she is suited for domestic service.

Bowen's stories dramatize the moments before and after epiphany, not the revelation itself. The reader is thus made to share the writer's process of testing the limits of what can be known and what can be imagined and constructed. Bayley calls this experience "the writer's secret" and argues that the story's meaning to the author "has itself become the justification of the tale, its subject, the reader's sense of fascination and curiosity" (39).

The inconclusiveness in "The Confidante" and "Flavia" comes from the interplay among the characters' responses to one another. Veronica's insidious ploys fulfill Penelope's self-effacing wishes, while Caroline's unselfconscious duplicity satisfies Bernard's self-deception. This web of manipulation points to a rupture between the world of Henry James and one still shaking from World Wars I and II. Beginning her career in the twenties, a time marked by all sorts of liberation for women, Bowen infused her short stories with an energizing spirit that stands in marked contrast to the loss and despair expressed by her male colleagues of this period. Unlike Hemingway or D. H. Lawrence, who depict the despair of war and its accompanying loss of innocence, Bowen celebrates that loss of innocence. This is not to say she denies war's waste; rather, her stories acknowledge progress while mourning the casualties.

This duality, often dramatized as a condition of unsettling social change that offers neither escape nor explanation, gives her comedies of sex and manners their underlying melancholy. If Italy seems a wondrous and fantasied escape from English manners and morals in "The Contessina," it also encapsulates the repressions that make escape necessary. In stories that convey the anxieties of wartime, such as "Careless Talk" and "Oh, Madam," there is always humor to relieve and express the anxiety originating in the characters' recognition that they have no one but themselves to blame for the loss of innocence that leads to an open-ended but insecure future.

Rebellion in the Drawing Room

In Bowen's drawing-room comedies, literary and historical changes are actual reversals of what was previously possible for female characters. In "The New House" and its sequel, "The Lover," Bowen takes motifs of haunting and constraining homes and uses them to shape a woman's liberation. In "The New House" Cicely Pilkington escapes her assigned role as angel of her brother's hearth. Just as they are about to move from their childhood home, Cicely discovers she must "get away before this new house fastens on to me" (57). In her decision to marry and thus attempt to escape her bondage to family homes, another Jamesian parable of the spinster's doom is revised.

"The New House" recalls the claustrophobic house of Dr. Sloper in "Washington Square" while undercutting its representation of patriarchal power. The identity, prestige, and stability Herbert Pilkington associates with his new house are undercut by its being a suburban imitation manor that "sneer [s] at him" (56). This reversal supports Cicely's rebellion. In contrast to the solemn gloom with which Dr. Sloper and his house are presented, Cicely's brother and his house are ridiculed, and she is given a self-determining voice. In those stories in which houses fail the characters' need for security and stability, the result is often an elegy of despair and dispossession; this story, however, as a comedy, allows the heroine to free herself from the feeling of having "been tied up, fastened on to things and people" (57).

"The Lover" shows Cicely, now married, continuing to kick up her heels and speak out. She upsets her brother with her good looks and confident sexual energy. Despite her apparent happiness, the twin stories contain a disturbing note. One line in "The New House" questions Cicely's liberation and happiness: Following Herbert's plaint that he needs his sister because he "can't get used to another woman at my time of life," the narrator describes Cicely as "suddenly superior, radiant and aloof; his no longer" but nevertheless "another man's possession" (58). This tag haunts the happiness in "The Lover" and gives us as much cause to worry about Cicely as about Herbert's fiancée, for while the honeymooners disdain Herbert's belief in women's "infinite sensibility" and "patience," Richard too insists that woman "is infinitely adaptable" (67). As Cicely responds, the narrator provides a foreboding note: "She has to be, poor thing (this did not come well from Cicely)" (67).

As Herbert leaves the happy couple "to review his long perspective of upholstered happiness with Doris" and "Richard's arm [creeps] round Cicely's shoulders," Bowen creates the ominous sense that marital happiness, like women's characters, depends on a traditional system of sexual manners and morals (69). Bowen's comic treatment of this theme questions whether progressive change is possible either within marriage and the family or through a literary critique of such structures. In an otherwise light comedy, "Shoes: An International Episode," conventional expectations of happiness and harmony oppress a young couple who barely know each other. The mistaken exchange of Dillie's brogues for spike-heeled party shoes signals the couple's frustrated efforts to understand each other beyond the socially constructed persona each presents and expects from the other.

In "The New House" and "The Lover" Bowen unveils a more devious side of the relationship between social and literary conventions by changing the method of portraying women's jailer from James's Grand Guignol horror to farce, for as we are given to like Richard, to approve of Cicely's decision to marry him and escape her oppressive brother, we comply with literary manipulation. In true comic spirit, we share the narrative's approval of the heroine's happiness. As we are led into the intellectually and emotionally satisfying game of satire, it is easy to forget the gloomy condemnations of James's melodrama. But playing comedy against Gothic evil, Bowen creates a heroine caught between conventional, easily recognizable oppression and the struggle to recognize the coercion hidden in relationships, the seductive power of so-called happy endings.[36] Along with Bowen's heroine, therefore, the reader enters unknown and perhaps precarious terrain. Bowen's comedies of sex and manners show us how the oppressive side of marriage and the family has its roots in the way our social codes control sexual expression in the literature we read.

The Old Order Strikes Back

In "The Man of the Family," "Aunt Tatty," "The Parrot," and "The Cassowary" anachronistic sexual codes seem more powerful than ever.

Although clearly set in the twenties when Bowen wrote them, these stories evoke the atmosphere of an earlier time. With this technique Bowen questions the sexual values of her own time as well as the past, once again using the register of Henry James's fiction to set the context.

In "The Man of the Family" the sexual codes of an old order clash with the pragmatic and freewheeling concerns of the new. Caught in the middle of this ironic commentary is William, an Oxford student whose education results more from his family's intrigues than from academic study. Those intrigues concern his titled but poor aunt, Lady Heloise Lambe; her adventurous daughter, Rachel; his untitled but wealthy Aunt Luella Peel; and her daughter, Patsey, "not modern at all" and finally engaged at 32 (441). Because Aunt Luella has often proclaimed him "the man of the family," William takes his position seriously and tells her that Patsey's fiancé, Everard, known by intimates as Chummey, is a "nasty" gold digger. Like James's Strether, William and his fine sensibilities are tested by the more pragmatic concerns of women. Unlike the innocent American, however, William is not taken in, either by the dashing Rachel, who, like James's Mme de Vionnet, needs "a good home," or by Aunt Luella's moral decrees.

The issue of power drives the characters and plot of "The Man of the Family." It is clear that however "nasty" the ironically named Chummey might be, he is the crucial pawn in Aunt Luella's plan to marry Patsey off and sustain the family. William's rite of passage identifies the manners and morals of one era as the instruments of power in a later age.[37] In the homes of Aunts Luella and Heloise, neither duplicity nor corruption can undermine family honor and duty; rather, they only point up the necessity of family stability. This morality—which places family stability above all else—does not change with time; as Rachel knows, it is infinitely malleable to suit any crisis in the old order. The failure to recognize such flexibility leads to a moral vacuum, as when Rachel recalls the time she agreed to run off with Chummey, who was then married: "I'm sorry, William, but morals are like clothes and I'd scrapped one lot and hadn't found others to suit me" (447).

Although the morality of the old order is designed to use people, its elaborate system of manners salvages some humanity from its pragmatic and cruel code of self-preservation. Rachel clarifies this idea for William and, in the process, articulates women's role in defending the system: "I honestly do believe that manners (or people not having them) undermine happiness far quicker than morals" (447). William's romantic notion about being heir apparent to a stable domestic order is thus called into question by the way good behavior is dependent on women's ability to find social and economic security.

Women are the avatars of sex and manners in another story, "Aunt Tatty," in which passion is domesticated by family concerns. When Eleanor takes her beloved to meet her provincial mother, trouble erupts in translating her urban habits into country customs. Accused by Paul of being ashamed of their love, Eleanor responds, "It seems so unreal. It's got no background. It isn't what one could possibly build up one's life on" (266). True love here must pass the test of domestic order, that is, to be subdued by it. In the process, however, the purpose of sexual love is questioned as the lovers are asked to fit their needs into the "background" of family order.

In Bowen's fictional world, domestic codes represent a defense against passion's anarchic power. Whether passion is experienced, as in her stories about courtship, or fantasized, as in "The Parrot," it is treated with comic irony. In this latter tale of a "magical interlude," an exotically hued and caged parrot escapes from Mrs. Willesden's fastidious household into the sensuous garden of her mysterious neighbors, the Lennicotts (122). For Mrs. Willesden, the fact that Mr. Lennicott is a novelist confirms the rumor that he and the woman he lives with are unmarried and thus justifies her fear that the demimonde of art threatens the more respectable "house of shut-out sunshine and great furniture" (122). Even though Mrs. Willesden complains that she could not finish Mr. Lennicott's novel because "it was so very dull," his "quizzical Spanish face" and disdain for those who "are full of moral indignation" menace his neighbor's cloister (119, 118). Ironically, the Lennicotts do not represent escape for Mrs. Willesden's parrot. A glimpse of the novelist's home reveals that both households are equally concerned with domestic propriety. The story is thus self-parodying: As a writer so concerned with the codes of domestic life, Bowen is as much as admitting the comic proportions of her own obsessions.

Passion is valued yet debunked as a threat in "The Cassowary," in which two sisters love a missionary missing in Africa. The suppressed passion of Phyllis and Nathalie seethes as a force more powerful than it would be were it expressed. The intense emotion of the sisters is hidden by their obsession with decorum. Nathalie tells Margery, the outsider, "You see, things are so difficult—life in a family. We've never spoken of this among ourselves. . . . Love's so embarrassing, isn't it? . . . [I]t was the only solution, his not coming back. . . . Scenes are so dreadful; we've never had scenes in our family" (321).

In this comedy of domesticated sexual feeling, family decorum silences the women. Although she wrote this story in the twenties and its time setting is unspecified, Bowen, by portraying the sisters as relics from a Victorian parlor scene, shows that the silent woman is no anachronism: "The girls were elderly as girls, though young as spinsters; speaking socially, they were awkwardly placed in years. They were tall, 'rousses,' each with a high-up stare . . . through pince-nez. . . . To this . . . brilliantly blank look . . . they owed a slight air of vacuity, 'artistic,' sometimes fumbling, generally elegant. In resemblance they varied between a Burne Jones and one of those Gallic drawings of English tourists. Their way of speaking—rapid, slurred, imperious, was such that one had always difficulty in understanding them" (314).

Bowen expresses the tension between anachronistic sexual codes and women's desire for sexual expression through the figure of the outsider. Margery's entry at 19 into the Lampeter household is her rite of passage—"how to behave in a grown up world" (316). What she learns, however, is not that there will be a melodramatic or romantic conclusion to the lovers' estrangement but that once exposed, romantic love is tranquilized. After years apart, Nathalie and her missionary express themselves "decorously, like husband and wife for a week parted" (324). The darker, dangerous side of passion is left in darkest Africa, presented as a myth to be treated as a joke, and thus tamed. In this way, Margery's brother responds to the sisters' narrative "flippantly":

> I wish I were a cassowary . . .
> On the plains of Timbuctoo,
> I should eat a Missionary,
> Coat and hat and hymn-book too. (318)

The comic aggression in this limerick, typical of "*Preparatory* school humour," defends against a more insidious male-authored text—the myth of a woman pining for love (319). While the "boys" romp in the wild, women are saved from their aggression by waiting voicelessly and selflessly for men to rescue them.

Of course, this strategy also protects men from being entirely domesticated themselves. In the language of jokes, "The Cassowary"

34

both replicates a tale of betrayed passion and exposes it as a sham. Like any good joke, it plays on conventions of serious tales—here a remote, empty house suddenly occupied by people who seem to be living a secret story, possibly "under a cloud" (315). The story that shocks Margery is that the house cannot contain the aggressive woman. Nathalie escapes to rescue the man she desires, "freeing herself with a movement from some imaginary constraint" (322). The imaginary constraint, or "cloud," turns out to be the sisters' dependence on the myth that they need to be rescued. With the story's conclusion, the joke is on the boys and men, whose search for adventure or a higher calling was an escape from women's passion and the domestic codes designed to contain it.

Sex and Manners beyond the Drawing Room

Other comedies of sex and manners dramatize the ironic relationship of men to those same domestic codes they need to contain their own aggression and use to control women. Bowen uses the desires and experiences of the young to convey the spontaneous feeling that calls for deeply imprinted codes of conduct: "I rely on immediacy and purity of sensations and indubitably the young are unspoiled instruments" (*MT*, 81). In "The Contessina" brutality results from the clash between men's sexual desire and the codes of conduct that constrain and protect both men and women. Evoking a Chekhovian seaside resort, with young ladies "all in white" and laconic tourists in the background, Bowen shows the grim side of male passion (137). Born outside the pale of English manners and morals, the Contessina is a target for the passion of Englishmen. Like Africa, Italy stirs the romanticism of the English just as it inspires their bad jokes; the Contessina, "fresh as a young petal, as brown as old, old ivory," therefore represents the exotic "other" they desire to possess at no cost to themselves (142). Viewed by Mr. Barlow as "just the sort of little girl I like," the Contessina is not subject to the sexual manners governing courtship at home (142).

In a scene recalling the pratfalls of farce, Bowen connects English boys' humor and the aggression behind the ideology of conquest. As the impeccably white-flanneled Mr. Barlow allows himself to be overwhelmed by the charms of the "peculiar [ly] delicious" young Italian woman, we witness a near rape (142). Though drawn entirely in comic moves, the story is also shocking. It points to a brutal morality: Exploiting women is legitimized by society's sexual rituals. In his most imperious manner, Barlow blames his victim for her fall from innocence. Dramatized as light comedy, a young woman tripping on a rocky beach becomes the center of a high moral drama: "The front of her dress was soiled irreparably cut right through at the knee and stained with blood" (145). The comedy is sustained, however, as two clashing sexual codes are shown to bolster yet undermine each other: They are each equally dangerous and absurd. The Contessina's incorrigible flirtatiousness, a by-product of sexual manners for women in her society, satirizes the romantic self-deception that brings Englishmen to Italy in the first place. At the end, she turns for protection to Barlow's friend Harrison, telling him, "You row like a god. . . . Do you like Italian girls?" (146).

The question is answered by another story set in Italy, "The Good Girl." Here an English girl is prey to the double standard twice over as she is treated to the advances of an Italian suitor and the hypocrisies of her English friends. Monica is never given a chance to sort out her own feelings. Her friend Dagmar is afraid that her "rich uncle" will be offended by Monica's innocent late nights, but then Monica is rejected by her Italian suitor, who must marry a rich cousin in order to support his family. The cost of virtue for Monica and the Contessina is the suppression of any sense of themselves other than what they are expected to be.

Women in all Bowen's fiction are victimized by a sexual ideology that offers them two self-defeating options: to fulfill men's fantasies of their sexual destructiveness or to marry and yield desires for self-expression. "The Dancing Mistress" shows what happens to women's creative and sexual energy when even the dubious outlets of upper-middle-class domestic life are unavailable. The dancing mistress is an artist whose only possibility for creative expression is teaching young girls to sublimate their energies into fine manners. The story focuses on an afternoon dancing class in which Joyce James exhausts herself by leading the girls through "Marche Militaire" and on to the more demure waltz. The musical transition from an invocation to aggression to an invitation to seduction parallels Joyce James's emotional odyssey. As the music changes, her frustrated energies turn into hatred for one pupil, the "overdressed" and inept Margery Mannering (255). Joyce's intense attention to Margery becomes an act of displaced passion;[38] it signifies the rage erupting at the disjunction between the rituals Joyce

James teaches to celebrate privilege and her own sense of brutal deprivation.

The story traces Joyce's sadistic pleasure in torturing Margery to the aftermath of her exhaustion. Except for her rage at the girl, the story would be a parody of middle-class sex and manners. But as it stands, both sex and manners are displaced by the strange relationship between Joyce and the girl. Joyce's encounter in the taxi with the one man who represents her conventional sexual options, the "fervent" Lulu, is a sexual anticlimax; therefore, her outlet for expressing passion is her waltz with Margery. The dancing teacher's obsession with the girl is expressed in a sentence that allows no conjunction, only a semicolon, which suggests an inseparable and insuperable connection: "She couldn't do without Margery Mannering; she wanted to kill her" (257). By the time Joyce leads Margery in a humiliating lesson in the waltz, with all the other girls and their mothers and maids watching, the scene takes on the qualities of rape. Bowen's imagery and rhetorical strategy represent a dialectical pattern of sexual aggression, failure, and brutal revenge.

Fighting off her fatigue through her command of the girls, Joyce rebuffs the intrusive Lulu, who plies her with his "Swiss-Romano" seductive talk: "You are so beautiful. I would give my soul, my body, all that I have" (258). The scene parodies middle-class sexuality, as Joyce has eyes only for the hated Margery, who is "bumping" disastrously through her waltz "with her partner all limp" (258). As failures of sexual and creative outlets meet, Joyce finds the perfect scapegoat. "I shall have to take you myself," she proclaims to the girl, and what follows is a travesty of sexual conquest: "The thump of Margery's heart was like the swelling and bursting of great black bubbles inside her. . . . Her hot body sagged on Miss James's cold bare arm. Her eyes, stretched with physical fear like a rabbit's, stared through the clouding spectacles at the mild white hollow of Miss James's throat. . . . Miss James's hand like a cold shell gripped the hot hand tighter" (259). With few words from the antagonists, but through their body language, the narrative depicts the displaced sexual energy of one powerless woman asserting power over another.

In countering the heightened emotion and suggestion of melodrama, the dense realistic detail beings the story close to the reader. What makes it so suggestive is the unnamed but carefully mapped Dublin setting reminiscent of James Joyce's *Dubliners*. Seen in this context,

Miss Joyce James is the artist worn-out and demonized by the constraining codes of a particular cultural and historical moment. But her position, like her name, is the reverse of that of Mr. James Joyce. A taxi ride to a train leading backward to a home without a future is a regressive version of James Joyce's journey to artistic fruition. James Joyce purges himself of the suffocating Dublin each time he restores it to view, giving the short story a new life. Joyce James finds she is stuck in "her own place," which provides no outlets other than a casual affair with a parodic Latin lover and bitter triumph over the despised but compelling Margery Mannering, who represents the strict social codes of Dublin. Joyce James's dream of a "new life, the self's," is aborted by her tedious realities but is transformed in another dream, one in which she dances with Margery Mannering to the beat of her rage: "'I'll kill you, I'll kill you,' she said like a knife. Something burst behind Margery's stretched eyes; she fainted. . . . Joyce smiled in her sleep" (262).

Like James Joyce, Elizabeth Bowen found in the cultural codes of Ireland a source of creative energy. Perhaps because Irish history, as she observed, is so violent, it sheds light on the more subtle yet equally restrictive manners and morals of English society. Whether the clash is between secular narcissism and the cloistered self-centeredness of the church, as in her story "All Saints," or between bourgeois complacency and academic pretensions, as in "Sunday Evening," the scene may be provincial England but its archaeology is Irish, that is, for Bowen, the contradictory sexual morality of Anglo-Ireland.

Using language to reveal as well as to mystify, as a system of exposure as well as of defense, was fully understood by Bowen as a strategy for survival in the genteel world of her native Ireland. She was raised in the culture of the big house, with its paradoxical combinations of geographic and social isolation and "intense centripetal life"; its lavish style of living was pursued in "greed, roughness and panic" (*BC,* 20; *MT,* 27). For her own survival, Bowen learned to read the spoken and unspoken languages that translated the "impersonality" and "hypnotic stare of the big house" into rules that, like the social codes in her stories, shaped her life but whose origins and rationale remained elusive (*MT,* 26). The rationale, of course, belonged to vigilant adults who allowed their children, like those in "The Dancing Mistress," to grow up "*farouches,* haughty, quite ignorant of the outside world" (*MT,* 27). Like the young people in Bowen's novel *The Last September* or in her story "Sunday Afternoon," Anglo-Irish children were raised to be insulated from the outside world so that they could replicate their elders' detached and oppressive rule.

The Language of Social Politics

Bowen's stories treat the effects of this mysterious language from various perspectives, ranging from tragic to comic. In the early stories "Lunch" and "Mrs. Windermere" conversation is used to express and disguise the narcissism of characters who prey on the neediness of others. The others are outsiders who look for reassurance that they are accepted by the fast-talkers but quickly discover they must defend themselves from language that threatens to reduce them to a momentary amusement. At the very beginning of "Lunch," Marcia ensnares an innocent bystander with her language of familiarity and contempt: "After all . . . there are egoists and egoists. You are one sort of egoist, I am the other" (59). Leaving him in the lurch at the end, she justifies her exploitation of the outsider: "I was right; . . . there are two sorts of egoists, and I am both" (63). Revealing by turns her total self-absorption and her use of others, Marcia spins a web of self-justification and self-deception. Her talk, which is mostly about her talk, describes her rhetorical power: "You see, generally I talk in circles . . . and when the conversation has reached a climax of brilliancy I knock down my hammer, like an auctioneer, on somebody else's epigram, cap it with another, and . . . [b]y that time everybody is in a sort of glow, each believing that he or she has laid the largest and finest of the conversational eggs" (61). Regardless of content, talk is used by Bowen's characters to create a defensive space.

In three of her fine World War II stories—"Careless Talk," "Oh, Madam . . . ," and "The Dolt's Tale"—Bowen connects self-deception and the dangers of political deception. In a time when neither words nor events reveal their meaning, conversation disguises the terror of the unknown, denying fear while revealing it. In "Careless Talk" two men and two women at a fashionable restaurant try to understand the war by exchanging names of people they assume one another knows. What the conversation reveals, however, is the "hope it didn't matter my having told you that," conflicting with the anxiety that it does matter, both politically and personally (670).

"Oh, Madam . . ." is a monologue spoken by a maid to her employer about the condition of their recently bombed London house. Attempting to reassure her employer in nonstop talk, the maid reveals her own anxiety that her subservient position is the only thing that seems permanent and fixed amid the destruction of material reality. The maid's obsequious monologue is thus a kind of self-protection, the concern for Madam and the house concealing her own vulnerability. She is the invisible other, bearing the burden of responsibility for keeping England intact while Madam rushes off to more comfortable quarters, perhaps to meet friends for lunch, as in "Careless Talk." "Oh, Madam . . ." owes its design to Katherine Mansfield's story "The Lady's Maid," written 20 years earlier. Also a monologue, Mansfield's story reveals the emotional subjugation of a servant as she speaks of sacrificing her chance at marriage to her tie to her "lady." In reassuring and controlling her employer, she, like Bowen's maid, also infantilizes herself, choosing her relationship with her lady over any adult sexual relationship.

"The Dolt's Tale" is also a comic monologue, but one that depicts the self-deception resulting from the narrator's assumption of social equality. The dolt is taken in by failing to recognize "any difference between our Income Tax johnnies and the Gestapo" (744). The melodrama of mysterious events is a metaphor for the dolt's relation to his mercurial hosts. He is implicated in their spy plot, not as an agent directing action but as a voyeur excluded by not having the master code to the images and language that dupe him and thus keep him in his place as powerless outsider. Like women and children in all Bowen's work, the dolt is kept powerless by social codes that seem easy to master but remain elusive and overpowering, because the invitation to join is really a discourse designed—like Marcia's conversation in "Lunch," the jokes of adolescent boys, and Joyce James's dancing lessons—to maintain control over the ever-shifting terrain of the prevailing social and political order.

Children's "Disconcerting Questions"

> Two things are terrible in childhood: helplessness (being in other people's power) and apprehension—the apprehension that something is being concealed from us because it is too bad to be told.[39]

Bowen's child characters are made helpless and apprehensive by only one thing: the death or disappearance of a parent. What is particularly terrible for most of them is that their plight remains unresolved. If a parent dies, grief is unabated, but even when parents live and stay, both their presence and their absence are still feared. Very early on, Bowen's children discover they may be unable to expect fully the parental nurture and support on which their lives depend. The power that gives and sustains life carries with it a power to destroy, the fear of which takes two forms: First, the all-powerful parent may withhold support; second, he or she may turn out to be not so invincible, hence dependable, after all. Bowen's children experience their needs as so insatiable they could actually destroy the source of their strength. It is no wonder, then, that when parents die or disappear in Bowen's stories, the grief of children is unrelenting, for coupled with the child's sense of loss is the guilt of feeling somehow responsible. A special group of stories, gathered from Bowen's entire oeuvre, highlights this cycle of dependence and fear by presenting it from the perspective of either the child or from an empathetic narrator.

Though parents in these stories may disappear forever or only momentarily, their children's agony is always so unbearable that it lingers into adulthood. Some of these stories dwell on the young child's fear, others on the coping strategies accompanying the formation of adult character. In both "Coming Home," in which a young girl returns from school to find her mother is not there, and "Tears, Idle Tears," in which a boy cries his heart out because his father has been killed in World War II, the child's anxiety and grief represent what Bowen posited as her definition of the short story: "a crisis in itself" (*MT*, 128). Because the child's desperate need for unconditional, unending parental presence and nurture is unmediated by a larger social network of friends, school, or the world outside the family, it is so compressed that its expression inevitably occurs as an explosion. In working out a method to dramatize and explore this subject, Bowen also discovered one that would shape all her stories:

> The tale without lyricism or passion desiccates into little more than a document. The poet, and in his wake the short-story writer, is using his own, unique susceptibility to experience. . . . The short story is at an advantage over the novel, and can claim its nearer kinship to poetry, because it must be more concentrated, can be more visionary, and is not weighed down (as the novel is bound to be) by facts, explanation, or analysis. I do not mean to say that the short story is by any means exempt from the laws of narrative: it must observe them, but on its own terms. Fewer characters, fewer scenes, and above all fewer happenings are necessary; shape and action are framed for simplification. . . . [a]t no point in the story must electrical-imaginative current be found to fail. . . . There (ideally) ought to be nothing in such a story which can weaken, detract from, or blur the central, single effect. (*MT,* 128).

In their subject and form Bowen's stories about children combine crisis, compression, passion, and vision. The vision involves looking back at her own childhood experience and reimagining it as the felt moment of a child's crisis. She states emphatically, "I reject stories which reek to me of myself by exhibiting sentiments—or betraying them. . . . I am dead against art's being self-expression" (*MT,* 128). Even when her stories are "transposed autobiography," as she said of "Coming Home," the "ring of emotion" that is with her "before the characters" is questioned and reshaped (*MT,* 121, 129). Only at this point does she feel, "'Yes, this affects me—but it would affect "X" more.' Under what circumstances; for what reason?" (*MT,* 129).

Unbridgeable Distances

Studying "Coming Home" enables us to see how Bowen transposes autobiography into the method responsible for her most powerful work. "Coming Home" is particularly revealing because the grieved-for parent neither dies nor disappears. But it does "ring" with the emotion of a child anticipating and fearing such an event has happened. On the day her essay is read aloud to unanimous praise, Rosalind anticipates her greatest triumph as she savors her mother's response. Anticipation, however, turns immediately to apprehension and then panic and horror as the girl discovers her mother is not at home. The trajectory of the child's experience of grief, loss, guilt, and finally anger at her mother escalates until it threatens any other perspective. Mother and child are saved, however, when Rosalind's mother reappears in the most natural way. The child's need is subordinated to a state of normalcy that validates the child's experience while granting the mother an autonomous existence beyond the child's need.

The story achieves a powerful empathy between the reader and the child by locating our own subjective experience within the child's. By withholding almost all comment, the narrative stays within the child's consciousness. Even when Rosalind's mother appears at the end, we view her from her child's perspective. Even as we may welcome her mature wisdom, we are forced back into the pain of a young girl feeling the unbridgeable abyss of a mother's distance. We are led to understand how Rosalind's fear that "Darlingest" has abandoned her turns into sweet revenge, forcing a distance between them. Yet there is little triumph for the child, since the mother not only takes separation for granted but welcomes it. The story thus celebrates a necessary pain: The distance between mother and child is the only guarantee that neither one will be swallowed up, incorporated into the other's subjectivity.

Although "Coming Home" is a very early story, Bowen has already worked out a dramatic style in which she uses her own enduring childhood emotion to understand a more universal experience. When Bowen was seven years old, her father suffered a mental breakdown; consequently, she and her mother went to live with relatives in England. The event was never explained to her, and she wrote poignantly of the terror and loss she felt. Although her father eventually recovered, by the time he was able to reconcile with his family, Bowen's mother was already ill with cancer; she died when Bowen was 13. Perhaps because mother and daughter were so close in their years alone together and because Bowen had already suffered the loss of her father, the mother's illness and death left an indelible mark on her consciousness. No doubt suspicions that something terrible was happening at the time of her father's breakdown were replayed with her mother's fatal illness. Bowen later wrote of "the tensions and mystery of my father's illness, the apprehensive silences or chaotic shoutings" that made her "tough" but also afflicted her with a lifelong stammer.[40]

The unanswered questions of her parents' illnesses informed Bowen's world view. Transported without knowing why from Ireland to the English coast, from villa to villa, she coped by asking, "Who *had* been the inhabitants, so mysteriously gone?" (*MT,* 280). These questions form the foundations of her fiction. The death or mysterious disappearance of a parent gives impetus to children's disconcerting questions about their place and personhood in the private, often-secret world of adults. Unanswered, these questions point to the unknowable core of each person's character and forevermore make the world a precarious place. In almost all Bowen's long and short fiction, adult and child characters wish for the return of absent parents as they struggle to establish intimacy and yearn for security throughout their lives. It is this struggle that defines the formation of character for Bowen. She understands it as a culturally bound, human event, and the questions she herself asked as an apprehensive child in Dublin and in England are those her child characters ask again and again.

What is so affecting in "Coming Home" is the child's acceptance of herself as separate from the mother on whom she depends to give her a sense that she is indeed alive and whole. The home itself, a physical structure, functions as an extension of the mother's body. Rosalind agonizes:

> How could she ever have left Darlingest? She might have known, she might have known. The sense of insecurity had been growing on her year by year. A person might be part of you, almost part of your body, and yet once you went away from them they might utterly cease to be. That sea of horror ebbing and flowing round the edges of the world . . . might seep out a long wave over them and they would be gone. There was no security. Safety and happiness were a game that grown-up people played with children to keep them from understanding. (97)

The push and pull of these feelings suggest a wish to retain maternal presence.[41] And yet as Rosalind pushes her mother away at the end, she expresses the need for her own subjectivity. The story maps the circular voyage of consciousness that makes this separation possible. As fear of loss gives way to anger at the mother's betrayal, the child creates a perfectly sound reason for rejecting her mother and yet having her where she wants her. Children's questions are disconcerting because they place parents in a no-win situation, always threatened by the child's insatiable demands for unconditional love. Failing to receive that which cannot be given, the child retaliates against even the best-intentioned parent. No amount of parental love is sufficient to break this cycle.

"The Visitor" and "The Return" show the child's imaginative capacities for testing parental vulnerability and the stability of the self in relation to the world outside. Roger, in "The Visitor," plays "the imagination game," wherein he protects his mother in a house with garden walls "so high" they are inviolable (126). His game cannot protect him, however, from the specter of his mother's impending death. Once again the child's perspective conveys the fear of endangering one's own life if the mother is lost. The story's elaborate symbolic design, reminiscent of Katherine Mansfield's imagism, traces Roger's rite of passage into knowledge of death and his own isolation. His primary activity when he visits the Misses Emery is to sort apples in their cozy apple room. Later, in the garden, as he gazes up into an apple tree, his fear is exposed: "I *must* know, I can't let them tell me. Oh, help me, let them not have to come and tell me! It would be as though they saw me see her being killed. Let it not have to be!" (133). Coming from a child, this statement is remarkable. It recalls the words of 11-year-old Leopold in Bowen's novel *The House in Paris*, who attaches his sense of self to the mother who abandoned him at birth: "Why am I—What made me be." [42] Bowen's empathy for children allows them to articulate the metaphysical questions underlying human potential for growth. Roger's statement declares his ambivalence about wanting his questions answered and fearing he is somehow responsible if his mother dies. It is as though the achievement of personhood includes the wish for and fear of omnipotence. The most ordinary language expresses extraordinary emotion, the force of which is validated by the sign of knowledge and experience—the apple tree. With the greatest economy, similar to Mansfield's use of the aloe plant, Bowen dramatizes the child's confrontation with the terrors of nature's cycle. In this way she shows that his pain is natural and signifies growth.

"Tears, Idle Tears," a later story, confronts a child's grief at a parent's death and the child's painful entry into individuality. Seven year-old Frederick is the same age Bowen was when her father disappeared, and her story shows the child's grief controlling him so thoroughly that he becomes "his own shameful and squalid enemy," an "outcast" (482). Frederick's grief is not new, however; his father has been dead since Frederick was two. Veering between "extreme silence" at the moment of his father's death and howling despair much later, Frederick represents an expression of loss so extreme it gives "the horrors": "[I]t is as though he saw something. You can't ask him. . . . It's as if he knew about something he'd better not" (484). Bowen presents the child's experience of parental loss as a necessary step to discovering an ongoing intersubjectivity with others.

This story's great achievement lies in the balance between Frederick's grief and his mother's taciturn response. Although at first Mrs. Dickinson appears indifferent, even callous toward her son, a mediating narrator reveals that the mother's self-control is as much a survival strategy as the child's outcries. In contrast to the stories discussed earlier, in which experience is filtered through the child's consciousness and parents are revealed only from that perspective, here Bowen introduces a narrator who presents the mother apart from the child's needs. If the narrator's casual tone mocks the mother's "courage" and "new intractable virgin pride," it does so only to highlight the insensitivity of her friends, whom she alienates with her "so few demands on pity" (484).

Once again images of nature depict how individual experience is effective only when one recognizes the value of the world outside the self. Here, the natural world intercedes between the needs of mother and son. Frederick gains his composure only after seeing "with joy" a tree, a duck, and then a girl who offers him an apple, thereby restoring his appetite for life (484). The story ends with the narrator's comment about Frederick's memory of the event years later, showing how, as grief passes, the child overcomes his deep dependence on attachment: "Frederick could still remember, with ease, pleasure and with a sense of lonely shame being gone, that calm, white duck swimming off round the bank" (487). This empathetic voice coincides with the signs of nature to distinguish the mother from child as subject and object while performing an act of reparation. The mother is portrayed as the object of her child's need, but as the subject of her own needs as well. In this way Bowen joins Katherine Mansfield in refusing to characterize women only as nurturers, always acquiescing to biological and societal imperatives beyond their control. Like Mansfield's character Linda Burnell, who may have no choice except to bear children, Bowen's mothers have yearnings unrelated to their children. Bowen's stories are remarkably powerful because their empathy extends from the child's needs to a denial that women achieve fulfillment and identity only by wishing to satisfy those needs.

Bridging the Distance

In "The Return" Bowen dramatizes the interdependence of mothers and children through a relationship between a woman and her maid. Bowen tells us that both "Mr. and Mrs. Tottenham were impossible. They were childless, humourless and dyspeptic" (29). But it is Mrs. Tottenham who faces up to her "impossibility" as she confides in her maid, Lydia. Lydia·is no mere listener. Her own unease drives her to ask intimate and irritating questions that reflect their relationship but lead to a catharsis for each woman. At the end, when Mrs. Tottenham bursts into tears, Lydia is "terrified" and feels "hard and priggish and immature," but "[t]he place was vibrant with the humanity of Mrs. Tottenham. It was as though a child had been born in the house" (34).

This last sentence does not validate the conventional association of domestic harmony with maternal happiness. If anything, it draws attention to the tensions between Lydia and the woman on whose goodwill she depends for support, for unlike those children who are dispossessed by the loss of parents, Lydia is the agent of her own becoming and of the older woman's self-revelation. As each woman discovers herself, she first sees herself in the other and then separates in order to survive. In the relationship between the miserable, self-absorbed, and childless woman and her isolated maid "The Return" reenacts the most extreme kind of separation between mother and child. The acknowledgment of this separation enables the growth of Mrs. Tottenham's humanity.

"The Game Is Up": Letting Go of Childhood

There is a group of Bowen's stories in which the drama of separation takes the form of various kinds of rebellious behavior she called "farouche." In two of them, written in the twenties, Rachel, 12 years old in "Charity" and just turned 15 in "The Jungle," storms her way through adolescence. Through her tentative girlhood friendships, Rachel distinguishes herself from her mother and older sister and hence feels a loss of identification. This primary loss is then reexperienced: It occurs first in her friendship with Charity in the story bearing her name and then again when she rejects Charity and bonds with Elise in "The Jungle." The formation of female subjectivity in relation to other women is the pivot on which Rachel's emerging self-awareness turns. In "Charity" Rachel develops a sense of herself as belonging to and yet being alienated from her family. This awareness is occasioned by her on-again, off-again feelings about her friend. Conveyed through an economy of half-spoken sentences, secret words, and intense, private fears and excitement, the intimacy and misunderstandings between the two girls compress their ambivalent feelings toward their families, needing them and yet needing to separate from them.

In "The Jungle" Rachel is at boarding school, where the girls chafe against each other's different growing pains and against the constraints of school. Discovering a wild place that is also a kind of nest where she can let herself go, Rachel learns that her sense of self requires another person. Thus, she invites Elise to join her there even though they have almost nothing in common. What they do share is the experience of needing another to face the loneliness of becoming oneself.

In both characterization and method these stories resemble Katherine Mansfield's "Prelude." Like Mansfield, Bowen uses the natural world expressionistically to convey the emotional experiences of women: Rachel "had felt a funny lurch in her imagination as she entered the Jungle, everything in it tumbled together, then shook apart again, a little altered in their relations to each other, a little changed" (231). Placed at the beginning of the story, this observation forecasts the girls' process of attachment, separation, and adjustment to the social order that will put the final stamp on their characters, for no matter how free the girls feel in their "jungle," their adolescent exercise in self-exploration and expansion will be limited by the expectation that they will develop into women suitable for the prevailing domestic life—as does Rachel's sister, Adela, the model flapper in the earlier story who becomes the model young wife in the later one. At the end of "The Jungle," when Elise falls asleep next to Rachel, their untamed bower becomes a kind of cocoon, "contracted round them, then stretched to a great deep ring of unrealness and loneliness" (241). This is no paradise regained for "the round cropped head like a boy's"; rather, it is the entryway to feeling "all constrained and queer" (241). The girls' sleep is the hibernation before awakening to civilizing domesticity.

In another story written in the twenties, "Pink Biscuit," Bowen compresses into a single incident a young woman's induction into society. Visiting a childless aunt during a school holiday, Sibella is forced to assume some household chores when the maid takes sick. Going grocery shopping for the first time, she is happy to be finally alone but also acts out a minor yet pointed rebellion against household servitude. Making her way around the grocery store, she becomes ravenous and sweeps a display biscuit into her pocket. The moment she eats it, however, she is overcome with guilt and remorse. The story ends on a comic note, with Sibella's attempt to make retribution rebuffed by the clerk who tells her the biscuits were intended as samples. What is not so funny, though, is Sibella's lesson. Spending all her money on a bag of biscuits to make up for her "theft" marks her fall from youthful innocence into what will be her real world: domestic space.

If Sibella and Rachel and her friends must eventually submit to domestic culture, they are also allowed a brief rebellious interlude immediately before doing so. In "Maria," "The Easter Egg Party," and "The Little Girl's Room," all written in the thirties, young girls rebel against constraints on their developing individuality. Read in context with the earlier stories, these comic portrayals effect a storm before the mordant calm of what we now know lies in store for Bowen's women. In all three stories the girls are left in the care of older women who serve as gatekeepers of domestic civilization. Spinster sisters in "The Easter Egg Party" and a step-grandmother in "The Little Girl's Room" resolve to educate their young charges to become exemplars of "British integrity" (426). The stories cheer on the girls' resistance to "having their character 'done,'" but their "red Revolution" reflects only a wish, for however intensely Geraldine refuses to become a "wonder-child," Hermione disobeys the rules, and Maria menaces her saviors, the gatekeepers will not be daunted (408, 434, 426).

In these stories mothers are either dead or absent, a narrative strategy that heightens the lethal effects of the older women and the loss of unconditional acceptance and nurture. Having internalized their civilization's imperatives to be its moral guardians, the earlier generation of women becomes its crusaders. It is in the dramatic contrast between the oldest and the youngest generation of women that "The Little Girl's Room" illustrates the potency of maternal absence. With no maternal support, relying only on her natural limitations and defensive strategies, Geraldine finds a way to protect herself from the lessons of art and civilization built into her step-grandmother's Italianate estate. But passive aggression toward her tutors turns to more imaginative rebellion in the privacy of her room. Amid Botticelli wildflowers and Carpaccio saints, assuming "the mood of a d'Este princess," Geraldine conjures up and defies her enemies (430).

The story ends, however, not with Geraldine's triumph over her

step-grandmother's deadly good intentions but with the girl's integration with society. Showing that Geraldine's conjuring is both necessary
and imaginary, Bowen introduces the specter of the girl's mother as a
mediating force. With an attitude "less interested, more indifferent
than the rest, and w [ear] ing her old ironical smile," Geraldine's
mother tells her, "It's all up" (431). Although the mother's ability to
teach is far more potent than the artifacts of high culture and Renais-
sance civilization, the lesson is the same. Both mother and daughter
are lost to the process that absorbs women into culture. "But what can
one do?" Geraldine's mother asks, resigned to losing the battle against
turning Geraldine "into a horrible little Verrocchio over a fountain!"
(432, 426). If the mother dies from an overdose of high culture, the
daughter will be absorbed into it with the help of a survivor. Reigning
over "her dignified exile," Mrs. Letherton-Channing transforms her
imperial palazzo into a hothouse in which her granddaughter develops
into its most treasured artifact (426).

Like Geraldine, Maria is motherless and sent to a civilizing household in which the target of her pent-up energy and rage is a fussy curate
resembling Geraldine's besieged tutor. And like Geraldine, Maria suffers a short-lived and illusory triumph, for although she engineers a
plot that removes her from "the cheerful and homelike" rectory, we
know Maria's fate will be a version of Geraldine's (409). In this story
there is no maternal voice to prepare the girl for entry into civilization;
there is only the model of womanhood represented by her aristocratic
and self-protective aunt, Lady Rimlade. The narrator's tone, however,
is similar to that of Geraldine's mother in conveying the sense that
although the girl's rebellion should be enjoyed for all it's worth, essentially "the game is up."[43]

The most complex story in this group, "The Apple Tree," is also
one of Bowen's masterpieces. In a different perspective on emerging
womanhood Bowen transforms "an innocent pastoral image" until it is
"seen black through a dark transparency" (465). The apple tree here
signifies the painful course of girlhood, representing a strange and
deadly conspiracy between two conflicting ideas about Myra Wing's
character: (a) the knowledge of her guilt, which has stilted her development, and (b) her fear that she is innocent and should accept adulthood. The story hinges on the stifling omnipresence of an incident in
Myra's girlhood. The memory of a friend's suicide by hanging herself
from an apple tree is transmogrified into the spectral appearance of the
apple tree everywhere Myra goes. The tree materializes in such a way

that it prevents anyone from getting close to her and, in so doing, threatens to envelop her in its branches and suffocate her.

Although recently married, Myra is described by the narrator as "this mannerless, sexless child, the dim something between a mouse and an Undine, this wraith not considerable as a mother of sons, this cold little shadow across a hearth" (463). Such figuration reveals a female character stuck in the cocoon in which Rachel and Elise hibernate on their way to womanhood. Like these younger girls and like Sibella, Myra is motherless. Although this fact might not be so relevant to a married woman, that Myra is only 19 and that the incident on which her story pivots took place when was 12 draw attention to the arrested development of a motherless child.

Like "The Jungle" and "Charity," this story turns on a schoolgirl friendship. Presented as a kind of doppelgänger, Doria is totally dependent on Myra's friendship; however, their intimacy is destroyed by Myra's revulsion at those very qualities which make them alike, for Doria not only is an orphan but, like Myra, is "ugly, always in trouble," and ashamed of her unhappiness (468). Isolated because of Myra's rejection, Doria hangs herself. Yet she remains a part of her only friend in an even more urgent form: Her presence is contained in the ghostly apple tree, signifying the knowledge Myra has repressed. What has drawn Myra and Doria together is also what forms Myra's character: the fact that their friendship replays the pain of parental absence, the "disease" of insurmountable grief that so afflicts Frederick in "Tears, Idle Tears" (468). Within the girls' feelings of ugliness lies the tension between yearning for the wholeness of family intimacy and needing to separate in order to become oneself. Without maternal love and recognition and paternal power and security, the world is experienced as unbearable. Together, however, Myra and Doria form a bond that only replicates the emptiness between them, thereby dredging up the fear of a suffocating dependency. No wonder then, that these two are "always in trouble" at the school whose "very high wall" protects them from becoming themselves (468). Unable to live with or without each other, they remain children, one in death and the other in life.

The yearning for family and the acceptance of adult sexual identity are resolved in three ways, each dependent on the other. Myra analyzes what her husband means to her: "I thought he'd save me. . . . I felt so safe with him" (467). Confirming that Simon is more parent than husband, the narrator calls Myra "the child" (467). A "great ruddy man," Simon cannot be Myra's husband until the fantasy of the tree of repressed knowledge is purged (461). It takes a maternal figure, acting in collusion with the narrator's assessment of the problem, to exorcise childhood guilt and grief and restore Myra to growth. Mrs. Bettersley, an older friend of Simon's, saves the day by winning Myra's confidence and taking her away. We are not told what happens when they are together, but the narrator ends the tale with confidence in this fairy godmother's gifts: The couple "disappeared into happiness: a sublime nonentity" (470).

In exorcising the apple tree, Mrs. Bettersley saves Myra's life by transporting her from one romance to another, removing her from the childhood romance that grew suffocating as it lingered into adulthood. Myra's character is threatened by her expectation that marriage will keep her a child yet save her from her childhood. In her marriage, then, she is as passive as she was as a schoolgirl. "Excused" from social and community functions, her character seems "withheld" (462–63). Whether she is reclining in bed or sleepwalking, no matter how hard "she trie [s] . . . to obliterate herself," she represents a negative power that threatens the life of her husband's home and community (467). Refusing to relinquish her childhood trauma for married love, she weakens her husband and withholds the generative power of fertility. Unlike Sleeping Beauty, who is rescued by her prince, Myra in this romance must be rescued by her godmother in order to rescue, in turn, her prince and the world they will inhabit together.

The dramatic consequences of this three-way romance complicate the suffocating domestic arrangements in other Bowen stories. At one level, the fantasy driven by ambivalence is resolved in "The Apple Tree" by more realistic conventions; accepting marriage as a vocation follows only too well in the fictive trajectory from Jane Austen onward. But as with Cicely in the twin stories "The New House" and "The Lover," Bowen embeds an ominous note in Myra's happy ending: Having "disappeared into happiness: a sublime nonentity," Myra recalls Cicely becoming "another man's possession," for if Myra grows into marital happiness at the end, her story also marks that happiness as an end to women's resistance to the romance of happy endings.[44] Myra's pathway to womanhood through the good offices of a godmother does, however, release her from her fantasies of yearning and dread to become a power in her own right. That Myra must rescue Simon and his world marks her a female hero, her own subject and object.[45] The stories in this particular group can thus be read as being about women's growth and the ambiguous attainment of their own desires.

Three uncollected stories set at Christmastime show women torn between childhood fantasies and the temptations of a myth of domestic harmony. In "Happiness" and "Candles in the Window" young women are nurtured by family life to face the satisfactions and disappointments of courtship. In "Comfort and Joy" two adolescent girls comfort a soldier who receives a letter from his fiancée breaking their engagement.

How the tightrope between childhood freedom and domestic order is maneuvered forms the outcome of "So Much Depends," an uncollected story written in 1951. Here older women play the role of cautionary godmothers to a young woman in hot pursuit of romance. Seventeen-year-old Ellen spends a rainy week in a guest house, pining for a young man at a hotel nearby. Although alone, she is watched over by Miss Kerry and the widowed Mrs. Ordeyne, who figure as guardians and models for Ellen's entry into womanhood. Despite her decision to renounce love, Miss Kerry yields finally to a man whose idea of love is "teaching each other good sense."[46] Ellen, by contrast, following her beloved's devastating announcement that he is engaged to someone else, realizes the joy "to be not in love" ("Depends," 161).

Like Geraldine's mother in "The Little Girl's Room," Miss Kerry teaches by example that "the game is up." Her failed escape from a domesticating courtship plot represents the ominous end to Ellen's feeling at the end of being "queen and ruler" over her own story ("Depends," 161). Read together, these two stories form a conversation in which girls and women empathize, instruct, and warn each other of their fates in the marriage plots that will define their adult lives. As with all Bowen's work, these stories question domestic ideologies and their relation to the literary formation of character. The writer does not, however, imagine alternatives but instead recognizes that the idea of an "Eden where fact and fiction were the same" must be given up.[47]

Bowen's stories show reality as being less constricting than the self-absorbed childhood fantasies that threaten to incorporate the objective world in their wish to satisfy insatiable needs. The stories in this group are both accepting and resistant. Even where the narrative structure applauds childhood rebellion, it also prepares the way for initiation into the complex, ambivalent relationships of adult life. In other stories Bowen explores the varying consequences of this necessary entry into social reality and the strategies by which her characters negotiate their places in worlds they did not create but in which they are captive.

Comedies of Sex and Terror

In a number of stories written over the course of Bowen's career, plots about domestic life are transformed and comedies of sex and manners give way to comedies of sex and terror. The lid bursts off the social traditions that limit or deny her characters' self-expression; rage against betrayed expectations explodes in murder or stifling domination. Never completely expiated, however, the rage against betraying lovers, parents, children, the weaknesses of oneself, or the unpredictability of fate persists, endlessly playing itself out. Like a ballad whose refrain repeatedly encircles only the smallest variations of its theme, these stories lament the violence that propels them while recognizing its inevitability.

Rage in these stories materializes in myriad forms. It is transmogrified into the ghosts and haunted houses of "The Demon Lover," "Green Holly," "The Cat Jumps," "The Claimant," and "Pink May." It is also embodied by damaged people—each of whom mirrors the frustrations of the strong—in "The Girl with the Stoop," "Look at All Those Roses," and "Dead Mabelle." And those who see themselves as scapegoats wreak their revenge in "Making Arrangements," "Telling," "Mrs. Moysey," and "Hand in Glove."

The stories are terrifying because the characters' extreme feelings are expressed in terms that violate our protective conventions; these characters force us to feel their unresolved conflicts as uncannily familiar. In the tradition of Saki's stories, these tales are comic as well as horrific. Ghostly repressed fears mock the haunted, reminders that terror begins in the self with unacknowledged guilt. Whoever is frightened out of his or her wits is thus a deserving target, and Bowen's gleeful narrators are clearly a raucous contrast to the more decorous style of those who recount stories in which characters struggle to maintain their hold on the rational. Perhaps more than any of her other stories, the comedies of sex and terror typify Bowen's definition of the short story as "allow[ing] for what is crazy about humanity: obstinacies, inordinate heroisms, 'immortal longings'" (*MT,* 130).

Battles of the Sexes

Several of the stories in this group show men and women locked together, despite separation or death. In "Just Imagine" two child cousins, Noel and Nancy, conjure up scenarios that produce "a perpetual case of shivers."[48] As it turns out, their spine-tingling game prepares Nancy and Noel for the emotional setbacks of adult life. The delicious terrors of their childhood fantasies compress the splits between their future pleasure and pain.

Moreover, their childhood experience forges a bond that reflects the cousins' ambivalent desires and fears: "[T]he more her terror reflected back on himself and was split into rays against the facets of his personality, the sharper his pleasure became" (82). Separated as adolescents, they meet again only years later, when Nancy returns to London with her Argentine husband and Noel is engaged to marry. Restless and unhappy, Nancy invites Noel to her flat and seduces him into playing their game once again. Layers of smart-set sophistication and repartee unravel to expose the way "the night fears of childhood" have escalated into a paralyzing terror of their own passions (89). Combining farce, satire, and horror, Bowen ends the cousins' game by turning on the lights to reveal Nancy's husband looming over them. As he faces them down with all his love, jealousy, rage, and despair, he is monstrous to them because he represents their own unrestrained emotion. The real horror lies in the metamorphosis of the cousins' repression: "[Noel] thought of the nursery fire for ever put out, and of how one went on through the world growing colder and colder" (85).

During World War II, Bowen saw repression as a necessary response to the terror of everyday life when "[t]he outsize World War news was stupefying" (*MT,* 96). In "Green Holly" the tensions felt by those on the sidelines of world war are represented in a sexual battle. The contrast between quotidian events and the feelings of mounting hysteria and fear captures the feeling of both terror and repression. Compressing the tedium and anxiety of wartime into a farce of sexual terror, Bowen depicts a haunted country house in which men and women of the British army carry on their private and public wars in the guise of "doing something frightfully hush-hush" (719). Isolated by their war work, "their reappearances in their former circles were infrequent, ghostly and unsuccessful" (719). It is no wonder, then, that when this "skeleton staff" meet the ghosts of Mopsam Grange, they face mirror images of themselves (719).

The isolation of the group is matched by the acute loneliness of the ghost of a femme fatale. The time is Christmas Eve, and the group's feeble efforts to simulate glad tidings are interrupted by the appearance of this ghost, who is fated to repeat yearly her role in the suicide of the man who loved and felt betrayed by her. Just as she is compelled to betray, so must she fall in love, and in so doing she parodies the condition of the women on the team. From an inertia born more of isolation than of passion, these "intelligence" women have been involved with two of their male colleagues, one of whom, Mr. Winterslow, the ghost targets as her own prey.

The ghost's interest in the aptly named, unromantic Mr. Winterslow marks the story's primary concerns with the existential malaise submerged in romantic comedy and melodrama. Her attitude of "tender impartiality and mockery" parodies romance but also reveals the comic side of ghost stories (724). Ghostly presence here highlights the feeling of deadness produced by repressing intense feeling as a protection against the fear that war will end all existence, for between the ghost's "[f]lamboyance and agitation" lies "an extreme anxiety: it was not merely a matter of, how was she? but of, *was* she—tonight—at all? Death had left her to be her own mirror; for into no other was she able to see" (723). Before death, the nameless ghost sees herself only as a reflection of the men who love her; after death, she re-creates that love in order to exist at all. If romance wards off the terrors of war, it also reminds Bowen's women that wartime legitimates the peacetime conditions in which they struggle for a basic sense of being.

In playing out their own romantic comedy, Miss Bates and Carla mirror the ghost. However significant their war work, the threat of annihilation and the ambiguity of their intelligence work leave them in limbo. The ghost thus signifies the terrifying possibility that they, too, may not exist. The emotional tenor of this terror is irritation, a feeling of the self chafing against anyone handy because the response at least proves one's presence. Thus, Miss Bates, Mr. Rankstock, and Mr. Winterslow pick on one another with sarcasm and "cross-examination," the energy for which both validates and vindicates the self (722). But it is Miss Bates's frenetic and circular movements, "like something in a cage," and the boils erupting on Carla's skin that betray the rage disguised in the petty outbursts (721), for like the ghost's endless seductions and betrayals, these are signs only of frustration.

There are simply no viable outlets for the energies of women in this story. The ghostly woman and the living ones are doomed to fade away, each reflecting the others' fruitless passions. Moreover, the self-eliminating pattern of their characters is matched by that of the men. Like the corpse of the dead lover on the stairs, Mr. Winterslow and Mr. Rankstock are inert, moved neither by the women's passions nor by war. Unlike the women, however, the men willingly "fade . . . under this fog-dark but glass-clear veil of hallucination" (725).

The most powerful words spoken in the story are those of Miss Bates, as she strikes out against the inertia of dead men. Reading an alternative tale into the character of the corpse, Miss Bates creates an "enchanting inverse": "'From his attitude, it was clear he had died for love. . . . [T]he hand that had dropped the pistol had dropped a white rose; it lay beside him brown and crushed from having been often kissed. The ideality of those kisses, for the last of which I arrived too late'—here Miss Bates beat her fist against the bow of her snood—'will haunt, and and by haunting satisfy me'" (726). Life cannot imitate art, and the invention of this romantic fantasy is only momentarily satisfying. Whatever emotional truths are contained in the ghostly lovers' melodrama are only partly translatable: The ironic urge of the living characters speaks of their need to keep their feelings submerged. The diminished emotional and material experience of the war, visible in the holly without berries, exposes the problem of validating one's sense of self at any time. The ghosts are terrifying because they remind Bowen's characters that, in wartime, the horrific is the prosaic and reflects the constancy of horrible emptiness.

In several stories sexual revenge fills the void left by repressed emotion. In "Making Arrangements," "The Cat Jumps," "Dead Mabelle," "Telling," and "The Demon Lover" men avenge their betrayed expectations with "a very wild kind of justice" on women who will not play their assigned roles (177). Written in the twenties, "Making Arrangements" reveals the connections between literary and social traditions and shows how stories of sexual betrayal validate social codes that entrap women in men's failed dreams. These codes hold women responsible for betraying the privilege of "being cognate parts of a [man's] whole," a privilege that "should justif[y a woman's] existence to her" (174).

When Margery Blair writes to her husband, Hewson, for the dual purpose of getting a divorce and her clothes, she betrays her one role in his life: that she "was becoming to him," that is, a reflection of his efficient, methodical, and self-congratulatory "finality of completeness" (173). That she "never quite knew what [he] wanted [her] for" is insignificant against the evidence that he buries his passion in decorum. Rage unhinges Hewson's stiff upper lip when he realizes Margery will no longer be his prestige ornament. As her clothes lie on her bed, "shudder [ing] as he came," Hewson tears them up in an orgiastic frenzy, symbolically raping and murdering the woman who satisfied him only as long as he felt no passion.

Margery's clothes represent her socially constructed identity as well as her escape from it. As Hewson takes the clothes quite literally to stand for the identity and purpose he provides her with, he misreads his wife in much the same way Ford Madox Ford's "Good Soldier" does all the women in his life. Though Bowen's good husband finally expresses the destructive passion buried in his largesse, he is as enfeebled by the effort as Ford's unreliable narrator. The sequence of attenuated events—from which Margery remains conspicuously absent—highlights her clothes as a disguise that protected her on the escape route to self-discovery: "These were all his, his like the room and the house. Without these dresses the inner Margery, unfostered, would never have become perceptible to the world. She would have been like a page of music written never to be played. All her delightfulness to her friends had been in this expansion of herself into forms and colours. Hewson had fostered this expansion" (177).

Margery is like a "chameleon," "shadowing behind all her changes an immutable, untouched, and careless self" (175). Like so many women in Bowen's stories, she is a mystery, basically unreadable because she is forced by social and economic necessity to conform to codes of identity that have little to do with the self she could discover outside her marriage. The gap between these codes and Margery's sense of herself is clarified in the contrast between her "sentient" silks and "sullen" velvets and furs and Hewson's paralyzed feeling (178). Hewson's destruction of the clothes is supposed to protect him from knowing her, but as he becomes entangled in their "quivering" sensuality, he is exposed as a prisoner of the very passion his codes of decorum are designed to deny (178).

Hewson's murderous eruption is ultimately more comic than terrible. The image of him "ankle-deep" in his estranged wife's torn clothes as "something black and snake-like . . . wound round his feet and nearly entangled him" makes him the comic butt of his own terror (178), for Margery's anthropomorphized wardrobe is the worthier adversary, performing like a seasoned ghost. The female sexuality Hewson thought he saved himself from comes back to haunt him after his futile efforts to exorcise it backfire, revealing that the "civilized man" is impotent (177).

"Dead Mabelle," written in the same period as "Making Arrangements," also explores the threat of female sexuality to the "arrangements" of man's civilization. Through a shift in social class, Bowen shows how the male will to dominate is a function of a world in which a man's work betrays his insignificance. William Stickford is a bank clerk, "intelligent, solitary, self-educated, self-suspicious," and sexually repressed, all of which qualities are expressed in his tedious and claustrophobic bank work (277). His only outlet becomes an obsession with the films of Mabelle Pacey. The story tracks the emergence of his eroticism as a sexual will to dominate the woman who inspires his transformation. Because Mabelle is a movie star, however, she exists only as an image for William. When the news breaks of her murder, her image haunts him, encouraging both his sadistic fantasies and the pleasures of being tortured by the dangerous sexuality of a cinematic ghost.

The story's tension builds from the convergence of two events that create an eerie sense of causality: (a) Mabelle's murder immediately after finishing her most seductive film and (b) the focus on William's increasingly violent response to her images. Technically, Bowen creates this tension in the way she sequences Mabelle's murder in relation to William's mounting infatuation. As a result, the ingenue's death appears as both cause and effect of William's violently repressed eroticism. The first sentence of the story announces Mabelle's "horrible end" as well as a "sense of foreknowledge" (276). This sense of violent inevitability conflates the public's frenzied response to her last and most provocative film and William's sexual arousal as he sees an earlier but typical Mabelle vehicle. The rest of the story then charts William's growing obsession with and appropriation of Mabelle's image. In a world in which William has little power, he can use his male gaze to construct a figure whose reflection of his desire makes him feel powerful.

The "delighted horror, horrified delight" inspired by Mabelle's films result from the power of male sexual fantasy to generate and sustain a culture's icons (276). Aroused by each image projected in the darkened theater's shafts of light, William is no passive observer. He creates his own scenarios in which the "abstract" celluloid images of "passion and purity, courage, deception and lust . . . rebounded to his perception" (278, 282). But the irony of this male-generated popular culture is that William is never fully in control of his creation. At the end, when it would seem Mabelle exists only in silver nitrate, and then only as long as her films are profitable, his image of her becomes overpowering: "You might destroy the film, destroy the screen, destroy her body," but "[s]he was there, left, right, everywhere, printed on darkness" (283–84).

For Bowen, culture and psychology are jointly responsible for the violent impasse between men and women. Neither Mabelle nor Margery is an autonomous creature who threatens men with her actual behavior. Rather, these women exist as projections of male desire and dread, the effect of a culture's sexual ideology on male and female consciousness. Because of the power invested in them by anxious men, women become terrifying creatures, overwhelming their creators with an ironic and therefore comic vengeance. "The Cat Jumps" shows how one woman is victimized by male fear and how another makes such fear her own. Bowen wrote "The Cat Jumps" in the thirties, along with many other stories told from a female point of view. In one sense it is a classic Gothic tale of horror, about a house that haunts its present occupants with its history of Mr. Bentley, a previous owner who murdered his wife. The story is also richly comic, however, in its satire of sophisticated people who pride themselves on their reasoned responses to the irrational but are then overcome by their own inexplicable fears. Like "Dead Mabelle," this story depends on the convergence of public and private fantasies and shows them to have their source in sexual wars.

As a haunted house, Rose Hill is a media event, the creation of newspaper headlines that work like silent-film titles to simplify and highlight an ambiguous story. Unlike William Stickford, however, stuck in his place, or Hewson Blair, ossified in his, the Harold Wrights are upwardly mobile, educated, sociable, and self-satisfied. None of this, however, saves them from the fates that befall William and Harold, for their "bright, shadowless, thoroughly disinfected minds" turn on them, exposing powerful hidden fears (362).

As in "Green Holly," an emptiness provides the horror that grips the house party at Rose Hill. And as is true of Mopsam Grange, the void at Rose Hill is filled by ghosts who haunt the occupants with sensations of sexual violence from the past.[49] Thus both terror and comedy derive from empty lives being filled up with a passion so boundless that it seems to live on beyond the death of its original victims. The violence of this passion, moreover, equals the efforts of the house party's members to protect themselves from it in their obsession with "unprejudiced," uninhibited disbelief (362). Passion in this story, however, is not rapturous desire for another person; rather, it is rage and revenge at the other, whose own passions are experienced as threatening to life itself. At first concealed by heated but intellectualized talk, this rage cannot remain closeted. It emerges, as in "Dead Mabelle," as uncontrollable and omnipresent, reminding Rose Hill's inhabitants of their own primal needs and conflicts.

Despite frenetic activity, from tennis to "frank discussions," despite a disinfected and whitewashed exterior and interior, the past infiltrates Rose Hill. At first it is felt through intermittent smells of stale cigarettes and sultry perfumes; then people are startled by one another's movements or erupt in unaccountable fury while one casual acquaintance reads another's manner as "cruel" and, finally, as murderous in intent (365). Each response is infused with what Bowen calls "sex-antagonism" and points to a "dark interiority," the characters' conflicted desires and fears, which cannot be explained away by their references to "Krafft-Ebing, Freud, Forel, Weingiger and the heterosexual volume of Havelock Ellis" (365–66).

The house party at Rose Hill ultimately succumbs to private but collectively formed terrors. As the tale of murder is narrated intermittently, in bits and pieces, it mirrors Mr. Bentley's drawn-out dismemberment of his wife's body. And so the tale of horror teases its listeners like a slow-working intoxicant. Its result is like the climax to a seduction in which fear, replacing passion, reaches new heights of frenzy and release. The women lock themselves in their bedrooms for protection against the specter of Mr. Bentley, whose persona they now perceive in every man's behavior, from Edward Carteret's talk of cutting up a cat to Harold Wright's "vague movements" (369). But rather than attributing this fear to some kind of folly on the part of her pretentious and smug characters, Bowen in her narrative voice withholds irony, suggesting that her characters' experience reflects a kind of psychological reality to which she invites us to respond empathetically.

Just before the end of the tale, when Jocelyn Wright hysterically envisions her husband breaking through her locked door with murderous rage, Bowen shifts from satirizing the characters' fears to validating them: "The door opened on Harold, looking more dreadfully at her than she had imagined. . . . Therein he had assumed the entire burden of Harold Bentley. Forces he did not know of assembling darkly, he had faced for untold ages the imperturbable door to his wife's room. She would be there, densely, smotheringly there. She lay like a great cat, always, over the mouth of his life" (369). This passage confirms the "sex-antagonism" of Bowen's women and men and shows it to consist of fears no rational explanation can allay. As Harold Wright becomes the alter identity of Harold Bentley, we are encouraged to generalize about man's "darkly assembled forces" (369). For in one man as in the other, murderous actions are the logical consequence of a rage resulting from the death threat of women's suffocating sexuality.

This story gives a different perspective to the comic images of a man's entrapment in a woman's sexuality in "Making Arrangements" and provides a social context to the mythological overtones of horror stories. In an image remarkably similar to that in the earlier story, a woman's clothing signifies her sensuality. Retreating to her bedroom, "Jocelyn dropped her wrap to the floor, then watched how its feathered edges crept a little" (368). The difference is equally telling, for the woman's clothing is dangerous to her sense of herself. In its opulence, the sensuous wrap represents a social construction of sexuality that does not originate in the woman's self-definition but does link her to other women. Like Margery's lamialike clothing, Jocelyn's reveals the price of her privileged life. As paid for by her husband, Margery's elegant clothes represent a snakelike stranglehold on her—her indebtedness to her husband's generosity. But as Hewson's abuse of his wife's wardrobe shows, there are greater expectations attached to this sign of a man's power than mere ornamentation. A husband, as Hewson's failed expectations reveal, is entitled to have his wife satisfy his every desire, even when that means satisfying his lack of desire. When she fails, he exacts payment, making her seem no more or less important than the objects that represent her to him. His retribution, in turn, makes him important and powerful to himself as he reclaims the objects to do with them what he will.

What is ultimately so horrible for Jocelyn is that the uncanny resemblances between past and present show her to be an object of a man's creation. Like Mabelle, she is an image produced and threatened by a male fantasy that conflates her economic and sexual value to him. "The Cat Jumps" achieves this economy in an image that connects it to both "Dead Mabelle" and "Making Arrangements." As the tale of the Bentleys is spun out, we discover that "'[h] e put her heart in her hat-box. He said it belonged in there'" (367). Harold Bentley's motives are not given, but as his action literalizes Hewson's plan to pack up Margery's wardrobe, it transforms a woman's "heart" from a romantic image into a symbol of social and economic reality, and a woman into an object. Ironically, a woman's heart is a romantic image so long as it is domesticated by economic dependence on her beneficent spouse and is subject to his disposal. The problem is that Margery, Jocelyn, and Mrs. Bentley cannot be emblems of their husbands' economic success without becoming "heartless"; turned into objects, they cannot feel. But without feeling, women's sexuality becomes even more threatening, making its demands and power felt even in those very objects which represent their dehumanization.

When a woman defies her mythic sexuality with different kinds of needs, she must suffer poetic justice—her "heart" is cut out and interred in an appropriate coffin. Like a safety deposit box, Mrs. Bentley's hat-box secures her value as a nontransferable commodity while ensuring that her husband is secure from the threat of her being lost or stolen or, worse, being alive to "be there, densely, smotheringly there" (369).

A man's rage against his own impotence and women's elusiveness is dramatized in the character of Terry in "Telling." Terry is inadequate, a man whose "hands wouldn't serve him, things he wanted them to hold slipped away from them" (326). Spurned by a woman, he is driven to murder her, an act proving only that he, like William Stickford, cannot have the woman of his fantasies. But Terry is also like Hewson Blair, for brutalizing a woman shows only his lack of passion and fear of it. The joke here is thus in exposing the impotence of a misogynist, for at the end of the story, when Terry is about to prove his manliness to his father by showing him the knife he used to kill Josephine, he discovers that, like his manhood, this all-too-easily-recognizable phallic symbol is lost.

Terry's impotence, like William Stickford's, has a distinct social context. His inexpressiveness, the inability to tell his tale, is an affliction Bowen usually reserves for female or child characters who suffer the losses of family and home. Terry's family does ignore him, and his running after them to proclaim his triumph shows that neither his failures nor his act of retribution is welcome in this bastion of upper-middle-class decorum. In this sense Terry is not a repugnant fiend like Harold Bentley. Indeed, the narrator generates sympathy by presenting his point of view for him, serving as adoptive and supportive parent to the child who, because he is not welcome in his own world, cannot represent himself.

The joke, then, is not just on Terry but on the staid world that rejects and drives him to murderous rage. Like Portia in Bowen's novel

The Death of the Heart, the awkward child explodes decorum by demanding unconditional acceptance from those who prefer to modify everyone's emotional needs to fit drawing-room manners. What saves Portia is the diary that gives vent to her needs while exposing the inadequacies of the adult world. Without any narrative skills to transform his demands into creative and critical self-expression, Terry finds that the only outlet for his rage is violence. As a result, he orchestrates grim plots for those who exclude him from theirs, for as he imagines, once the murder becomes known, his brother Charles won't be able to return to school and his sister Catherine will never marry. If Terry cries "Nothing, nothing, nothing" at the end, when his father asks him what he is trying to tell, he need no longer rely on telling his tale, for he has brought down the world that made him what he is.

Vengeance of the Lost Soldier

In "The Demon Lover," justifiably one of Bowen's most famous and widely anthologized stories, a soldier avenges the grim fates of war. Written during World War II, the story embeds the psychological horrors produced by a Blitzed city in a plot about "sex-antagonism," but, in a rare move for Bowen, the haunting presence is a man. The result shows how rage transcends time and space. This man cannot simply murder his lover and be done with it; he instead carries her off in a way that suggests her terror will last forever. Strictly speaking, there is no comedy in this tale, but its extreme terror invites laughter that both expresses shock and is its antidote.

The subject of "The Demon Lover" is a woman returning to her house during the Blitz to retrieve some possessions. The empty house is now haunted, however, by the presence of a mysterious letter from her fiancé, who perished in World War I. Alarmed, she runs out of the house and takes a waiting taxi, only to discover that the driver is the ghost of her fiancé. The story ends with Mrs. Drover screaming endlessly as the taxi "made off with her into the hinterland of deserted streets" (666).

The story is quite short, only six pages, and part of its terror derives from the compression of its events and effects. The narrative line follows Mrs. Drover's attempts to explain the letter, whose mysterious appearance is like an emotional bridge between the two world wars.[50] Spanning the period of the stories discussed in this group, the letter thus also works as a puzzle containing the secret explanation of the rage each of the men in these stories expresses toward women. For this reason, it is useful to quote the letter in full:

> Dear Kathleen: You will not have forgotten that today is our anni versary, and the day we said. The years have gone by at once slowly and fast. In view of the fact that nothing has changed, I shall rely upon you to keep your promise. I was sorry to see you leave London, but was satisfied that you would be back in time. You may expect me, therefore, at the hour arranged. Until then . . . K. (662)

The letter binds Kathleen Drover to a promise she has no way of fulfilling. "Presumed killed" in action for 25 years, her fiancé nevertheless expects her to drop whatever she has made of her life to fulfill his need to see her (664). The letter assumes betrayal because it allows for no other reality than his. Despite its polite language, his right of retribution is contained in his expectation that she be there regardless of her needs. And indeed, his appearance in a form symbolizing the infinite depths of his rage creates the story's terror. Kathleen Drover's everlasting terror is more clearly predetermined than the fates of Mrs. Bentley and Mabelle, for it is clear that she would always be compelled to build her life around her promise to him to "need [to] do nothing but wait" (663). Ultimately, Mrs. Drover is driven by a male fantasy of her total devotion and by the rage that presumes she is doomed to fail. What is therefore so terrible is the sense of a setup—that she is damned to a lonely hell if she waits for her fiancé and doomed to be with him if she does not.

In her efforts to recapitulate the events leading up to the letter, Kathleen Drover reveals that the intervening years have indeed belonged to her fiancé. Her recollection of the moment he departed for the war front shows no chance for her to agree with or dissent from his expectation that she will wait. Her one attempt to clarify his demand is only a series of tentative phrases: "But that was—suppose you—I mean, suppose" (663). Because Kathleen has no ability to assert herself, "that unnatural promise" makes its primacy felt and defines her character (663). Thus she experiences "complete dislocation" from sexual love, and after she does finally marry, her life is marked not by the joys of family life but by illness and an expression of "controlled worry," a tic that also signifies "assent" (662). Given this profile, it is clear that Kathleen's fiancé had nothing to worry about, no need to doubt her bondage to him. What, then, is his terrible retribution about?

Kathleen's capture by her fiancé at the story's end merely activates what is implicit in his character from the beginning. Kathleen recalls that at their last meeting she "had not ever completely seen his face," that she "imagined spectral glitters in the place of his eyes" (663). Already a ghost, the soldier is also cruel, even at this intimate moment: He presses her hand to his chest but does so "painfully," so that "[t]hat cut of the button on the palm of her hand was, principally what she was to carry away" (663). If her character shows the indelible mark of his domination, he remains unknowable except through his demands on her; he is a mysterious, omniscient instrument of fate who even when he comes back to haunt her cannot be described, despite there being "not six inches between them" and doomed to spend "an eternity eye to eye" (666).

The horror to which Mrs. Drover and readers respond is the recognition of an unknowable and therefore unmanageable oppressor. But he is neither godlike nor even heroic. Although assigned to protect his nation from invading evil, this soldier is himself an evil power. Suffering the ravages of one world war, he reappears in the next as an angel of death avenging his own suffering. The spectral soldier is thus not a self-made evil but the product of historical forces. His unverifiable death becomes a metaphor for the world wars that are certain only in their havoc but whose losses can never be fully tabulated and whose causes can never be entirely explained or understood. Because World War I was left unresolved, its casualties untold and its beginnings confused, it becomes a terrifying ghost in this World War II story. Neither Mrs. Drover's reconstruction of the past nor her ghostly fiancé's interpretation of it is a viable epistemological tool. If World War I was the war to end all wars, Bowen re-creates it as extracting a terrible promise, a promise the war's incomprehensibility makes it impossible for its survivors to fulfill.

This ghost is not terrorizing the woman because she fails to fill the emptiness in his life. Terrorized himself by historical forces he cannot redirect, much less understand, he imposes a promise on his fiancée that will provide the one stabilizing element in his life and death. But this victim of history is also one who helped create and perpetuate it. As a man, he is empowered by historical precedent to govern; if his efforts end in war, failure turns to rage. Thus the soldier carries off his woman to share the terrors of history. Just as the past invades the present, his consciousness overtakes hers. This process is so complete that, as the "K" of his signature shows, Kathleen is haunted by becoming his reflection. Like his hidden face at their earlier parting, the letter represents him only as she responds to it. Like her memories, the letter is a ghostly artifact, a sign that as a survivor of two wars she has internalized their terrors and guilt. Accordingly, she is terrorized at the end by being the passive victim of a ghastly history.

In the postwar period Bowen could look back with a more cynical view of these horrors and the vengeance they breed. In "The Claimant" the female narrator survives an allegorical fight to the finish between two men over the house they both claim, but she is victimized by their rage. The narrator's tone is weary as she assesses a battle that kills the combatants, one already a ghost and the other an old man. Their war leaves her in dire straits, having to sell the land over which they fought. Thus the sense of a stable, knowing, and knowable self is lost in the battles over proprietorship and propriety.

The Decorous Rage of Women

In "The Cheery Soul," "Reduced," and "Hand in Glove" decorum is threatened by inscrutable women who reflect its hidden violence. "The Cheery Soul," a World War II story, subjects the vulnerable figure of the soldier to a woman's revenge. This soldier is unlike the demon lover, who conceals his character behind a text that reshapes history by controlling a woman's life. Instead, the soldier in "The Cheery Soul" writes his own story, a first-person narrative that ironically reveals no understanding or control of what is happening to him. Because his need for succor manipulates him into believing it, he is completely taken in by a story without an identifiable author. Like "Green Holly," this story is set at Christmas, a time when the dislocations of war intensify a need for human connectedness, a sense of belonging. Thus the narrator responds eagerly to a "word of mouth" invitation to spend Christmas at the home of the Rangerton-Karneys (643). Instead of holiday cheer, however, he finds the house empty except for a refugee aunt and a piece of paper in the kitchen on which is written a mystifying message: "I AM NOT HERE. To this was added, in brackets: 'Look in the fish kettle'" (645).

These ghosts are terrible because they never present themselves; they leave clues to the possibility of violence but no material evidence of it. What terrifies the soldier, therefore, is the sense of a mystery that cannot be identified, much less solved. Thus, when the narrator follows the clue to look in the fish kettle, its "ominous hollowness" reveals only another written message: "Mr & the 2 Misses Rangerton-Karney can boil their heads. This holds 3" (645). Applying strict methods of ratiocination, the narrator conducts an inquiry into these nonevents but remains mystified. Even the police only hint at an explanation. As with the narrator in "The Dolt's Tale," what the soldier ultimately discovers is the discordance between language and meaning, that horror derives from unresolved ambiguity. Unlike the narrator, both the cook and the aunt avenge themselves against such ambiguity by authoring their own: The cook dies without explaining her messages, and the aunt speaks in innuendos, both of them victims and signs of war's incomprehensibility.

"Reduced" plays with Henry James's plot in "The Turn of the Screw," in which a governess develops an intense relationship with her charges. Bowen, however, reverses the site of ambiguous evil. In her story the hold of a governess on her pupils is sufficiently threatening to their mother to revive suspicion that, although acquitted from the charge, she may be a murderess. Written in the thirties, "Reduced" uses terror to satirize the world of parvenu sophistication. Miss Rice, like an icon of an earlier time, is invited by the Carburys to add gentility to Pendlethwaite, their house, whose "uninviting books must have been bought in lots, and looked gummed in the shelves" (471). But as the title suggests, this inconspicuous consumption must fail because Godwin Carbury is "careful, savagely careful about money"; his great bargain turns out to be a very risky venture (471). Hiring a woman of dubious character does not render him powerful and good like his namesake, the celebrated Victorian liberal William Godwin. Instead, Miss Rice's "perfect technique" only revives suspicion about her, undermining his authority and "charity" and exposing his pretensions (472, 474).

Like Terry in "Telling," Miss Rice can never disclose her real story and is controlled by the doubts about her character. Here too those very doubts create a subversive story that ultimately determines the fate of those who attempt to control her. Allowing her suspicions to overwhelm her admiration of Miss Rice, Mrs. Carbury entraps herself while also ensuring that the governess has no way out, for at the end, the Carbury children, who may be inspired by the "influence" of Miss Rice, shake the self-deluded world of Pendlethwaite by threatening to leave with her if she is fired (479). Yet as they speak to their mother, another muse inspires the girls' "mutiny" against the entrapping tales of their home (479); they glance at a copy of Jane Austen's *Emma*. Like themselves, Emma can grow up only if she abandons those plots which mold other people's characters to her self-enclosed world (480).

Designed to protect against the uncertainties of the future, the insular world of Bowen's characters is like a house of mirrors. Its reflecting and repeating images of the self conjure up a sense that what is so terrifying is that infinitely regressing distortions represent a future made ghastly by one's own repetition of the past. "Hand in Glove" is set in Ireland, a place where Bowen felt history does not so much repeat itself as supply minor variations on the same old themes. Thus what is particularly eerie about this story is its 1904 setting, written by Bowen in the postwar period: The disjunction in time reflects the way modern Ireland remains haunted by cultural attitudes and constraints from an earlier time. Especially during the war, when Bowen visited Ireland for the Ministry of Information, she felt the Nazi threat was ignored in order to go on as always. She illustrates this pointedly in her aptly named story "Unwelcome Idea," in which one Irish character registers irritation at the war effort for having "stopped the Horse Show," while another "doesn't seem to blame Hitler at all" (576).

Such self-enclosure is evident in "Hand in Glove" in the names of its Anglo-Irish heroines: Ethel and Elsie Trevor are the orphaned and penniless nieces of Elysia, the widowed invalid Mrs. Varley de Grey. Unable to direct their "coming out," Mrs. Varley de Grey offers as inspiration her memories of courtship "back in the golden days" (771). In this moribund society her recollections are as serviceable as recycling her antique trousseau. With a few "spangles," the material of yesterday's society works just as well in the present (768). The aunt's clothing is thus a metaphor for the powerful codes that direct women's lives in Irish county society. As the trousseau marks the "splashing" but disastrous marriage of Aunt Elysia, so its remnants predict disaster for her nieces, who are obsessively driven by the dictum to marry at all costs (767).

"Hand in Glove" dramatizes a tug-of-war between Aunt Elysia and Ethel over the not-so-Elysian fields of the marriage market. As Aunt Elysia's memories are revived, so is the competitive edge that is the side effect of women driven desperately to marry. At first in collusion over "trap[ping] a man," they ultimately collide over possession of the key to success: the keys to the trunk, which holds Elysia's pure white gloves (774). Just as Ethel is about to grab it, one of the gloves, an agent of Aunt Elysia's avenging rage, writhes and clutches at her, causing her "to choke among the sachets and tissue" (775). Recalling the snakelike clothing in "Making Arrangements" and "The Cat Jumps," the glove exposes the comedy of terror in the original Temptation story. The secret knowledge Ethel accepts so uncritically leads to her fatal fall. As she falls into her aunt's trunk, Ethel grotesquely parodies the fate of the woman whose initial foretells her own—Eve. Ethel is killed by the clothing that was designed to make a woman fit for civilization by covering her up.

The "Nerve and Core" of the Avenging Imagination

In Bowen's comedies of terror, when vulnerable or damaged people have no outlet for their rage it turns inward, eroding the will to survive and involving others in its self-destruction. Whereas "The Girl with the Stoop," "Love," and "Mrs Moysey" illustrate the terrible power of the weak, "Pink May" and "Look at All Those Roses" reveal their prevailing despair. Both "Love" and "The Girl with the Stoop" take place in a seaside summer town where "[s]imply to live here is not fully to live" (563). "Shy and vague," Tibbie in "The Girl with the Stoop" appears to have no will, yielding instead to her "destiny lines," which are always read the same way (565, 567). Lack of curiosity combined with an "indeterminate" view of life makes her easy prey to the devouring will of the crippled Francis, who compensates for his physical limitations by his ability to "plot" (563, 567).

In his wheelchair and expensive garb Francis is a horrifying parody of the man whose only function is to offer economic security to a woman who stoops because she has no options besides marriage. The action centers on a battle of their wills to survive. Whereas Francis needs Tibbie to restore his life to some kind of natural state, the only life offered to Tibbie involves yielding to a man who can support her. Although her engagement to another man seems perfectly natural and an alliance with Francis does not, Tibbie's response to Francis is a commentary on her fate in any marriage: "I'd be afraid. . . . You sort of eat me up" (569). Tibbie's escape from him shows how she is fated to remain in someone's power. As she gets up to leave, "[i]t was as though wires moved her" (570).

Like "The Girl with the Stoop," "Love" produces its comedy of terror by showing the grotesquely diminished lives of isolated people who cling to each other in their will to survive. Composed in the thirties, both stories effect a mood of depression, reflecting the social and economic condition of the time. The contrast between Francis's grand suite at the Palace Hotel and the otherwise gloomy resort town calls attention to the image of Tibbie washing her stockings and the pressure on her to marry well. The hotel in "Love," by contrast, "*is* a poor-looking place" (Bowen's italics), one whose only residents are a mad old woman and a younger man who takes care of her (539). These two are relics of "the crash," protecting each other from their impoverished reality in a mutually fixed fantasy (545).

"Love" presents an apocalyptic vision of a world whose social and economic props have collapsed. What remains is a desert in which "no sun . . . made everything look unnatural," a description that includes the hotel. Once the playground of "a rich gentleman [who] could have bought England," the hotel is now boarded up, lost, like the Major's money, to sand (539, 545). Bowen's vision of a civilization in crisis comes in the decade following T. S. Eliot's response to World War I—*The Waste Land*. Her imagery recalls his but offers a different perspective. Within the desolation and debris of Bowen's wasteland is a vision of contentment, one she argues is possible only after the fall not only from but also of a paradise that is man-made.

"Love" presents two views of survival in an impoverished and imperiled society. Combining gallows humor and farce, the story sets up an unlikely meeting between two young women making the best of an inexpensive holiday and the mad heiress and her caretaker. As Miss Meena's story unfolds, however, it positions the younger women as wanderers in the desolate aftermath of the nightmare that halted the older woman's life. Pushing their way into the abandoned hotel, the narrator and her friend Edna find a strange kind of refuge in a world formed out of greed and violence, the ossified remnant thereof providing the only safe harbor for its heiress. The young man who reluctantly gives them tea reveals that he and Miss Meena Tope have retreated to the hotel where she once reigned "like a queen" (545). The onetime "headquarters" of speculators is now "a loony-bin," a monument to their mad recklessness (545, 541). Like a dream turned nightmare, their spoils "melted away like snow," an image that recalls the lifeless sand on which the hotel is built and suggests that the runoff will include not only liquid but also human capital (545).

This wasteland cannot be regenerated. Unlike Tiresias, Eliot's prophet and sage, Miss Meena is neither blind nor hermaphroditic, but she is mad and desexualized, a sacrifice to her father's fall. Despite her powerlessness, however, "her people are all on to get her shut up"

(544). Miss Meena is thus like the girl with the stoop and like Edna, who, her friend observes, is "shut up, just like a clam" (539). A woman's fate in Bowen's wasteland is to be contained. Miss Meena's only protection and chance at autonomy are, ironically, to replicate the shell that contains her but now allows her to live a completely antisocial fantasy, for Miss Meena not only thinks she protects Oswald from the charge of murder but behaves like both a child and a mother, thus defying all the discrete and discreet boundaries of her society's definition of a woman.

The comic and terrible vision of Miss Meena suggests ambivalence about the social construction of gender. The madwoman in the haunted hotel is saved from "her people," who "wouldn't care what she suffered," by a man who would rather participate in her fantasy than join the world that has created their condition (544). Together, however, they cannot regenerate or transform that world. The price of not playing the social and sexual roles they are assigned is to enclose themselves in a fantasy as solipsistic as the one that made "all these windows blaze . . . down on the sand" (545).

Bowen explores her ambivalence about gender roles in "Look at All Those Roses," "Mrs Moysey," and "Pink May" by showing how women sustain those values which stifle them. Of the three stories, "Look at All Those Roses" is the most dramatically terrifying; its comedy lies in its excesses. As in "Love," there is a confrontation between women from apparently different worlds. Also written in the thirties, the story conveys a depression experienced by two characters as a persistent "negative" mood that "oppresses one with fatigue and a feeling of unreality" (512). The women here feel "bound up in the tired impotence of a dream" to a "future [that] weighed on them like a dull burden" (512). Like the travelers in "Love," Edward and Lou encounter a more dramatic version of their own reality by gaining entry to a house haunted by past injuries.[51] Here too a father has abandoned a daughter he has brutally hurt and has done so in a house where she is "the nerve and core" (515).

Particularly horrifying is the suggestion of a crime that is imagined as retaliation against the kind of despair for which there is no antidote, much less revenge. Vulnerable herself in an unhappy relationship with a married man, stultified by her own "obsessions," Lou avenges herself along with the crippled Josephine by imagining "that Mr. Mather lay at the roses' roots," perhaps murdered by his wife (519, 517). The concordance of Lou's avenging imagination and village gossip provides the basis only for melodrama, however, not for a story about a woman freeing herself from a man's rage by expressing her own, for the imagery suggests this kind of power in a woman is grotesque. Like the roses she grows, Mrs. Mather "disturbed with fragrance the dead air" (514). This "shabby amazon of a woman" is drawn as though she would be unnatural, indeed threatening, without the man she is supposed to need (514).[52] She therefore represents a warning to Lou, who can only feel irritation with her own inability to imagine a life alone.[53] Like Miss Meena, the women in ''Roses'' are ultimately locked into a plot in which they "must have lost contact with the outer world completely" (514).

No matter how melodramatic or fantasied any Bowen story might be, its effects go beyond the conventional because it explores human instability within social and historical contexts. This grounding refutes the criticism that Bowen sometimes works purely for effect. Neither topical nor mythic, her stories, as Bowen testified, are no mere entertainments: "[T]he short story is not a mere ease for the passing fancy; it offers no place for the unobjectified sentiment."[54]

Bowen's model for the significance of the "objectified sentiment" as a mode of observation and assessment is her experience of having lived in England all her adult life. From this perspective she saw the way in which the excesses and deficiencies of Anglo-Ireland were present in the more modified English soil. Her ghosts, therefore, could be said to make the trip from Ireland to England with ease, the logic of which is present in the plots of her comedies of terror. Here extreme desire is matched with dread, personal obsession with public manners. According to Bowen's own stated theory, "Fancy has an an authenticity reason cannot challenge. The pure fantasy writer works in a free zone: he has not to reconcile inner and outer images" (*CI*, 44). Bowen's characters in these comedies of terror are damaged by the clash between their need to conform to images of social acceptance and those unconsciously conceived images which represent rage at a dominating culture. Thus in the story "Pink May" one woman who is trying to escape the tedium and frustrations of both war and a bad marriage is haunted by the ghost of another woman, who, like "a puritan" serving the interests of social propriety, brings her subject to despair (716).

"Mrs Moysey" concerns a woman who hides the trophies celebrating her greatest satisfaction, understanding that to the world, her desire is grotesque. Although her pile of chocolate boxes remains in her closet, she finally displays her hunger publicly by turning two young children into her addictive equals. With this equation Bowen shows how a woman clashes with two conceptions of herself. In a world that lives off her good nature, her socially adaptive impulse to be nurturant coincides but clashes with her desire to absorb what is sweet. The image describing the result is disquieting in its horror and humor: an engulfing maternal beneficence—"the blond and the dark head [of the children] pressed deeper into the crimson capaciousness," chocolate dribbling from their mouths (345).

Bowen's use of melodrama shows the collision between a wish to "let go" of "obsession" and "wanting to keep everything inside [one's] own power" (519). At the same time, it shows her own ambivalence toward anarchic rage. John Bayley explains how this would work: "Melodrama is an excuse, a concealment, a kind of substitute for the truth in a story; and yet although it is not the true thing it points towards it, giving a presence to what in a masterpiece of narrative must necessarily be intangible" (165). The intangible for Bowen is expressed as ghosts that reflect her characters' fears of being entrapped by their own rage. Often projected onto another, rage is reflected back as weakness and vulnerability. The terror derives from an anxious sense that social and historical forces manifest themselves in tangibly felt experience and yet the truths of this experience cannot be captured in language and thus communicated rationally. The comedy derives from the extremes Bowen's characters go to either dodge or yield to the effects of history and social codes.

Elegies of Loss
and Dispossession

Many of Bowen's stories are distinguished by a sadness generated by loss of home, human connectedness, or the sense of an authentic and autonomous self. Characters yearn for a time when the family and its home could fulfill their need for purpose and identity, but they also suspect that this is never to be. Torn between romantic nostalgia for wholeness, security, and stability and denial of their often-disappointing history, they understand but ignore the way a perfectly knowable past foretells their difficult future. No comedy relieves their horrific pain; no ghosts anthropomorphize the lingering effects of history or stultifying social codes. Instead, pervasive suffering in these stories originates in the characters' own politics of survival, depicted as the manners and morals to which they cling for a sense of order and prestige. Ironically, the stability these codes gave to earlier generations creates a sense of disorder in characters who rely on them as a saving grace in the face of war, economic collapse, or dislocation.

No less startling than Bowen's ghost stories, these elegiac tales achieve their effect by embedding oppressive social and historic forces in the very nature of the characters. This technique reflects Bowen's theory of character as shaped by historical processes. Because their desires and fears are not projected outward as haunting presences, answerable through disconcerting questions, or mystified by the sense of an unknowable history, these characters bear the burden of their own responsibility in creating the events that threaten their carefully ordered lives.

"Secluded behind Glass"

In "Sunday Afternoon" the narrator's assessment of an Irish lawn party during World War II illustrates the tone and method of these stories:

> The coldness had been admitted by none of the seven or eight people who, in degrees of elderly beauty, sat here full in the sun, at this

sheltered edge of the lawn: they continued to master the coldness, or to deny it, as though with each it were some secret *malaise*. An air of fastidious, stylized melancholy, an air of being secluded behind glass, characterized for Henry these old friends in whose shadow he had grown up. To their pleasure at having him back among them was added, he felt, a taboo or warning—he was to tell a little, but not much. (616)

This lawn party is an artifact, "secluded behind glass" from its violent Anglo-Irish history and from the current global war it simply will not face. These people protect themselves by retreating into the rituals of gentility. "The grace of the thing done over again" represents the triumph of genteel continuity over brutal contingency; however, choosing to live in a fictional past rather than face up to the stark realities of the present only ossifies these people (621). Assuming no responsibility for the history that was and is, they construct their lives as an "eternalized Sunday afternoon," as though "their spell" can be touched by "nothing dreadful" (617, 616).

Like the tea party that ignores World War II, or the "meetings for good causes" that deny the imminence of World War I in "Ivy Grips the Steps," parties in "The Tommy Crans" celebrate security and stability as though life were untouched by historic events or personas (691). Every time the Anglo-Irish Tommy Crans lose all their money, they give their "perpetual Christmas party" to celebrate "how Life came back again and again to beg their pardon" (353). Their rites of continuity signify their recklessness. Forced to sell every house they buy, they just move on, incurring more debt but perpetuating the illusion that drives so many of Bowen's characters: that houses endow one with an integrated sense of self, whether they be the well-kept Italianate villas of "Sunday Afternoon" and "Requiscat" or the impoverished estates of "The Needlecase" and "Ivy Gripped the Steps." In these stories, therefore, to be dispossessed by war or economic depression is to break the very backbone of that society which gives one a reason for living.

If the older generation will assume no responsibility for a misguided past, it becomes the burden of their heirs. In "The Last Night in the Old Home," as in "The Tommy Crans," young people cope with the losses their parents have bequeathed to them. The story concerns the last moments in a family home about to be dismantled and auctioned off. Although there are hints of reckless spending, the story does not focus on individual responsibility. Instead, it identifies the way a family home contains the seeds of its own dissolution. Filled with relics from the past, home signifies nostalgia for continuity. But as the children of this home reveal, continuity must be disrupted if they are to liberate themselves from a repetitive and stifling past. Thus Delia, Henry, and John feel that even now, "home had lasted a day too long" (374).

Their matter-of-fact tone is as much a defense against the weight of continuity as their house is a defense against change. Thus, Delia's indifference to home and family destroys "some fiction of innocence [that] had always unnerved her" (372). This fiction, like the childhood letters saved by her mother or the parties in other stories that are frozen in a timeless world, is preserved because it certifies family unity and legitimates the value of the past. But there is a price to be paid for living the present as if it were the idealized past. As their "odd" sister Annabelle demonstrates, being her parents' "homegirl" means her role in that fiction afflicts her with being unable to "grow up" (372, 371). Instead, she is her parents' living relic, preserved as a monument to their "brave" if "sinister . . . brightness" (373).

Like the children in "The Last Night in the Old Home," Nancy Crans cannot afford to remain innocent and, like them, realizes that "to know everything" is no guide to "how we are ever to live" (352). But unlike the others, she cannot extricate herself from the bondage of family, home, and history. An adopted child, she bears the double burden of having no inherited identity but also having to compensate for the sterility of her adopted parents. Nancy's identity is submerged further in her effort to reconstitute the Crans through the fiction that theirs is an unbroken history. Assuming the obligations left to her by her adoptive parents, she marries a man for "his thousands" so that "[t]he Tommy Crans would go on for ever and be continued" (353–54). His money will salvage his in-laws and reestablish a home base for them, but it cannot regenerate their old order, as Nancy's pregnancy ironically shows, for instead of reproducing the Tommy Crans, bound by timeless conventions and relentless historical myths, Nancy's child inherits the world of the self-made interloper, a character capable of determining his own destiny.

The re-creation of selfhood through the myth of the family home is put to the test and then quite obviously demolished in wartime, for no matter how Mrs. Vesey's tea party in "Sunday Afternoon" denies the possibility of external danger, the characters must face their own fra-

gility. Unlike Nancy Crans, who marries wealth as an antidote to instability, Maria in "Sunday Afternoon" is attracted to instability as an
escape from the wealthy's "aesthetic of living" (616). Giving full
weight to her feelings, Maria "seemed framed, by some sort of anticipation, for the new catastrophic *outward* order of life—of brutality, of
being without spirit" (620).

Like Delia in "The Last Night in the Old Home," Maria registers
the "brutality" of having to live as a hothouse flower, an ornament of
a moribund society denying its role in its own dissolution. If she joins
"a world at war," however, she only proves that her "whole existence
has been in contradistinction" (620, 622). She will replicate her ancestors' "savage" world; she may escape from the languid state of the tea
party into "action," but then she will lose the very fantasy that gives
her identity (622). At the end of the story, Henry says good-bye to
Maria by calling her "Miranda" and telling her, "This is the end of
you" (622). Like Shakespeare's Miranda in *The Tempest*, Maria is about
to affirm her own identity, indeterminate as it is, by leaving the world
of fantasied order and facing the disorders of the past and present. Like
Delia, she will gleefully enter a world in which the "fiction of innocence . . . went—pouf!" (372).

Maria and Henry, a man visiting Anglo-Ireland as a reprieve from the
Blitz, offer critical perspectives on the denial of history. An Anglo-Irish
insider whose wisdom comes from living abroad, in England, Henry
suffers the loss of his illusions about the privileged world he left. Losing his "valuables" in the Blitz revives his sense of the supreme importance his civilization attaches to its homes and possessions as signs
of a tangible identity traceable to a knowable past (619). Like his
namesake in "The Last Night in the Old Home," however, Henry also
senses his losses may be gains, for the "morbid value" of a house and
its things also recall the deadliness of the world represented by Mrs.
Vesey's tea party.

Bowen also felt that in times of crisis, possessions and homes encourage one to survive. In her preface to *The Demon Lover*, her collection of World War II stories, she described how "the passionate
attachment of men and women" to their personal belongings represented a "resistance to the annihilation" threatening their lives (*MT*,
92). War, in Bowen's vision, is the final blow to a romanticized past
that had given her characters a sense of "extraordinariness in the fate
of each of us" (622). Negotiating between the unsettling history of
their homes and homelands and their comforting fantasies, Bowen's

characters become indeterminate, that is, hypothetical constructs testing the possibilities beyond the myths of their inherited past. Her stories thus theorize character as being in flux, as though loss and dispossession destabilize it but also create the contingencies that allow character to be reimagined.

"A Day in the Dark" questions the way in which character can be imagined out of an unsettling history. The story concerns a woman creating a narrative about which she declares, "I refuse to fill in [the characters'] outline[s] retrospectively: I show you only what I saw at the time" (780). But Barbie's observations are mediated by her attempts to clarify her own history, played out "on the margin of a passion which was impossible" (780). Set in postwar Ireland, the story connects Barbie's emotional dislocation to her homeland's constant irresolution. Emerging from a position of neutrality in World War II, Ireland teeters on the chaotic margins of civil strife. Like her homeland, the outlines of Bowen's characters are ambiguous and tendentiously driven by her ambivalence toward prevailing Irish values. At the end of the story, Barbie, like the characters she imagines, is "not among . . . the scenes of safety," indeed far "from . . . every hope of solitude" (782).

"Glassless" Houses

Set in London during the Blitz, "In the Square" depicts a scene of danger and dissolution. No longer "secluded behind glass," the discreet world of the upper middle-class is now "exposed" by "glassless windows," (616, 609). The dispossession of war brings the end of social civility. People's lives are indeterminate because the siege of Britain has made their fates uncertain and even interchangeable. Magdela returns to her London house to find it occupied by strangers: her husband's army secretary, who is also his mistress; caretakers; and unidentified others occupy the house once prized for its privacy and exclusiveness. War, by contrast, makes sure that "there was nothing muted. . . . One got a feeling of functional anarchy, . . . fittings shocked from their place" (610). Gina, Anthony's mistress, is presented as lacking "fine feelings"; her imagination is insufficient "to be surprised by the past—still less, by its end" (613). But her lack of historic sensibility is countered by Magdela's snobberies, which are shaken by a recognition that the war has, at least for the moment, turned her world inside out. Chairs "worn rough" mark an invasion and occupation of a home originally designed as a sanctuary for a class that now feels it is left with "nothing except one's feelings" (610, 615).

Significantly, the enemy originates within Magdela's house and is cultivated by the "fine feelings" of a class attached to the myth of stability and exclusivity. To show the insecurity this myth disguises, the following statement is repeated twice: "[T]he place seems to belong to everyone now" (615). What Magdela does not recognize, however, is that she is threatened not only by the invasion of her space but also by her "dead room" (610). Instead of saving her, this ancestral sanctuary makes her "the replica of so many others that you could not count" (610). Like Nancy Crans, Magdela aims to reproduce her world in herself, and this world, like Mrs. Vesey's tea party, is an "extinct scene [that] had the appearance of belonging to some ages ago" (609).

The world of the British upper classes, as Bowen showed so dramatically in her World War II novel *The Heat of the Day*, is threatened as much by its narcissism as by bombs. Stella Rodney, the heroine of that novel, runs away from the Anglo-Irish estate her son inherits when she realizes the price of its privilege and "inherent wrongs" is to be so "utterly out of reach" (*BC*, 453).[55] Exclusive and inbred, it produces only a "society of ghosts" (*HD*, 173). The only reason "In the Square" ends on a happy note is that Magdela has "no plans"; the impact of national and worldwide crisis on her personal life offers an opportunity to rethink her fate (615).

In several stories of the thirties Bowen shows how the middle class stifles itself by clinging to anachronistic myths of stability. In "Attractive Modern Homes" and "A Walk in the Woods" she imagines women "riveted into society" and "walled in alive" without alternatives (491). Charting the fortunes of an upwardly mobile class, Bowen diagnoses an acute depression within prosperity. In "Attractive Modern Houses" Mrs. Watson loses her sense of herself when she moves away from the town where she was born. As in the portraits of ghostly women in *The Heat of the Day*, she retreats into a silence that expresses dread of her new home. She feels that the barren estate is "not like a village, it has no heart" (522). At the most acute moment of her alienation, however, she is rescued by a new definition of community. When her husband finds her on the ground after a fall, she tells him that isolation has made her discover it is "natural" to sustain not their former compulsive socializing but the relationships growing out of intimacy and understanding.

"[A] woman who did not picture herself," Mrs. Watson almost dissolves in her home, which "isn't anywhere" (524, 526). Like Magdela, she is vulnerable without the secure boundaries of a traditional home in a self-absorbed community. It takes a threatening experience to make both women understand that such security is also entrapping. Like Carlotta, "riveted into society" in "A Walk in the Woods," they are "like something wrecked and cast up on the wrong shore, . . . one of those women going through life dutifully, and at the same time burning themselves up" (489, 492). An exchange between Mrs. Watson and her husband exposes the kind of limited relationship defined by a family home and marriage impervious to change:

> "We're the same as we've been always."
> "Yes," she said, "but it didn't notice before."
> He changed colour and said, "You know I . . . I think the world of you."
> "Well, you've sort of got to, haven't you?" she replied unmovedly. "Why aren't the two of us having a better time?" (527)

For Mrs. Watson as for Magdela, the marriage relationship becomes a threatening space. Magdela's house is taken from her not by Gina but by her husband, who installs his mistress in the space he governs. With unquestioning deference to her husband's promotion, Mrs. Watson moves from her beloved home and discovers that "the whole structure seemed to be very frail" (521). But the fragile structure of domestic life threatens men as much as it does women, for at the end of the story Mr. Watson disappears. He turns out to be as disembodied as the ghost that "comforted" him in its "persistent aliveness," a sign of Mr. Watson's undaunted but self-destructive belief that domestic life is stable because it never seems to change (525).

Although Mrs. Watson is saved by another woman's gesture of friendship, the story shows Bowen's ambivalence about the strength of domestic tradition. Favorably, the friendship between two women transforms a barren landscape into a new community. But its suburban location nevertheless isolates it from the center of political and historical processes. Although this factor saves domestic life from the vicissitudes of change, it also keeps women from imagining that they can participate in the political arenas that shape their lives. Mrs. Watson knows herself only as a housewife until the very moment her husband calls her "batty" (526). Keeping her character suspended without signs of alternatives, the story ends with her realization that she is "just noticing" her character.

Stifling Houses of Mirrors

The traditional relationships that stifle characters in Bowen's stories are linked by opaque and ambiguous language to myths of nurturing and sustaining homes. Three early stories—"The Storm," "Joining Charles," and "Requiescat"—and a World War II story called "A Love Story: 1939" explore the language of these myths and its effect on character. Like several of Bowen's comedies of sex and manners, "Requiescat" recalls Henry James, using abstract, overlapping, and unfinished dialogue to suggest an ambiguous interdependence in human relationships. But whereas the comedies celebrate rebellion against constraining relationships, "Requiescat" mourns the inability to recognize constraint, a limitation exacerbated by the characters' language of restraint. The story rests on the assumption that the Majendie marriage was happy, but as it unfolds, "Requiescat" reads less like a requiem for than an inquest into the marriage relationship that can only produce an uncertain verdict.

As the story nears completion, we are told that the romantic villa on Lake Como at which the story is set is "as sunless as an evening garden" (46). Although easily taken as a metaphor for the widow's bereavement, the image also identifies a romantic but destructive view of marriage that is figured in the all-too-exquisitely-ordered and self-contained honeymoon house. Like the characters' language, the carefully tended villa is a sign of those codes of decorum which protect Bowen's characters from confronting their deepest desires and fears. As in "The Confidante," these codes are voiced in a language that reflects the characters' temptation to know what they already suspect and yet to deny that knowledge. Thus, as widow and brother-in-law meet to discuss the "business" of Howard Majendie's bequests, each one questions and yet skirts the other's relationship to him. Ellaline and Stuart Majendie tiptoe as on eggshells around the knowledge that their mutual jealousy kept each of them from having a more complete relationship with the man who was husband to one and brother to the other.

Positioned at the center of the story, this triangular relationship expresses the characters' desire for total possession of the beloved. As in the oedipal conflict, the desire for another is intensified by a rivalry that not only constitutes its own relationship but is as important as the relationship with the beloved. Because "Requiescat" focuses on the characters' uncertainty about what they are willing to recognize and articulate about these complex relationships, it also shows how their language constitutes their characters. For example, Ellaline and Stuart's defensive rhetoric reduces them to the elusive sum of their abstract and unfinished questions and answers, as the narrator shows: "He wondered what she thought he thought of her" (44). The possibility for infinite regression here implies that character becomes increasingly unstable as long as it depends on another to imagine and sustain it. The use of the reticent "wondered" in a sentence that diffuses the intensity of each character's desire to be affirmed by the other actually parodies the expectation that marriage affirms exclusive love. As Ellaline's widowhood reveals, marriage also leaves her less than sure what she is worth to anyone, much less herself.

It is no wonder this story suggests a Berkeleyan universe, with its setting and dialogue suspended outside an identifiable historical moment and its characters threatened not by social or economic upheaval but by the solipsism of their self-enclosed relationships. The only time Ellaline comes to life is when Stuart rebuffs her. She creates herself by creating her own pain, "gripping . . . branches of the climbing rose" until "[t]he thorns ran deep into her hands" (47). Like the honeymoon villa in which the story is set, this gesture of romantic suffering underscores the fragility of the characters and the ephemerality of their desires. All the detailed beauty of the villa cannot deny the sense that it mocks two kinds of romance: the ancestral home and an exclusive love relationship—fantasies of nurture and sustenance that, in Bowen's fiction, suffocate characters.

In "The Storm" another Italian villa suggests a nightmare of suffocation and dissolution. Like the mirroring images in "Requiescat," the villa's "infinite rooms . . . too like one another" threaten to "crash again at any moment into darkness" (184). With no boundaries to distinguish one from the other, the rooms are like the married couple who vacation there, each mirroring the other's dependence on and invasion of their sense of themselves. The marital relationship here breeds a fear that results from relying on possessing one's spouse to validate the self. Together, the couple without a last name (she has no name except "Rupert's wife") add up to nothing more than the sum of "how ineffectual they both were, how they neither of them knew what they wanted, how suspiciously they watched one another, jealous of a gleam of certainty" (183). Instead of fostering a romantic dream of wholeness and stability, this house of mirrors reflects a nightmare of self-confrontation and with it the sense that neither husband nor wife exists without the other, equally insubstantial self.

"The Storm" presents no way out for Rupert and his wife; their only remedies replicate their problem. Whereas Rupert's wife longs to free herself from "the super-imposition of Rupert," Rupert needs "to evade *her*, to escape utterly" (181, 183). They discover, however, that only mutual fear of each other gives them substance (187). Rupert seeks God's presence to affirm his existence but sees only ghosts who signal his own emptiness. His wife's "urgency . . . to stamp on time her ineffaceable image" is a ghostly sign of her fears (187). Like myths of ancestral places, their ghosts represent "testimony" only to the characters' unfulfilled need to create each other as evidence of their own existence (188). But equally, as each one "projects" his or her needs on the other, they negate each other (187). The result affirms the failure to create the self in the other, for at the end, "[t]hey contemplated one another's outlines speechlessly; . . . and mutually pitiful[ly]" (188).

In Bowen's fiction the effort to create oneself in another only denies subjectivity instead of affirming it. Even in her earliest stories, such as "Daffodils," characters feel "a poignant disappointment and relief" when intimacy fails, because the desire for separateness and autonomy is just as urgent (27). As the story "Joining Charles" illustrates, to merge with another in order to fill up one's emptiness not only is self-deluding but destroys the boundaries keeping these characters intact and the contingency inviting change. Like "Requiescat," the dialogue here is opaque, expressing the characters' inability to fully acknowledge their desires and fears. Recognition is thwarted by a romantic vision of home but intensified by the separation of husband and wife.

As in "Requiescat," the story enacts an oedipal configuration to suggest the presence of a hidden and forbidden desire within a traditional family relationship. The triangle no one can face positions the mother at one point and her children and their solipsistic fantasies of family homes at the two other points. From the start, we know that Louise is deeply attached to her mother-in-law and withdrawn from her husband. She dreams that she misses her boat and is also losing her place in her mother-in-law's home; the former is a wish for freedom, but the latter reflects fear of being on her own. The story suggests the precarious fate of a female character caught in a relationship that, because it defies the primacy of marriage, cannot be expressed. The other side of the triangle in this story is equally threatening to marriage and to female character. Submerged in the more conventional references to Louise and Charles's marriage is Charles's domination of his mother's home. The effect on Louise is calamitous. Her presence is felt only as she is constituted through Charles: She is mostly called "Mrs Charles," and his family "used to try and read him from her secret, sensitive face" (226). Charles is also present as "he looked out at Louise . . . from the family talk" or when "Mother looked at her; out of the eyes looked Charles" (225, 227). The logical consequence to Charles's dominating presence is expressed in his wife's response to the idea of having his child: "Louise had a spasm of horror. . . . For the first time she looked at the baby's face and saw it was Charles's" (229).

Fear of sexual violation is suggested in this statement and in others, including those about Louise's fear of Charles's cat, the embodiment of its owner's sexuality and cruelty. But along with feeling that "[i]t's death to be with [Charles]," Louise also fears the loss of "Mother," who "possessed her entirely" (226). Presenting both fears simultaneously and therefore as equally important suggests they combine to produce fatal loss. To lose the mother "that she did not think she could live without" and be "enfold[ed] materially" in marriage means her sense of being individual and autonomous is destroyed (226, 223). The young wife may dissolve into the fantasy of being only an extension of her husband. Leaving to meet Charles, Louise thinks, "Either I am dreaming . . . or someone is dreaming me" (229). The warmth she enjoys at her mother-in-law's house is stifling; like so many homes in Bowen's fiction, it is not a haven or a place to express personal identity. As in "The Needlecase" and "Attractive Modern Homes," the White House is a monument to absent men and the women sacrificed to them. Although "Mother" tenderly offers her support on the grounds that "[m]arriage isn't easy," the dominance of the son and husband requires a conspiracy of silence so that his wife may disappear unnoticed as she is submerged in him (230).[56]

Set in Ireland at the start of World War II, "A Love Story: 1939" shows how silence and reticence enshroud people and their homelands. Characters in three different relationships struggle desperately to remain intact at the moment history proves the futility of their efforts. Mrs. Massey comes to the neighborhood hotel with her daughter,

Teresa, to drink herself into a stupor over the death of her lover, a young soldier. Clifford and Polly Perry-Dunton are there hiding out from the war, while Frank and Linda are lovers meeting secretly. By the time Frank and Clifford help Mrs. Massey and her daughter home it is clear that neutral Ireland is an appropriate sanctuary for all of them, denying dangers both within and without.

Danger in this story is embedded in the nature of the characters. The "atrophied" Polly Perry-Dunton's "rape of Clifford" is made possible by "[h] er will . . . detect [ing] the flaw in his will" (501). Defined as "static, depleting intimacy," this union encourages Polly's "passive, moronic unseeingness" and produces only "claustrophobia" (501, 500). Equally oppressive are Mrs. Massey's feelings about her lost soldier, as her daughter reveals: "She'd rather him dead than gone from her" (509). The soldier is not the only victim of Mrs. Massey's overwhelming grief; her daughter is denied any feelings of her own. Among the three couples there are no viable alternatives to their destructive dependency. Linda and Frank avoid dependency in their affair but sacrifice intensity, intimacy, and individuality. Linda's game of "patience" only reduces her to a mere shadow of Frank's idea of "how foolish it was, in love, to have to differentiate between women" (507, 510).[57]

Lack of an individuality that differentiates personas from one another forms the greatest danger to Bowen's characters. Whether this lack results from being dominated or from being indifferent to one's needs and desires, the characters in this story can disengage themselves from neither others nor a historic past that binds them. The failure to differentiate is so total that the three couples become almost interchangeable. Even the narrator's straightforward language is no more effective and therefore no different from that of Teresa or Linda. What is being mourned in this group of stories is the loss of interdependence with others and with the historic past and crisis of the moment. Clearly this loss is not positioned simply in terms of individual psychology, for the story links it explicity to cultural and political conflict. As "A Love Story: 1939" shows, in its violation of national and cultural boundaries World War II threatened the loss of individual and cultural freedom. Bowen observed that Ireland's neutrality might save it from invasion, but it would suffer nevertheless. Neutrality isolated Ireland from the mutually enabling responsibility of fighting for the right to retain cultural distinctions and national boundaries. Like Bowen's ancestral homes, the Irish homeland reflects the internal politics that determine its place in the external world.

Songs of "Disheartened" Houses

In Bowen's stories the politics of interdependence are also experienced in personal relationships. In "The Evil That Men Do—" and "No. 16" women are tempted by the language of artists to change the way they think of themselves. In the first, a poet's letter to a woman who attended one of his readings provokes her doubts about marital happiness she has taken for granted. Appealing to a romantic sense of having a hidden self, his letter describes her as "a nymph coming out of a wood," "defensive," and "hurt" (84, 83). In effect, the poet's imagery remakes her, but the transformative power of his language endangers the integrity of her sense of self. The narrator tells us the poet "snatched at" her; his aesthetic gesture turns out to be far more assaulting than being "intruded" on by the ordinary needs of her family (84). The woman, whose name we never learn, is saved by a mixture of O. Henryesque twists of fate and her own ironic double vision: The poet is run over by a truck before he ever receives her reply, and her growing dissatisfaction is mitigated by her recognition that marriage provides her with both "solitude" and love (87).

In "No. 16" Jane Oates, a writer herself, is threatened by another writer's self-pity. Thrilled by Maximilian Bewdon's laudatory review of her first book and his invitation to lunch, Jane is then crushed by his discouragement. Like the poet in "The Evil That Men Do—," Bewdon makes the woman his subject. Here, however, his language remakes her in his image. Instead of a romantic portrait of a woman needing rescue, in this story the artist re-creates her as a reflection of his own weakness. That this is death for the woman artist is confirmed by Bowen's use of the name Bewdon, sufficiently like Bowen to call attention to her concern about the status of the woman writer: "[H]e lying, she kneeling twisted beside the sofa. They looked like a suicide pact" (553). The only encouragement Jane receives is to become a female version of her mentor—a tormented artist, wasting away from neglect.

The O. Henryesque twist in this story does not save the woman. Arriving home, Jane finds a telegram warning her about Bewdon's illness, suggesting in effect that her own illness makes her like her mentor. Like the woman artist, the woman as audience is at risk in a male artistic tradition. As its title suggests, "The Evil That Men Do—" concerns the fate of a woman rendered nameless as she is denied autonomy, whether as a wife or as the artist's artifact. Reading herself from one perspective and then the other, she internalizes an image of herself as "little wee wife"; she is caught between the artist's assumption that he "know [s] her so well" and the exquisite gifts her husband buys her to represent what she means to him (88, 83).

Both stories identify the "sinister advantage over one of being able to see the back of one's head" as not having to look a woman full in the face (83). The impersonal "one" is none other than these male artists who thrive on their romances of the misunderstood and misguided woman. Such romantic constructions, however, cannot save either artist from the dread that weakens and holds him captive, as Bewdon's home suggests: At "Medusa Terrace . . . the masks . . . had lost their features: the pilasters crumbled; front doors boarded up" (547). The male artist's view of women, like that which turned Medusa's pursuers to stone, produces exactly what it is trying to avoid: an artist "frustrated and spent" from projecting his fear of failure onto his subject (550). These artists succumb to myths of their powers to shape a woman's nature. The female subject is manipulated into submitting to the language of the artist because it shares the vocabulary of those codes which already shape her sense of herself.

"Songs My Father Sang Me" is a female subject's elegy to the failed artist who created her. It is both a woman's eulogy to the father who made her in his image and a dirge about the historic conditions that drove him. Unlike the two earlier stories, "Songs" celebrates the woman's ability to create her own work of art, a narrative that dramatizes her father's inescapable and problematic influence. It does so, however, with a compassion that liberates her. The form of the story captures the father's influence as it shows the historical events that molded his psychology. On a casual date during World War II, the daughter hears a World War I song her father used to sing. As she tells her father's story to her date, past and present, father and daughter, and two world wars blend, each the image of the other but each demanding its own distinctiveness.

Although the nightclub setting recalls the romance of the woman's parents' and her story incorporates theirs, her story is not the sum of theirs. As her mother raises doubts about her daughter's paternity and the daughter discovers herself by coming to understand her father, both women struggle to separate from "war and love" narratives that make them objects of male fantasies: "[D]reamlike caricature [s]" of "anxiety . . . dissolved in a haze of smoke" (654, 650). The father tries to save himself by running away from the overpowering sense that he "lost" England, which, he says, "lost me" (657). In their failed efforts to connect, men and women in this story are lost to each other and to any permanent and stable reality. The experience of living through the war and its aftermath produces only restlessness, failed fresh starts for the father, and for the mother, dissolving into "look [ing] like nothing" (654).

The daughter's narrative counters the father's hopelessness and the mother's breakdown. She not only gives them the power and integrity of their dreams and failures but refuses to perpetuate them in fantasies inspired by another world war. By contrast, characters in other stories are "lost" when they have no other narrative to give them substance. In the story "Firelight in the Flat," an ex-officer and his wife are lost in mutual self-delusion in the period between the wars. Imprisoned by his "bitterly retrospective" hopelessness and her inability to "get on without him," their lives lack purpose (439, 435). His moment of glory in the past is canceled by an economic depression that makes both past and future seem like hapless illusions. Unable to rely on either myths of privileged stability or an empathetic narrator, they cannot escape their disabling fantasies. The narrator vacillates between cynicism and sentimentality, reducing the already-diminished lives of the characters to a slice of life that "counted for less and less" (435). In contrast, the narrator of "Songs My Father Sang Me" powerfully takes hold of her own life by interpreting her parent's story in the wider context of historical conditions.

"The Needlecase" links the story of a woman's life to the narcissistic fantasies of those whose power derives from a society's belief in the romance of tradition and privilege. The story's setting in the economically turbulent thirties highlights the carelessness and intransigence of a landed gentry whose fate depends on maintaining the traditional order of the ancestral home. From Danielstown in *The Last September* to Doddington Hall in "Ivy Gripped the Steps," the ancestral home may fall victim to economic and political trouble, but it is also immortalized by myths of its power. "The Needlecase" concerns two sisters who depend on their brother Arthur to marry sufficiently well to keep them in the house that is their launching pad to prosperous marriages. In a melodramatic turn, they discover how close they are to disaster when the dressmaker who restyles their old party dresses turns out to be the mother of Arthur's illegitimate child.

"The kind of house that easily looks shut up, and, when shut up, looks derelict" is the legacy of an inbred society that has lost the capacity to regenerate itself (453). The young heirs in this story cannot help but perpetuate the history of economic and emotional waste to which their own destinies are sacrificed. As Bowen portrayed so clearly in *The Last September,* the young cannot have much of a future if the empire-building vitality of their forebears leads only to the privilege of keeping up appearances. Toddy and Angela's altered party dresses represent not the possibility of replaying a romantic history but rather the alteration of the brutal events composing their family history. As the artist entrusted with making such denial credible, the dressmaker inscribes her own tragic story as well as the ironic fate of the house she serves. In addition to the tools of her craft, her needle case holds the portrait of her son, that is, the image of his father. A sign of his father's irresponsibility, the boy is the natural heir to a decaying house whose codes of conduct decree him to be illegitimate and therefore not an agent of revitalization.

Here as elsewhere, Bowen uses codes associated with an earlier time to make the connection between the destiny of women and their retrogressive economic and social positions. The narrator tells us that the house is "like a disheartened edition of Mansfield Park"; the driving forces behind that nineteenth-century structure are alive and dominant here (455). The imperatives taking Jane Austen's Mr. Bertram to the West Indies parallel the economic reasons spurring Arthur's courtship of the heiress. In Bowen's story, the reason the house is so disheartening is that the codes making women dependent on their fathers' and brothers' goodwill and fortunes are still so vital. This unrelenting pattern eclipses women's ability to make their own lives and fortunes. The economic privation that connects Arthur's "fallen woman" and his sisters also isolates them and prevents any impetus for change (457).

Despite its melodramatic ironies, the story rigorously assesses the literary and social traditions in which Bowen works, for as in Mr. Bertram's case, nowhere are the values Arthur represents more apparent than in his absence. Like Mr. Watson's emotional distance in "Attractive Modern Homes" and that of Louise's husband in "Joining Charles," Arthur's absence (he never appears in this story) is crucial to the fate of his sisters and to Miss Fox. By centering his character outside the story's frame, Bowen makes it clear that, in his social and economic system, Arthur is the subject whose actions turn his sisters and Miss Fox into objects—relics of an unyielding order. Although the story shows an unstated understanding between the women, it also affirms the unbridgeable distance between Miss Fox and the world of the sisters she serves. She will not marry into upper-middle-class life as Fanny Price is permitted to do in Jane Austen's novel, and this negative parallel offers a significant social critique. The precarious position of Arthur's sisters lends a poignant cast to the silliness of the Bertram sisters, while the grim fortunes of Miss Fox point only too clearly to the fairy-tale quality of Fanny Price's fate.

Bowen does, however, show how women can take advantage of a loophole in their economic and social systems. With men absent, women interpret their own story. When Miss Fox narrates the events leading to her "fall," she says that "Mr. Arthur . . . let . . . drop" one of her "dummies" (459). Read metaphorically, the statement shows not only that the dressmaker's position is the rationale for Arthur's treatment of her but also that she, like the enigmatic milliner in the story "Ann Lee's," gains from her position a screen behind which her character can be what she wishes (459).

Losses Suspended in History

In "Ivy Gripped the Steps" the numbing effects of a long war question a nation's myths of privilege and continuity. On leave in 1944, Gavin Doddington revisits the home of a woman whose view of history 30 years earlier marked him for life. Standing in front of Mrs. Nicholson's now-vacant house, he cannot feel anything. His apathy is a result of her having used him years ago as a plaything to prove she could ignore change and "live in the present day" (695). He acquires the reverse of her "protective adaptability" by exchanging feeling for an "infantile passion for explanation" (688, 702).

Like "Songs My Father Sang Me," this story is ringed by two world wars, but the characters' dispossession and losses place them in a wider historical process. Gavin's "frozen" feeling is symptomatic of a society that believes, as Mrs. Nicholson says, that "there *is* one reason for learning history—one sees how long it has taken to make the world nice" (703, 696).[58] Her view assumes there is one idea of civilization to which all people aspire and which is accessible to all. The implementation of this vision requires a denial of domination, a belief that "even savages really prefer wearing hats and coats" and that they have the right to change so long as they become like Mrs. Nicholson (696). But her "enchanted" circle is not alone in denying the expression of individual subjectivity (690). It is supported in this by the country estate of Gavin's parents, which stands "outside the zone of electric light" and "belonged, by its nature, to *any* century" (696–97).

As Gavin travels between his parents' impoverished estate and Mrs.

Nicholson's nouveau riche milieu, the striking external differences between the two worlds betray a kind of underlying unity that characterizes Bowen's vision of England on the brink of two world wars:

> This existence . . . was unprogressive. It had stayed as it was while, elsewhere, history jerked itself painfully off the spool; it could hardly be more depressed by the fateful passage of armies than by the flooding of tillage or the failure of crops: it was hardly capable, really, of being depressed further. It was an existence mortgaged to necessity; it was an inheritance of uneasiness, tension and suspicion. One could preassume the enmity of weather, prices, mankind, cattle. It was this dead weight of existence that had supplied to history not so much the violence or the futility that had been, . . . but its repetitive harshness and its power to scar. This existence had no volition, but could not stop; and its never stopping, because it could not, made history's ever stopping the less likely. (697)

This passage could easily serve as Bowen's description of Anglo-Ireland, not just a rendering of English landed society. The ethos she sees in both societies is the commitment to a continuity guaranteed by an intractable social system. This commitment invites a fusion of "rentier" and county society, personified by Mrs. Doddington wearing Mrs. Nicholson's cast-off dresses (690). But internal unity only further endangers this island nation threatened by external siege, for as the metaphor of beautiful dresses suggests, covering up "the violence or the futility" only produces decay within. A society that makes itself "effectively sightless" is "balanced up and up on itself like a house of cards: built, it remain[s] as precarious" (686, 700).

The ivy gripping this house of cards also grips the people who live within, suffocating them with its "austere, religious idea of their own standing" (691–92). Bowen repeats various forms of the word *brutal* to describe the way a society's view of its role in history produces "a civil and indifferent little boy" (702). But the story is not simply critical of the society and individuals that make each other in this story; it shows how Gavin and his parents and Mrs. Nicholson are victims of the values they perpetuate. The rituals celebrating "the high dream" of self-made men and landed gentry signify a society "without function"; self-enclosed, it fails to see its violent history coming home to haunt it (691).

An ornament of this world, Mrs. Nicholson is an extension of the nameless wife in "The Evil That Men Do—." Just as that woman wanted the poet's fictional portrait to fill her empty life, so Mrs. Nicholson uses Gavin; his lack of feeling simply reflects being used up by the unfeeling woman he adores. The terrible sadness with which the story ends is Bowen's response to the moment when this world has come to a stalemate. As World War II grinds on in its fifth year, Mrs. Nicholson's prophecy of coming to the end of history may be fulfilled, but, as her early death shows, in a form that shows her world to be obsolete. Gavin is her heir, "a gentleman," but preserved "under an icy screen," like some relic of a history that "had only not stopped where or as she foresaw" (709).

During World War II Bowen crystallized her views of historical processes and character. Just as she had seen the interdependence of character and event in her chronicle of Anglo-Ireland, *Bowen's Court*, so she imagined people suffering from a war whose causes they inherited but were helpless to do anything about. Her most celebrated story of World War II, "Mysterious Kôr," is an elegy to the city, which for her encapsulates the life of a civilization. The title derives from Rider Haggard's ancient city, where *She*, the larger-than-life Queen Ayesha, ruled and mourned the loss of her lover. Bowen had read *She* when she was 12, and at the height of her career spoke of its indelible influence on her creative imagination. Her story envisions two lovers afraid of losing each other as they wander through London, a city nearly lost to war, "like the moon's capital—shallow, cratered, extinct" (728).

Unlike Rider Haggard's "forsaken" city "with no history," Bowen's London could be said to suffer from too much history (729). The persistent references and meditations on the historical events Bowen knew firsthand provide a critical commentary on Haggard's fantasy. Her story does not criticize his attempt to view history in the form of fantasy, for it combines a poetic or imaginative view with critical commentaries on history and the war.

With its origins in her experience of reading as a child, this story fulfills a significant part of Bowen's theory of the short story. It springs from a strong impression from which derive those images conveying "the valid central emotion and inner spontaneity of the lyric" (*CI*, 42–43). It is both pleasurable and disturbing, compressing painful moments into an aesthetic whole. In "Mysterious Kôr" images of mundane material reality alternate with surreal images suggestive of dreams. For every reference to "this war" and a "two-roomed flatlet" in London, there are lyrical images of "the abiding city"; conversely, with every reference to moonbeams, we are reminded of searchlights (731, 730). Imagination, experience, and meditation function together as critical checks and balances on a view of human history composed of passionate involvement and dispassionate disenchantment.

Bowen here concludes that responsibility for historical consequences is achieved only through empathy. Both romantic and ameliorative, her view also recognizes the contradictions and disorders of the lives and events portrayed. Thus, while she mourns the failure of human connection, she also refuses to impose an order that would stifle the ambiguity and open-endedness of human experience. Her elegy therefore mourns "the loss of . . . mysterious expectation, of . . . love for love" but recognizes that these are "small thing [s] beside the war's total of unlived lives" (739).

The man and two women who are the only characters in "Mysterious Kôr" are both isolated and connected in several ways. The story creates a tense relationship between the characters and their response to a moment in history, a moment that seems to stretch endlessly, like the light of the moon, across the human landscape. They feel equally crowded out by a war-torn city and "dissolved" by a moonlight that transforms the concrete into the "immaterial" (729, 728). They look to one another for warmth and connection while at the same time refusing it. Lovers who "seemed to have no destination but each other" wander the moon-drenched city (729). But Pepita and Arthur are also subject to more material concerns: They have nowhere to spend the night except for the flat she shares with the very conventional and dense Callie. Appalled by Callie's attempts to be hospitable when the only thing required of her is to disappear, the lovers chafe at each other; Pepita crawls angrily into bed with Callie, while Arthur spends a restless night on the couch. In the concreteness of their discomforts resonate the dreams and nightmares that provide both hope and anxiety.

The three characters each take turns responding to their historical and personal situation romantically and critically. Pepita yearns for the solidity of Kôr's monumental structures and its predetermined "finality" but also for the "ideality" of its "fanciful" open-endedness (740, 732, 738). She is annoyed at not being able to be with Arthur but dreams of him being "the password, but not the answer" (740). Betwixt and between connection and isolation, dependence and autonomy, Pepita is a character in flux. Renting a sofa bed from Callie, she has no permanence, either in her attachment to Arthur or in his dream of postwar stability. Callie too has her contradictions. Shy and repelled by human closeness, she also represents an idealism and "innocence" that give way to a more concrete sense of "wanting . . . what's human"

(732, 738). The clash between the women's idealism and pragmatism is mediated by the presence of Arthur. His own combination of romanticism and convention points to the way each woman responds to personal and historical disaster.

In creating these alternating dualities, Bowen defines her characters by their responses to historic circumstances. Thus Arthur says, "[T]here's no such place," while Pepita insists, "[W]hat it tries to say doesn't matter: I see what it makes me see" (730).[59] In their mutual misunderstanding the two women and the man register differences that, in reasserting their individuality, regenerate them in a time of loss and dispossession. It thus becomes clear that whatever apocalyptic view of history the Battle of Britain encourages, Bowen sees a regenerative capacity in the contradictions and ambiguities that situate characters in historical processes. With its symbolic, poetic structure, the story places the momentary, concrete dislocations of war in both social and mythological contexts.

Two stories, written immediately after the war, "Gone Away" and "I Hear You Say So," provide a postscript to Bowen's view of history. Each story questions, in a combination of hope and despair, what the future will bring. "I Hear You Say So" takes place a week after VE Day in a London victorious but uneasy about the aftermath. With panoramic vision, the narrator takes us across a park in northwest London to touch base with several people from different social classes. Providing a gloss on the hopeful song of a nightingale are the voices—hopeful, skeptical, cynical, and reflective—of people so overwhelmed by the war that "[e]ven Victory's nearly been too much" (755). Questioning what is "normal" after all the losses and barely comprehensible gains, they form a collective view that traditional British caution may be the sanest step toward a knowable and manageable future (755).

"Gone Away" is an apocalyptic tale of Mr. Van Winkle's return to his village after a holocaust. The village is empty of people except the Vicar; everything about it is unnatural, including the buildings, which are only mock-up facades like a movie set, and the weather, in which the sun shines relentlessly. Paired with "I Hear You Say So," "Gone Away" presents an alternate vision of caution gone awry. Too much planning has resulted in a civilization bored to distraction with sameness. On the day when the regular ticking of its machinelike structure stops, everyone runs away. Having been regulated to the point where "Brightervillians had ceased to talk, being able to think of nothing further to say," they are panicked by the sudden silence of their utopia (763).

Both the cautionary tale and the dystopic fable end similarly. On hearing the nightingale, a young widow in "I Hear You Say So" breaks with the hope of "a magic recapturing of the past" to face the future as a mystery (757). At the end of "Gone Away," the Vicar and Van Winkle are surprised to hear a cry in the void. It turns out to be an old woman in a wheelchair; her good humor and insistence on having her tea put civilization back on course. Her voice and those of the young woman and the nightingale signal the end of sameness and stasis. Calling for individuality and interdependence, however mundane, these voices present an alternative to the chaos and violence of the past and the mechanization of the future. Recognizing both loss and dispossession at the center of their lives, the women in these stories seize the opportunity to revise the plots that controlled them. Crippled and old, the woman in "Gone Away" maneuvers her chair ahead of the perplexed men trying to keep up with her. Feeble yet persistent, she imprints her humanity on a desolate landscape: "Overhead, in the colourless crystal sky, there appeared a cloud the size of a man's hand" (766). In her turn, the young widow becomes a "fugitive" from being cast as "the angel at the foot of her own bed, never staying long under any kind of roof, always wanting to be in an hotel or apartment house where she was no one's business" (756). The tragedy of her loss is superseded by an unknowable future in which she is freed from being the angel of domestic life. The end of this story inscribes a new possibility for female character in the English literary tradition: She is unknowable because the future is hers to invent.

Three Masterworks

Although several of Bowen's stories have been hailed as masterpieces, three in particular deserve separate attention because they combine all the techniques and narrative modes she described as necessary to her craft. The icy but decaying halls of a Palladian mansion in "The Disinherited" evoke a "scene [that] burned itself into" Bowen's creative consciousness (*MT*, 129). "Summer Night" connects the fates of two women—who never meet —in a single image of a "leaf-drowned castle ruin" (605); the story "approach[es] aesthetic and moral truth" (*CI*, 43). And in "The Happy Autumn Fields" "the idea of the past draws" one woman to a scene 100 years earlier in order to unveil "the illusion" that conceals history's "dismay and apathy" (*MT*, 57). In each of these stories Bowen combines her elegiac and satiric modes with a jolt of comedy.

"The Disinherited" connects two unlikely stories. In one, Davina, the penniless but aristocratic niece of Mrs. Archworth, takes her new friend Marianne, the recently transplanted suburbanite, on a midnight ride in which they discover the limits of their emotional horizons. The narrator keeps a deeply ironic distance from the women and everyone they meet, while weaving intricate connections between autumn's decay and the personal losses of all concerned. Bursting through this delicately nuanced web, almost exactly at midpoint, is the brute force of a very different story. Prothero, Mrs. Archworth's chauffeur, writes the same letter every night to his dead lover. Like a relentlessly throbbing pain, the chauffeur's repetitive language of desire and dread drives through Davina and Marianne's story of denial and defense. If Prothero's talk seems to rip the more delicate story apart, it is also trapped by being woven into the other.

Each scene, place, narrative mode, and voice intensifies the others. As "The Disinherited" connects strands of seemingly dissonant worlds, characters, and plots, it dramatizes their separateness. This method is also true of the way Bowen sets up the relationship among these characters, these houses, and her readers. It is as though each house and character stands in bas relief in a way showing that any attempted relationship between them will ultimately be felt as invasive. The more each one is revealed to us, the more the house or character seems to recede into a kind of mystery. Prothero's narrative, for example, exposes his rage and despair again and again, but the repetition obfuscates the man hidden behind the assumed identity of the chauffeur. In drawing these narrative connections Bowen conveys the sense, as she said of Katherine Mansfield's stories, that "nothing is more isolated, more claustrophobic than the dreamfastness of a solitary person no one knows."[60]

The tension Bowen sets up among Aunt Archworth's manor house, Marianne's suburban estate, Lord Thingummy's decaying country house, the hut where Prothero meets his lover, and Prothero's room over the garage suggests the desperation and self-absorption of the characters. As none of these houses turns out to be a safe haven, however, together they suggest a pervasive social bankruptcy.

With the introduction of Prothero and his tale of murder and loss of identity, the narrative tensions are relieved only by an inevitable disintegration wrought by the entropy enfolding all people and places. Bowen's weave of the class-bound and the classless produces a picture of a society decaying as a result of having entrusted its future to a failed promise. "The Disinherited" shows a landed aristocracy incapable of assuming responsibility for itself, much less for anyone else; the story's upwardly mobile middle class is lost on its way to nowhere. Together, they represent a frozen society that disintegrates at the first disturbance. In this milieu the chauffeur's chameleonlike presence and obsessively repeating narrative disturb—both critically and comically—the myths of constancy and equilibrium contained in the other characters' stories. The man disguising his energy and identity in chauffeurs' livery trades sexual favors and mutual contempt for the cigarette money that keeps the restless Davina going. But it is the narrative he rewrites every night that brings terror to their comedy of sex and bad manners and to the elegiac tale of the dispossessed and lost.

The story sets up an immediate clash between the new country-suburban estate and the old-town Victorian manor. Despite Mrs. Archworth's efforts to be gracious to Marianne, it becomes clear that they, like their houses, are inherently incompatible. Their differences are further highlighted by Lord Thingummy's decaying Palladian mansion, which appears midway through the story and miles away from the others. The story, however, hinges on Marianne's and Davina's need for each other. Davina, who lives "with and on her aunt," has worn herself out in unsatisfactory love affairs and other expensive habits (377). Stifled by a myth of privilege, her energies are reduced to tics— compulsively clicking her finger and thumb, she paces the floors of her aunt's house and the surrounding country as though searching for outlets but confident its empty horizons will yield none.[61] She makes friends with the unlikely Marianne, a middle-class housewife who, like Mrs. Watson in "Attractive Modern Homes," has been transplanted from a community of friends and now feels very much alone in her new house. A source of pride but also of loneliness, the estate's "exclusive" modernism, with its "stigmata of intellectual good taste," repels Davina and chills Marianne (376, 378). The property may be new, but it suggests neither youth nor vitality. Its promise of a fresh start is as doomed as the original estate, which was broken up to make room for the more "functional" houses. The combined image of the story's three houses suggests an ecological disaster.

Together, Davina and Marianne escape their homes for one night. With bad directions and a nebulous invitation, they take Marianne's car to a party at Lord Thingummy's. But their midnight journey to discover adventure and change ends in failure. Neither a changing new world nor an ossified old one can offer direction for their still-inchoate desires. They are greeted at Lord Thingummy's mansion with "patterns of black ice," a sign that the spirits of a land and people are frozen (385). It is here that an old but worn-out landed aristocracy still feeds on those who cling to its failed promise of traditional order and prestige. The party is hosted by a former lover of Davina's, another aristocrat fallen on hard times. Oliver has been commissioned to catalog Lord Thingummy's library. Like every effort in this story, this too is a futile enterprise, both because Oliver is entirely unmotivated to do his job and because even if he were, he could hardly carry it out: After aeons of neglect, the books, undusted and unread, fall apart when they are touched.

The meeting among Oliver, Davina, Marianne, and a motley assortment of guests dramatizes their inability to escape "from poverty, each frozen into their settings" (387). There is no real opportunity to change, to connect, to find direction among dissolute aristocrats, wandering émigrés, and those who have failed to find passage from the lower classes. Miriam, who would like £100 to spruce up her tea-and-cake parlor, really knows that neither money nor company will get her out of her "hole of a place," that "everything's talk . . . and what does all that come to?" (399, 398). Bowen is critical of both a failed aristocracy and the compromises and purposelessness of an apathetic middle class. What Marianne discovers here is the "disorientation" resulting from having to trade her secure world for her husband's nostalgic dream of retiring near the college of his youth. She finds only the terrors of uprootedness, an experience that chills her as it "reflect [s] itself in the vacant glass of her mind." (405).

"The Disinherited" moves among several layers of dispossession and disintegration. The traditional values that once supported county aristocracy and old-town gentry have shifted. Although there are no explicit topical signs of a specific historical moment, the portrait of an impoverished aristocracy, of meager dreams of economic progress and the building of new suburbs, draws our attention to a time of economic and emotional depression and hopes for change and progress. Being unsettled and bankrupt emasculates the aristocratic Oliver and makes Davina heady with risk, but her self-destructiveness shows the weakness built into the foundations of her world.

That in this tale manners and morals do not lead to regeneration is most clearly stated in Prothero's narrative, which subverts that of Davina and Marianne by showing the delusions behind taking a risk and embarking on a fresh start. Whoever Prothero was before he murdered his lover and assumed the name on the passport of the man he shoved into a river in France, he was no better or worse off than he is with his new identity: "I always was what I am, now I am what I always was, what you said that time. Flunky" (393). Although he claims to be a "free man . . . snug as a monk," he is trapped by his obsession for a woman and by the failure of his England to allow social or economic mobility: "Now I don't want all that any more, now I don't want" (393). Compulsively repeating the same narrative night after night, he recites a litany of his entrapment.

In contrast to the world of endless possibilities D. H. Lawrence imagined for the classless Mellors and his aristocratic lover, Lady Chatterly, no new world emerges at the end of Prothero's love affair with his upper-class lover. His is a romantic dream doomed to failure. As in Lawrence's novel, the unhappy and frozen woman takes as her lover a man from the lower classes who should be unencumbered by the social constraints of her class. But as Bowen makes only too clear, the romantic idyll in the cottage in the woods is but a fantasy. Here the lovers use each other to destructive ends; the cottage in the woods is no escape from the freezing emptiness of the great country house, the claustrophobic warmth of the town manor, or the functional but cool design

of the suburban estate. The dependence of one class on another produces only murder, both literally and figuratively: Prothero murders his
lover and, in a sense, himself; his disguise covers a self that has no
substance or shape to call its own. The love nest is simply another
version of the grave. Prothero discovers not what he desired in romantic
love but only the inability to find satisfaction and the compulsion to
keep trying: "Love was just having to act in the one way. There was
just one way we could go, like both being in a tram. We acted the way
we had to" (393).

Even the act of murder, which should have brought closure to his
endless quest, is never over for Prothero. His anger at Anita's indifference to him revives each time he writes, "[T]o see you don't see that
I don't see you or want you" (397). Murder and desire are reinscribed
in the letter he rewrites "loud" every night, so that the dead Anita will
hear his plaint (397). Prothero is frozen in place just like Davina,
Oliver, Marianne, and the hapless Anita. Anita's grave, frozen over one
minute and dank and decaying the next, is one more place in which
dreams of desire do not stay buried but instead haunt the living. In
this story the characters are complicit in their own freeze and disintegration.[62] Davina and Prothero feel alive only in parasitic relationships
in which they slowly disappear as they feed off each other.

Placing Prothero's narrative at the center of the story adds a macabre
irony to the comic farce of Oliver's party. Like a mausoleum, Lord
Thingummy's mansion hosts a party of living dead. The guests' nihil-
istic chatter—about not "believ[ing] in anything" and the "White Russian with little stake in the future"—and Oliver's feeble attempt to
kiss Marianne are juxtaposed with Prothero's hopeless desire for emotional connection and a new start (398, 389). Like Virginia Woolf's *Mrs.
Dalloway*, this story contains two narratives about two sets of characters.
Although Bowen's characters, unlike Woolf's, interact directly, the
technique connecting them also suggests their irreparable separation.
Still, this is not a depressing story; comedy abounds even in its bleak-
est moments. As Oliver's guests fumble their way around the elephan-
tine halls of Lord Thingummy's mansion, their weary sighs parody
their failed seductions. Like her literary ancestor Maria Edgeworth,
Bowen depicts the grotesque consequences of a dissolute society,
showing it to be as absurd as it is self-defeating.

Another master story, set in Ireland, portrays self-deceived and self-
enclosed characters wishing for connection and regeneration. Perhaps
because war hangs like an ominous cloud over "Summer Night," even

fragile connections are seen as restorative. With the kind of wary affection reserved for incorrigible relatives, Bowen manages a complex portrait of her own homeland that exposes its romantic fantasies as misguided but also delights in their transformative possibilities.

The story sets up several interlocking contrasts in which comedies of sex and manners provide a critique of dispossession and loss. "Small" and decidedly modern in her stockingless sandals, the erotically charged Emma tears through the ancient, slumbering Irish countryside in her "big shabby family car" (583). She is on her way to meet her lover, "the big, fair, smiling, offhand, cold-minded" Robinson, a factory manager living in a rented house on the demesne of a ruined castle at the edge of a "sleepy" town (589). Stability and disturbance, old traditions and new money, and fantasy and restraint are at odds in every scene, personifying a world that is as ambivalent about trusting order as it is about seeking change. With its wartime setting, this society is one in which "[i]n the heart of the neutral Irishman indirect suffering pulled like a crooked knife" (588).

As in "The Disinherited," Bowen here interlaces three narrative strands, each providing a critical gloss on the others, each in turn questioned by its own internal tensions. Using Emma's trip as a unifying thread, the story weaves back and forth between the family she leaves behind at home and the two people visiting Robinson at his house. In each place people try to connect but remain separated by the very fantasies that associate them in narrative terms with characters they never meet. More elegiac than "The Disinherited," though it depicts neither violence nor depression, this story suggests that the war is a historically logical consequence in a world whose fantasies and absurdities may yet be saving graces.[63]

Ironically representing disruptive change, the usually "imperturbable" Robinson is challenged by an unexpected visit (588). Unable to resist his "anxious, disturbed attraction" to Robinson's "unmoved physical presence," Justin Cavey drops by with his sister, Queenie, only to feel shunted aside (589). Justin's "solitary arrogance," which prevents him from seeing anything except as it reflects the "screen of his own mind," disconnects him from others and from history (588). The "neutral man," he signifies his country and its self-protected isolationism. He carries on about the war being "an awful illumination; it's destroyed our dark; we have to see where we are. Immobilized, God help us, and each so far apart that we can't even try to signal each other" (590). Justin's impaired vision is a product of his neutrality, not his impartiality, and his "we" is fundamentally self-absorbed. This perspective keeps him from making connections, not only with Robinson but with his own sister and, finally, with his own place in the war in Europe. His neutral stance allows him to feel that "[o]ur faculties have slowed down without our knowing" (590).

Justin's blindness to the historic moment does not allow him to transcend it; such blindness is instead presented as a hysterical symptom of not wanting to take any responsibility for what is happening around him. Bowen offers another perspective, however, one that initially seems just as impaired but actually does provide what Justin is pleading for—a visionary "break through" (590). The deafness of his sister, Queenie, heightens her capacity to see "with joy . . . visions of where we are" (591). Hers is a romantic vision, but not a wish-fulfillment fantasy, for it creates genuine connections between past and present, passion and tenderness, and even unlikely characters.[64] Between Robinson and the middle-aged deaf woman, for example, springs an affinity neither has occasion to express openly. But it is conveyed in two parallel scenes that also link Queenie to Emma and to the past and future. The significance of Robinson's walk with Emma becomes clear only at the end of the story, when Queenie recalls another summer night many years earlier when she had walked with a lover in the same place: "His hand, like Robinson's, had been on her elbow, but she had guided him" (607). Now, 20 years later, "it was Robinson who, guided by Queenie down leaf tunnels, took the place on the stone seat by the lake" (608).

The narrative provisionally conjoins these characters, each "locked" into his or her solitary world (587). Emma notices the photos of Robinson's children that earlier captured Queenie's attention. Then, as Emma moves through Robinson's house and garden, it is as though she too is guided by Queenie, for she has a vision informed by that of the older woman. Emma's romantic enchantment with the demesne ruins comes to an end as she realizes that what is "adventure" to her is habit to Robinson, that if he does not break her heart, he has "broken her fairytale" (604–5). "Summer Night," however, ends not by dismissing romantic imagination but by verifying it, in the form of the "solitary and almost fairylike world created by [Queenie's] deafness" (587). Queenie's imagination is a saving grace; as she recalls her walk with her lover, "the transposition of this nothing or everything" becomes "an everything" (607).

Although the characters are at best able to effect the most tenuous relations, the narrative draws them together. About midpoint through the story, Emma's daughter Vivie colors her naked body with chalk tattoos, a romantic gesture in which she transforms herself into a cartoon that affirms and questions all the characters' fears and fantasies. In a time of war it signifies her Aunt Fran's fear that "the enemy is within,"that the dissolution of internal order by such "anarchy" as Emma's adultery and her child's play means that "[t]he blood of the world is poisoned" and "[e]ach here falls to the enemy" (599, 597). But if the childish gesture satirizes the older woman's fears, it also confirms them, for this "implacable miniature" of her mother, indulging her own "animal" senses, also wants "to run the night" that is "threatened" as well by enemies outside (596, 599). At the same time, the child's behavior validates her mother's frenetic drive for passion. Their staid, well-ordered house may provide a sustaining base, but it needs a woman's romantic yearning for sensual expression to keep it from "the touch of decay" that throws "lifeless reflections" on its occupants' lives (594).

Ultimately, however, it is the combination of romantic gesture and parody in Vivie's art that suggests the story's wish for renewal. Painting herself may seem like the ultimate narcissistic gesture, with her body as the canvas, both medium and signifier of pleasure and meaning. But the narrator's affectionate and comic description assures us this is not the case. In its very childishness, Vivie's naked, tattooed body dancing on her mother's bed charts the course from Queenie's romantic dream to Emma's broken "fairytale" (605). Drawing on her own resources just as the deaf woman does, Vivie endows her "lifeless" home with a warmth and vitality that derive from her mother's sensuality.[65] But then "Aunt Fran, as though the child were on fire," wraps her up in an eiderdown "until only the prisoner's dark eyes, so like her mother's, were left free to move wildly" (598). Embodying her mother's broken "fairytale," the child is wrapped up in the constraints of a traditional order that defends itself from the siege of history by putting down the "anarchy" of a woman's passion.

In contrast with the transformative possibilities of the women's imaginations, the obsessions of Justin and Robinson, like those of Oliver and Prothero in "The Disinherited," are enervating and self-defeating. The professed neutrality of the one is only a self-protective screen, while the business drive and easy cynicism of the other conceal a lack of passion. But unlike the women in "The Disinherited," who are defeated by the pervasive depression, the women in "Summer

Night" are energized at the very moment war threatens. As Aunt Fran realizes, "to wrap the burning child up did not put out the fire. You cannot look at the sky without seeing the shadow, the men destroying each other" (599). Thus the fires of man's war and of woman's passion converge. Destruction is held back not by neutrality but by a young girl who experiences herself as the source of imaginative transformation.

"The Happy Autumn Fields" may be Bowen's most haunting story. There are no ghosts, but the present has no meaning except as it is haunted by the past. As we have seen, this theme reverberates through all Bowen's work, connecting the construction of an individual's psychology to the reconstruction of the historical past. Because the past remains elusive, however, filtered through memory and myth, it is more felt than understood. It is experienced emotionally, a feeling that one's life is part of an old story. Bowen's characters paradoxically find that their feelings become more their own as they are transmitted by people who lived long ago. In stories like "Foothold" and "The Back Drawing-Room" feelings from the past manifest themselves as ghosts, while in novels like *Friends and Relations* and *The House in Paris* and in stories like "The Shadowy Third" and "The Cat Jumps" the past is relived as characters in the present replay unresolved tensions.

Past and present are not abstract constructs for Bowen; they are the sum of social, political, and cultural events, a climate that in turn shapes her characters' psychology. Therefore, whether the past is manifest as a ghost or as a character replaying an old scenario, the story signals a history that continues into the present. Perhaps the most clearly marked on this continuum of past and present are those stories which concern war, for no war results solely from the conflicts specific to its time. By its very name World War II is for Bowen the result of unresolved conflicts in the past simmering to the point where they blow up in the present. In many of her World War II stories characters are haunted by ghosts from the preceding world war, as in "The Demon Lover." Some reexperience the losses of the past only to remain lost, as does Gavin in "Ivy Gripped the Steps." And the narrator in "Songs My Father Sang Me" finds herself in the plaintive refrain of a World War I song that recalls her father's story.

In "The Happy Autumn Fields" past and present jolt each other with shocks of violent yearning and losses.[66] Reaching back into history further than ever before in her fiction, Bowen divides the story between a Victorian scene and the Blitz. Neither scene is weighted as the key to the significance of the other. Instead, the movement back and forth gives the sense that the yearnings, violence, and losses of one era begin and end in the other and that each one can be understood only in the other's light. Thus, the emphasis on order and stability in Victorian life is made understandable only as it is threatened by the violence that erupts during the Blitz. For example, the accident that takes the life a young man in the earlier time seems as much a result of the future tumultuous world war as of the horse shying in empty and peaceful Victorian fields. Conversely, the jolts of falling debris during the Blitz seem to originate in the hidden, seething violence of Victorian order. In this contrapuntal rhythm, as history boomerangs forward and backward, present and past haunt each other with the sense that neither is complete or knowable in itself; rather, present and past are part of an ongoing process in which each is regenerated and made understandable in the other.

Even more radically, the whole question of whether past and present history can be understood is vexed by the implied presence of the reader, for as Victorian and modern scenes interchange, we are encouraged to participate by reading the two strands as though they should add up to meaning, to answers unavailable to the characters confined in either setting. But as the final clues are offered to us, we—like the characters—are left only with questions.

The title, "The Happy Autumn Fields," is ironic. It refers to a romantic view of history that the combined tales question. As the story of the present interrupts the narration of the past, signs of pain and violence disturb the otherwise-tranquil surfaces of an idyllic Victorian scene and wishes turn to dread. The opening scene shows a Victorian upper-class family enjoying the privilege that gives them a sense of order, purpose, and stability. "Papa" leads his children across his vast fields while they follow his plans for courtship, marriage, and succession (671). The scene of long ago ends abruptly, however, when the narrator shifts from past to present tense: "We surmount the skyline: the family come into our view, we into theirs" (675). As the first sign of disorder, we are invited into the narrative, indeed to join the narrator in her desperate plea to Sarah to "Stop oh stop Henrietta's heartbreaking singing" (675). But we are all helpless to revise this disturbance in the Victorian tale, much less to understand it.

"A shock of striking pain" moves the narrative away from the lost past and transports us to the present (675). What is most "striking," however, is that the pain reverberates from the Victorian scene but is part of an event taking place a century later. A young woman who has returned to her London home during the Blitz to retrieve some valuables has taken a nap and is awakened from a dream as she strikes her knuckles on a piece of furniture.[67] Paradigmatic of the story's vision of history, this pain is the outgrowth of events in the past, for Mary's dream consists of that earlier scene and her pain is presented as both a continuation and a result of it. It is as though her "outflung hand" reaches back not only in time but also into a reality different from that limned by the palpable signs of war (675), a reality constructed by her empathetic dream of feeling the past. The pain felt vividly by the Victorian characters becomes fully realized only as the modern character reacts to it.

The narrative works in reverse as well, as we can see in Mary's off-hand relationship with her fiancé, Travis. Her responses to him become understandable to her and to us only in light of the Victorian courtship tale: "His possessive angry fondness was part, of course, of the story of him and Mary, which like a book once read she remembered clearly but with indifference. Frantic at being delayed here, while the moment awaited her in the cornfield, she all but afforded a smile at the grotesquerie of being saddled with Mary's body and lover" (677). Although both "books" appear to be about the same subject—courtship—Mary's compelling attraction to the older story reveals another kind of attachment and still another story. She wishes to become Sarah, whose own intensely close relationship with her sister, Henrietta, violently disrupts the Victorian tale and triggers Mary's response to it. The first sign of disruption occurs during the walking party, which, for Sarah, serves the purpose of meeting up with Eugene, her brother's friend and her suitor. But this most conventional tale is subverted by another, for Sarah yearns as much for Henrietta as she does for Eugene. Bowen does not skirt the sisters' passion for each other, as Sarah's musings show: "She must never have to wake in the early morning except to the birdlike stirrings of Henrietta. . . . Rather than they should cease to lie in the same bed, she prayed they might lie in the same grave" (672). A self-fulfilling prophecy, this prayer is ultimately as responsible for the conclusion of the sisters' story as it is for Mary's ambivalent desire for Travis and her urge to join Sarah and Henrietta.

Although the sisters' relationship fits well within the traditional order of the Victorian family, it has the power to destroy it, as Sarah foresees: "How could she put into words the feeling of dislocation, the formless dread that had been with her since she found herself in the drawing-room," the feeling that in this halcyon time "the seconds were numbered?" (681).[68] The language Sarah uses to express her feelings makes them more consistent with Mary's wartime story than with the carefully ordered tranquillity of her own story. Their separate tales therefore converge at the point of Mary's desire and Sarah's dread. Sensing that she too has been dreaming, Sarah helps to produce a narrative that connects the violent emotions seething within a domestic tale to the siege of the homeland in a world war. Despite the prescribed decorum in "Mama's" drawing room, Henrietta utters a war cry to the man who would carry off her sister: "She *is* never out of my sight. . . . Whatever tries to come between me and Sarah becomes nothing" (683). This outburst is immediately followed by an aftershock of the Blitz: "The house rocked [with an] enormous dull sound of the explosion," one leaving more than "a minor trickle of dissolution" in both houses (683). Henrietta's warning to Eugene is wielded "like a scientific ray"; it is a weapon that joins force with Sarah's earlier prayer to bring the Victorian courtship tale to a violent close and thus to connect it with the later war story (675). At the end of "The Happy Autumn Fields" we discover that Eugene is killed in a riding accident and Sarah and Henrietta probably remained unmarried and died young. Whatever other circumstances played a role in these destinies or in Mary's, the narrative directs responsibility at the sisters' wish to be united forever.

Although the sisters' union after death depends on a tale of Victorian sensibility, it is realized only in a story of "the anaesthetized and bewildered present" (*MT,* 98). Mary's story represents a yearning to overcome wartime's unsettling combination of "depersonaliz [ing] persons" and "an obsession" with "personal destiny" (*MT,* 97). In her essay about her stories of this period Bowen says that "during the war the overcharged subconsciousnesses of everybody overflowed and merged . . . and we felt, if not knew, each other" (*MT,* 95). At the same time, however, people's individual dreams "with which formerly matter-of-fact people consoled themselves by day were compensations" (*MT,* 96). Although Mary's dream compensates only momentarily for her decentered wartime life, it is a sign of an alternative: "What has happened is cruel: I am left with a fragment torn out of a day, a day I don't even know where or when; and now how am I to help laying that like a pattern against the poor stuff of everything else?" (684).

Mary's dream is part of "a pattern" that connects her with kindred spirits who populate a tale foretelling the violence and disconnections of her own "book." A model of twentieth-century themes of alienation and fragmentation, Mary's narrative can acknowledge, piece together, and reconstruct the violent past. Most important, it takes the modern, destabilized heroine to lend coherence to the fixed female characters of the past and to interpret their story. In some ways Mary seems too passive to be the agent of this discovery: After all, it is Travis who reads through the letters and papers of the Victorian characters, constructs their fate, and whisks Mary away from her house to fulfill *his* plans. His pragmatic view of reality and history, however, cannot connect past and present so that they cohere and make meaning. Rather, the connections that construct a whole story out of the bifurcated "Happy Autumn Fields" are made by the feelings flowing among Sarah, Henrietta, and Mary. The yearning of these women for one another conveys the sense that only together do they constitute wholeness. Realizing she is separated from Henrietta and Sarah forever, Mary feels she can "[n] o longer reckon . . . who she was" (683). They cannot be joined in life or in death; however, Mary and Sarah merge in a dream that reconstitutes conventional fictions of family life and courtship into a history of instability and violent ends.

Like the story's movements between past and present, the women's dream reverberates with each other's desires and fears, which are thus shown to be continuous, without beginning or end. The women's stories are entirely different from those which take their lead from Papa or Travis, and the women undo Papa's dynastic plans and Travis's fatalistic interpretation by creating a relationship outside the conventions of courtship, marriage, and family continuity. Indeed, the women's dream is so threatening to men's stories that it disrupts them by calling attention to the violence that signals the end of patriarchal family sagas. Thus Eugene's death is also the result of a traditional tale of dynastic succession and order, for as Mary's tale shows, the line from Victorian order leads to world war. The tranquillity of the Victorian scene is therefore truly an illusion, a "mist of love" that sows its own seeds of violence (681). The women's yearning represents an alternative tale, an escape from such violence. Papa's disappearance is a strong sign that his story is becoming anomalous even as he leads his children down his garden path.

On the one hand, neither Mary's nor Sarah's story represents a way out of violent history, especially as one tale seems trapped in the other and Sarah and Mary dramatize the similar conditions of women 100 years apart; moreover, although only Mary's house is fractured by war, the Victorian house is split apart by its internal tensions. On the other hand, violence is a saving grace here because it forces the women to recognize the disorder hidden in their lives. Out of the chaos of the present grows an empathy and understanding of the less recognizable turbulence of the past. In this story more than any other, it becomes clear that however constrained women are in the values and conventions of their time and place, only they are capable of composing a new story out of disturbing old ones. Mary and Sarah together wrest their stories away from Travis and Papa to create an altogether-new kind of tale. Building connections out of isolation and discontinuity, these two women point the way to a fiction that "give [s] scene, action, event, character a poetic new actuality" (*CI*, 43). They "cull the past from fiction" and in so doing, create an "idea of the past which draws us" because they unveil the secret yearnings of women as agents of history (*MT*, 58).

Notes to Part 1

1. Howard Moss, "Interior Children," *New Yorker*, February 1979, 128.

2. See, for example, William Heath, *Elizabeth Bowen* (Madison: University of Wisconsin Press, 1961); Edwin Kenney, *Elizabeth Bowen* (Lewisburg, Pa.: Bucknell University Press, 1975); and, most recently, Harriet S. Chessman, "Women and Language in the Fiction of Elizabeth Bowen," *Twentieth Century Literature* 29 (Spring 1983):69–85.

3. Preface to *Encounters*, in *The Mulberry Tree: The Writings of Elizabeth Bowen*, ed. Hermione Lee (New York: Harcourt Brace Jovanovich, 1986), 121. Writings from this volume are hereafter cited in the text as *MT*.

4. "The Bend Back," in *MT*, 57–58.

5. *The Faber Book of Modern Short Stories*, in *Collected Impressions* (New York: Knopf, 1950), 39. Writings from this volume are hereafter cited in the text as *CI*.

6. *Bowen's Court* (New York: Ecco Press, 1979), 19; hereafter cited in the text as *BC*. About houses in Bowen's work, see R. B. Kershner, Jr., "Bowen's Oneiric *House in Paris*," *Texas Studies in Language and Literature* 28 (Winter 1986):407–23; Richard Gill, *Happy Rural Seat* (New Haven, Conn.: Yale University Press, 1972); and Gary T. Davenport, "Elizabeth Bowen and the Big House," *Southern Humanities Review* 9 (Winter 1974):27–34.

7. "The Big House," in *MT*, 28–29.

8. John Bayley, *The Short Story: Henry James to Elizabeth Bowen* (New York: St. Martin's Press, 1988), 9, 11, 38; hereafter cited in the text as Bayley.

9. "The Mulberry Tree," in *MT*, 21. Gayle Greene discusses the liberating function of memory in the work of contemporary women novelists. Bowen is more ambivalent than either the nostaligic British writers or the revisionists cited by Greene (in "Feminist Fiction and the Uses of Memory," *Signs: Journal of Women in Culture and Society* 16 [Winter 1991]: 290–321). Memory can unlock an irremedial past for Bowen's characters, whose brutalities persist in contemporary social institutions. These brutalities may be recounted and critiqued, but they resist revision even in representation.

10. A. C. Partridge traces James's influence on Bowen in "Language and Identity in the Shorter Fiction of Elizabeth Bowen" (in *Irish Writers and Society at Large*, ed. Masaru Sekine [New York: Barnes and Noble, 1985], (169–79), as does Angus Wilson in his introduction to Bowen's *The Collected Stories* ([New York: Knopf, 1981], 7–11).

11. See Elizabeth Hardwick, "Elizabeth Bowen's Fiction," *Partisan Review* 16 (1949):114–21. George Kearns, however, in his review of *The Collected Stories*, shows how Bowen sympathizes with the way class and social codes entrap women in marriage and place them and others "precariously at the edge of the comfortable classes" ("Fiction Chronicle," *Hudson Review* 34 [Summer 1981]:300).

111

12. Joseph M. Flora, ed., *The English Short Story: 1880–1945* (Boston: G. K. Hall, 1985), 47; hereafter cited in the text as Flora.

13. "D. H. Lawrence," in *CI*, 158–59. For a discussion of Bowen's relation to modernism, see Clare Hanson, "The Free Story," in *Elizabeth Bowen: Modern Critical Views*, ed. Harold Bloom (New York: Chelsea House, 1987):139–51.

14. Preface to *Stories by Elizabeth Bowen*, in *MT*, 130.

15. Preface to *The Second Ghost Book*, in *Afterthought* (London: Longmans Green, 1952), 101–2. Writings from this volume are hereafter cited in the text as *A*.

16. For Bowen's relationship to other Anglo-Irish writers, see Frank Tuohy, "Five Fierce Ladies," in *Irish Writers and Society at Large*, 199–206.

17. Mary Jarrett sees houses as ghostly incarnations of the "imprisonment" Bowen's characters feel consciously or unconsciously in their human relations ("Ambiguous Ghosts: The Short Stories of Elizabeth Bowen," *Journal of the Short Story in English* 8 [Spring 1987]:71–79).

18. Preface to *The Demon Lover*, in *MT*, 98.

19. *The Collected Stories of Elizabeth Bowen* (New York: Knopf, 1981), 200, 202; hereafter cited in the text by page numbers.

20. Allen E. Austin notes that Janet's "suppressed desires produce the ghost of a woman, not a man" (*Elizabeth Bowen* [New York: Twayne, 1971], 100).

21. Frank Tuohy sees the destroyer as a sign of Anglo-Ireland cutting itself off from history (204).

22. Sean O'Faolain sees the comedy in this scene as Celtic high spirits (*The Short Story* [London: Collins, 1948]), while A. C. Partridge observes that Bowen's "wit chafes at the technical restrictions of her chosen form" (177).

23. In "Eire" in *The Mulberry Tree*, Bowen sees Ireland's neutrality as part of its historic ambivalence toward England.

24. Susan Gubar and Sandra Gilbert, in *No Man's Land: The Place of the Woman Writer in the Twentieth Century*, vol. *1*, *The War of the Words* (New Haven, Conn.: Yale University Press, 1988), and *Volume 2: Sexchanges* (New Haven, Conn.: Yale University Press, 1989), discuss a "war of the sexes" between men and women writers between World Wars I and II. Bowen's historical concerns are less universal than those of Gilbert and Gubar in that they are tied to social structures that define her characters by cultural and class markers.

25. John Hildebidle sees the men suffering an intense sense of loss despite their intrusion on the women's world (*Five Irish Writers: The Errand of Keeping Alive* [Cambridge, Mass.: Harvard Unviersity Press, 1989], 89–90).

26. Austin indicts Mrs. Fisk for her "essential inhumanity" (106).

27. Marry Jarrett finds Ann Lee's power lethal, as "the mysterious enslaver" (73–74). Clare Hanson sees Ann Lee's "implacability of character" as protection (145). David Meredith argues that the story focuses on the struggle

by a female artist for independence ("Authorial Detachment in Elizabeth Bowen's 'Ann Lee's,'" *Massachusetts Studies in English* 8 [1982]): 10.

28. "I Died of Love," in *Choice: Some New Stories and Prose,* ed. William Sansom (London: Progress, 1946), 131; hereafter cited in the text as "Died."

29. Helena Michie argues that the "otherness" of female character disrupts traditional family models that stifle women's sense of themselves ("Not One of the Family: The Repression of the Other Woman in Feminist Theory," in *Discontented Discourses: Feminism/Textual Intervention/Psychoanalysis,* ed. Maureen Barr and Richard Feldstein [Urbana: University of Illinois Press, 1989], 15–28). Patricia Yaeger shows how women writers subvert and reverse traditional plot and character formulations through inventive use of language. See *Honey-Mad Women: Emancipatory Strategies in Women's Writing* (New York: Columbia University Press, 1988). Bowen's enigmatic female characters suggest that any definitive plotting or unambiguous use of language could tie her female characters to expectations that would be constraining.

30. Nancy Armstrong traces this phenomenon to eighteenth-century conduct books ("The Rise of the Domestic Woman," in *The Ideology of Conduct,* ed. Nancy Armstrong and Leonard Tennenhouse [New York: Methuen, 1987], 96–141).

31. Eva Figes discusses the reality principle of economics and passion in *Sex and Subterfuge: Women Writers to 1850* (New York: Persea, 1982).

32. Nina Auerbach explores the literary transformation of the old maid in *Woman and the Demon: Life of a Victorian Myth* (Cambridge, Mass.: Harvard University Press, 1982). Bowen has too often been accused of "unexamined social assumptions" about her women characters' complicity in classbound traditions and expectations. See, for example, Rosalind Miles, *The Female Form: Women Writers and the Conquest of the Novel* (London and New York: Routledge & Kegan Paul, 1987), 30–31. I explore Bowen's critique of traditional plotting in *Elizabeth Bowen* (London: Macmillan, 1990). This critique places Bowen among the experimental, anticanonical writers discussed by Ellen G. Friedman in "'Utterly Other Discourse': The Anticanon of Experimental Women Writers from Dorothy Richardson to Christine Brooke-Rose," *Modern Fiction Studies* 34 (Autumn 1988): 353–70.

33. Janet Dunleavy discusses the aggression aimed at Mr. Rossiter in "The Subtle Satire of Elizabeth Bowen and Mary Lavin," *Tulsa Studies in Women's Literature* 2 (Spring 1983):69–82.

34. William Trevor, "Between Holyhead and Dun Laoghaire," *Times Literary Supplement,* 6 February 1981, 131.

35. "Flavia," in *The Fothergill Omnibus,* ed. John Fothergill (London: Eyre and Spottiswood, 1931), 61.

36. On the conventions of marriage plots, see Nancy K. Miller, "Emphasis Added: Plots and Plausibilities in Women's Fiction," in *Feminist Criti-*

cism: Essays on Women, Literature and Theory, ed. Elaine Showalter (New York: Pantheon, 1985), 339–60.

37. Edward Mitchell sees William as replaceable in his family because "marriage and materialism are the penultimate values" ("Themes in Elizabeth Bowen's Short Stories," *Critique* 8 [Spring–Summer 1966]:50.

38. Mitchell reads Joyce James as "perverse" (198), while Austin sees her response to Margery as her only sign of feeling, 97–98.

39. "Uncle Silas," in *MT,* 111.

40. "Origins," in *MT,* 270.

41. Of particular interest to the study of women writers are the feminist revisions of psychoanalytic models of parent-child relationships, especially the socially constructed role of motherhood. See Nancy Chodorow, *The Reproduction of Mothering* (Berkeley: University of California Press, 1978); Marianne Hirsch, *The Mother-Daughter Plot: Narrative, Psychoanalysis, Feminism* (Bloomington: University of Indiana Press, 1989); Jane Flax, "The Conflict between Nurturance and Autonomy in Mother-Daughter Relationships and within Feminism," *Feminist Studies* 4 (June 1978):171–91; and Janet Sayers, *Sexual Contradictions: Psychology, Psychoanalysis, and Feminism* (London: Tavistock, 1986).

42. *The House in Paris* (New York: Knopf, 1936), 65.

43. Dunleavy discusses the story as a satire of manipulative people; A. C. Partridge identifies Bowen's concern with class in her treatment of the poor little rich girl's snobberies.

44. Suzanne Juhasz, in "Texts to Grow On: Reading Women's Romance Fiction" (*Tulsa Studies in Women's Literature* 7 [Fall 1988]:239–59), offers an alternative view of the marriage plot as celebrating "the cornerstone for a politically healthy society" (240).

45. See Lee R. Edwards, *Psyche as Hero: Female Heroism and Fictional Form* (Middletown, Conn.: Wesleyan University Press, 1984).

46. "So Much Depends," *Woman's Day,* September 1951, 159; hereafter cited in the text as "Depends."

47. "Out of a Book," in *MT,* 53.

48. "Just Imagine," in *Best British Short Stories,* ed. Edward O'Brien (London: Jonathan Cape, 1927), 88.

49. Judith Bates discusses the existential elements of the story's horror in "Undertones of Horror in Elizabeth Bowen's 'Look at All Those Roses' and 'The Cat Jumps,'" *Journal of the Short Story in English* 8 (Spring 1987):81–91.

50. Julia Briggs sees the ghost as filling the "spiritual void left by the shock of war" (*Night Visitors: The Rise and Fall of the English Ghost Story* [London: Faber, 1977], 181); Daniel Fraustino argues that the story's place among Bowen's World War II stories suggests Mrs. Drover's unconscious yearning to escape an unfulfilling marriage and domestic life ("Elizabeth Bowen's 'The Demon Lover': Psychosis or Seduction?" *Studies in Short Fiction* 17 [Fall

1980]:483–87); and Douglas Hughes sees the ghost as a function of Mrs. Drover's psychological collapse as war repeats itself ("Cracks in the Psyche: Elizabeth Bowen's 'The Demon Lover,'" *Studies in Short Fiction* 10 [1973]: 410–13).

51. Hildebidle observes that this house, like all Bowen's houses, is "an active" if ominous character (110).

52. Bates interprets the story's horror as stemming "from what deviates from the normal" (84).

53. Jarrett identifies Lou's problem as abandoning her life if she abandons her "desire to control one's fictions" (78).

54. "Gorki Stories," in *CI*, 153.

55. *The Heat of the Day* (Harmondsworth, England: Penguin Books, 1986), 168; hereafter cited in the text as *HD*.

56. Although Partridge sees Charles as grossly materialistic, he also condemns Louise as cold and "repelled by the mother's self-assured sentimentality" (173).

57. Hildebidle notes that the three sets of relationships accentuate the way in which "love cannot have a story" in 1939 (100).

58. Partridge notes "how Edwardian wealth could strangle human values" but does not link the values of the Edwardians to either world war (180). For a historiographical discussion of personal and collective reconstructions of the past and its relation to memory, see David Lowenthal, *The Past Is a Foreign Country* (Cambridge: Cambridge University Press, 1985).

59. There is much debate about Pepita's vision. Whereas Mitchell sees it as "her desire to escape into nonentity" (49), Jeslyn Medoff sees it as a refuge ("'There Is No Elsewhere': Elizabeth Bowen's Perceptions of War," *Modern Fiction Studies* 30 [Spring 1984]:73–81) James M Haule praises Bowen's portrayal of women's loneliness in their relation to society but sees Pepita's vision as a powerful but incomplete solution ("*She* and the Moral Dilemma of Elizabeth Bowen," *Colby Library Quarterly* 22 [December 1986]:205–14). Austin sees Pepita's vision as "an antidote to the war's unreality" (119); Bayley identifies a moral and emotional toughness in the story that keeps it from lapsing into melodrama or sentimentality (166–78); and Hanson sees Pepita's vision as a surrealist image that "reveals her subconscious desires" (150).

60. "A Living Writer: Katherine Mansfield," in *MT*, 79.

61. Haule links Bowen's artistic debt to Rider Haggard's *She* to development of Davina's character.

62. Mitchell argues that "the established order" is "in a state of upheaval," but he does not specify what constitues that order (51); Austin sees the story portraying the pain caused by the inability to adapt to change. Peter Brooks argues that the desire for "a new story" represents "a narrative redescription of reality," a yearning for change (*Reading for the Plot: Design and Intention in Narrative* [New York: Vintage, 1985], 235, 285).

63. Eudora Welty finds this story "the most remarkable of a group of longer ones" ("Seventy-nine Stories to Read Again," *New York Times Book Review*, 8 February 1981, 22). And in his review of *The Collected Stories* Sean O'Faolain uses "Summer Night" to analyze Bowen's various prose styles ("A Reading and Remembrance of Elizabeth Bowen," *London Review of Books*, 4–17 March 1982, 15, 17).

64. Medoff and Hildebidle each maintain that the story shatters illusions, whether they are "a romantic ideal" (Medoff, 76) or an "illusion which has both the shape and emotional force of life" (Hildebidle, 104). Austin interprets the Major as denying the connection between public and private worlds (116). And Antoinette Quinn discusses Irish neutrality in "Summer Night" and "The Happy Autumn Fields" in "Elizabeth Bowen's Irish Stories—1939–1945," in *Studies in Anglo-Irish Literature*, ed. Heinz Kozok (Bonn: Bouvier, 1982), 314–21.

65. Partridge condemns Emma as "a superficial and impulsive Irish housewife" (178), while Mitchell sees her encounter with Robinson as a necessary antidote to the possibility that she will "destroy all preexisting values and standards" (52).

66. Walter Allen calls this "Bowen's most subtle, complex story" (261).

67. Brad Hooper argues that this is not a dream but is instead a narrative device to make Mary and Sarah "alter-sel[ves]" ("Elizabeth Bowen's 'The Happy Autumn Fields': A Dream or *Not?*" *Studies in Short Fiction* 21 [Spring 1984]:151–53; Austin refers to the Victorian tale not only as Mary's dream but also as a "script" she creates as an antidote to war (120).

68. For a discussion of the range of intimacy permitted women of the time, see Carol Smith-Rosenberg, "The Female World of Love and Ritual: Relations between Women in Nineteenth-Century America," *Signs: Journal of Women in Culture and Society* 1 (Autumn 1975):1–30.

Part 2

THE WRITER

Introduction

Elizabeth Bowen was both a student and an artist of the short story. Although she rarely acknowledged the influence of other writers on her work, from her reviews of other writers' stories and prefaces to their story collections we can discern the qualities she admired and trace her aesthetic discrimination to her own work. Because Bowen came to see the short story as an art form distinctly separate from the novel, she did not model her stories along the structural lines set by Henry James or Thomas Hardy, whose stories she saw as condensed novels. Those elements of their art she found useful serve her ambiguous language, which both reveals and leaves open to speculation the nature of the intense passions setting the atmosphere of her stories. From James she learned a kind of suggestiveness she felt ought to characterize short fiction. Intensely imagistic and impressionistic, the short story for Bowen must dramatically and poetically evoke the writer's sensation while maintaining a dispassionate narrative stance, thus preventing the story from sliding into mere sensationalism or inflated emotion. Hence her admiration for the "dispassionate understatement of Maupassant" and Chekhov's romantic detachment.[1]

An excitement permeates everything Bowen wrote about short fiction. She calls the genre "impetuous" and tense, suggesting a kind of rebellious spirit in relation to its older relative, the novel. Like the "farouche" characters who repeatedly upset her more decorous drawing-room comedies, Bowen's idea of the short story is brash and calls the older conventions into question. It is perhaps for this reason she felt form was perfected by the equally rebellious writers of Ireland and the United States.

In the selections that follow, we see a writer expressing an acute self-consciousness about crafting a medium distinctly different from the novel. Whether she is reviewing the stories of Maxim Gorki, Katherine Mansfield, or herself, she remains consistent in her view that the short story has "special criteria" that challenge readers to see the shape of fiction differently.[2] Overturning a primary feature of the novel, she develops the idea of a story's action as a drama taking precedence over character development. Instead of character, emotion shapes events, and even contemporary political issues are transformed into "dislocated and stabbing" feeling (*CI*, 46). Even setting or atmosphere, as she writes in the preface to *Encounters*, is given its frame by emotion.

Because both her forms and her plots challenge literary and social convention, Bowen would probably agree with Frank O'Connor, who in his study of the short story, *The Lonely Voice*, argues that at its most characteristic the short story is unique in prose fiction forms. He attributes this distinctiveness to the story's "intense awareness of human loneliness, this sense of outlawed figures wandering about the fringes of society."[3] We have seen this loneliness in Bowen's stories, from her portrayals of children caught at the edge of adult society, yearning to recapture a sense of oneness with maternal nurture, to the adolescents who are becoming aware that their own nascent sense of self depends on separation, and in the adults and ghosts who negotiate spaces inside and outside the homes that promise sustenance but leave them out in the cold. The moments of acute loneliness dramatized in Bowen's stories not only constitute the backbone of her form but, as O'Connor proposes, are ideological. By this, O'Connor means that the story itself, like its characters, is outside the realm of "the community—romantic, individualistic, and intransigent" (O'Connor, 21).

Short story theory still seeks to justify the form. This view differs from studies of the novel, which long ago recovered from defending its popularity against charges of "low" culture. Theories of the novel have long accepted the way each new work revises previous definitions of the form, and such theories therefore investigate the genre through the work of individual authors and even individual novels. In their search for a technically distinct vocabulary to describe the short story, theorists and critics of short fiction often inadvertently express doubt about the form they claim to admire. In studies with such titles as "The State of the Art," "What Is a Short Story?" and "The Margins of Narrative" scholars search for ways to legitimize a form of fiction long embraced by Bowen as one that combines "an immediacy and purity of sensation" with drama in a way unique to itself.[4] Having written 11 novels and some 92 short stories, Bowen knew from the inside which form satisfied which narrative urges.

The following selections from Bowen's nonfiction show how the artist herself develops definitions of the short story form, a form that captured her imagination for 50 years. In addition to those selections dealing with Bowen's theories and assessments of the short story tradition, I have chosen pieces that express her concerns with the cultural and family history she acknowledges as a primary influence. Thus, excerpts from "The Forgotten Art of Living," "Sources of Influence," and *Bowen's Court,* allow us to see the way in which her formal and thematic concerns and her historic sensibilities intertwine. Viewing the short story as an ongoing literary tradition with its own creative imperatives enables Bowen to distinguish this form from other literary genres and to demonstrate without a doubt the unique combination of elements that make the short story so powerfully evocative.

Notes

1. Review of *The Faber Book of Modern Short Stories,* in *Collected Impressions* (New York: Knopf, 1950), 39; hereafter cited in the text as *CI.*

2. "Gorki Stories," in *CI,* 153.

3. Frank O'Connor, *The Lonely Voice: A Study of the Short Story* (Cleveland: World Publishing, 1963), 19; hereafter cited in the text as O'Connor.

4. For current debates on short story form, see Susan Lohafer and Jo Ellen Clarey eds., *Short Story Theory at a Crossroads* (Baton Rouge: Louisiana State University Press, 1989). Bowen discusses the application of her theory in "Stories by Elizabeth Bowen" in *The Mulberry Tree: Writings of Elizabeth Bowen,* ed. Hermione Lee (New York: Harcourt Brace Jovanovich, 1986), 130.

From "The Experience of Writing"

Up to now, have talked about writing in terms of theory . . . evolved out of 30 years writing experience. In talking about practice—I must shake off shyness, because creative writing is—above all—an impersonal matter. . . .

. . . I began writing fiction at 19, still under the influence of . . . the wish to paint.

. . . The short story was good for me in two ways. 1) visual 2) the poetic stress on the moment. The impression for its own sake—spotlit, isolated—only slight need for rationalization and explanation. All my short stories have departed from a visual impression to which some poetic sign attached.

Excerpted from notes to a lecture delivered at Wellesley College on 10 March 1950. Reprinted by permission of the Henry W. and Albert A. Berg Collection, New York Public Library; the Astor, Lenox, and Tilden Foundations; and the Curtis Brown Group, Ltd., London, literary executors of Elizabeth Bowen's estate.

From the Preface to The Faber Book of Modern Short Stories

The short story is a young art: as we now know it, it is the child of this century. Poetic tautness and clarity are so essential to it that it may be said to stand at the edge of prose; in its use of action it is nearer to drama than to the novel. The cinema, itself busy with a technique, is of the same generation: in the last thirty years the two arts have been accelerating together. They have affinities—neither is sponsored by a tradition; both are, accordingly, free; both, still, are self-conscious, show a self-imposed discipline and regard for form; both have, to work on, immense matter—the disorientated romanticism of the age. The new literature, whether written or visual, is an affair of reflexes, of immediate susceptibility, of associations not examined by reason: it does not attempt a synthesis. Narrative of any length involves continuity, sometimes a forced continuity: it is here that the novel too often becomes invalid. But action, which must in the novel be complex and motivated, in the short story regains heroic simplicity.

An art having behind it little tradition is at once impetuous and halting, and is very affectable. Its practitioners are still tentative, watching each other: some positive and original mind is wanted to renew impetus, or to direct it. The short story as an art has come into being through a disposition to see life in a certain way. But the writer himself may stay unaware of this new disposition if he have not already seen it made evident elsewhere in art: only the rare writer does not look for a precedent. In England, the limitations of narrative prose with its *longueurs*, its conventions dangerous to truth, had appeared for a long time to be impassable: oblique narration, cutting (as in the cinema), the unlikely placing of emphasis, or symbolism (the telling use of the object both

Excerpted from *Collected Impressions* (New York: Knopf, 1950), 38–40. Reprinted by permission of the Curtis Brown Group, Ltd., London, literary executors of Elizabeth Bowen's estate. This preface was first published in 1936.

for its own sake and as an image) were unknown. The short story was once the condensed novel; it needed a complex subject and depended for merit on the skill with which condensation had been effected. The short stories of James and Hardy show, in their excellence, a sober virtuosity: they are *tours de force* by practised executants, side-issues from the crowded imagination. They show, *qua* the short story, no urgent aesthetic necessity; their matter does not dictate their form. Their shortness is not positive; it is nonextension. They are great architects' fancies, little buildings on an august plan. They have no emotion that is abrupt and special; they do not give mood or incident a significance outside the novelist's power to explore. Their very excellence made them a dead end: they did not invite imitation or advance in any way a development in the short story proper. That impetus that it needed, the English short story had to get from abroad. Rumour, the translation and easier circulation of foreign books, also a widening curiosity, brought Tchehov and Maupassant into the English view.

The influences of two foreign masters on an affectable new form have necessarily run counter to one another. Tchehov stands (or stands with us) for an emancipation of faculties, for a romantic distention of the form of the story to let in what might appear inchoate or nebulous. Maupassant stands for astringency, iron relevance. Tchehov opened up for the writer tracts of emotional landscape; he made subjectivity edit and rule experience and pull art, obliquely, its way. His work was a system of irritations beautified; he secreted over the grit inside his shell. His hero was the sub-man; he crystallized frustration, inertia, malaise, vacancy, futile aspiration, shy or sly pretentiousness. He dragged that involuntary sub-life of the spirit up into the impassive light of art. The suffering, too-intelligent and submissive bourgeois is typified in him; he came of that class which fosters its own annihilation, and which revolution cannot obliterate. He was, in art's sense, a political force in art, revolting against the aristocratic rejection of matter for manner's sake. He made his own manner, commanding it so completely as to suggest less discipline than it had—and this has, on the whole, made him a dangerous influence. He has been made to sponsor self-concern, licence, fortuity.

. . . In the short story, semi-poetic, amazement is not only not fathomed but not stated; but has to be made evident. The writer must so strip fact of neutralizing elements as to return to it, and prolong for it, its first power: what was in life a half-second of apprehension must be perpetuated. The extraverted short story—bare of analysis, sparse in emotional statement—is the formula for, never the transcript of, that amazement with which poetry deals. The particular must be given general significance. Narration is bound to be exact and impassive. . . .

. . . The first necessity for the short story, at the set out, is *necessariness*. The story, that is to say, must spring from an impression or perception pressing enough, acute enough, to have made the writer write. Execution must be voluntary and careful, but conception should have been involuntary, a vital fortuity. The sought-about-for subject gives the story a dead kernel, however skillfully words may have been applied: the language, being *voulu*, remains inorganic. Contrived, unspontaneous feeling makes for unquickened prose. The story should have the valid central emotion and inner spontaneity of the lyric; it should magnetize the imagination and give pleasure—of however disturbing, painful or complex a kind. The story should be as composed, in the plastic sense, and as visual as a picture. It must have tautness and clearness; it must contain no passage not aesthetically relevant to the whole. The *necessary* subject dictates its own relevance. However plain or lively or unpretentious be the manner of the story, the central emotion—emotion however remotely involved or hinted at—should be austere, major. The subject must have implicit dignity. If in the writer half-conscious awe of his own subject be lacking, the story becomes flooded with falseness, mawkishness, whimsicality or some ulterior spite. The plot, whether or not it be ingenious or remarkable, for however short a way it is to be pursued, ought to raise some issue, so that it may continue in the mind. . . .

. . . The fantasy story has often a literary beauty that is disarming; the one test one can apply is: does the *imagination* find this credible? Any crazy house against moonlight might, like the House of Usher, split right down to show the moon: there is assent at once, but no way to check up. Fancy has an authority reason cannot challenge. The pure fantasy writer works in a free zone: he has not to reconcile inner and outer images.

. . . The retreat from fact that private fantasy offers has been as grateful in life as its variations are fascinating to art. Man has to live how he can: overlooked and dwarfed he makes himself his own theatre. Is the drama inside heroic or pathological? Outward acts have often an inside magnitude. The short story, within its shorter span than the novel's, with its freedom from forced complexity, its possible lucidness, is able, like the poetic drama, to measure man by his aspirations and dreads and place him alone on that stage which, inwardly, every man is conscious of occupying alone.

. . . If the short story is to keep a living dignity, and is not to be side-tracked into preciousness, popular impatience on the one hand and minority fervour on the other will have to be kept in check. The present state of the short story is, on the whole, healthy: its prospects are good. It shows on the plane of fact a better documentation, on the plane of feeling less showy uneasiness. Manner, once threatened with over-elaboration, has been simplified, subordinated to subject. The attack on convention is being better directed. There is a revulsion against "rare" or inflated feeling—this revulsion, however, is sometimes dangerously strong. For it must be kept in mind that the short story, while rightly eschewing the false-poetic, cannot from its very nature be completely prosaic. Political bias, more and more appearing, has been to the good: it makes for a new heroism.

. . . This century's emotion, dislocated and stabbing, has at least this value: it makes a half-conscious artist of every feeling man. Peaks of common experience soar past an altitude-line into poetry. There is also a level immediately below this, on which life is being more and more constantly lived, at which emotion crystallizes without going icy, from which a fairly wide view is at command. This level the short story is likely to make its own.

From a Review of Gorki Stories

Short story writers form a sort of democracy: when a man engages himself in this special field his stories stand to be judged first of all on their merits *as* stories, only later in their relation to the rest of his work. The more imposing the signature, the more this applies. The craft (it may be no more) of the short story has special criteria; its limitations are narrow and definite. It is in the building-up of the short story that the craftsman side of the artist has to appear. Very close demands on the writers' judgment are made; the short story is not a mere ease for the passing fancy; it offers no place for the unobjectified sentiment, for the impulsive start that could not be followed through. It must have implications which will continue when the story is done. It may be a *tour de force*, but it must not be a by-product; if it reads like a by-product it is so much wast. Its disadvantages are an emotional narrowness that the writer would not permit himself in a longer work, a necessary over-simplification of characters, and a rather theatrical tensing-up of the dialogue—if there be dialogue. The writer who rates above all things verisimilitude and the all-around view, or who cannot sustain one mood till the writing rounds itself off, does better to leave the short story alone. It must be recognized that even in the short story of the greatest integrity there has to be a sort of concealed trick.

Excerpted from *Collected Impressions* (New York: Knopf, 1950), 153–54. Reprinted by permission of Curtis Brown Group, Ltd., London, literary executors of Elizabeth Bowen's estate. This review first published in 1939.

From the Preface to
Ann Lee's and Other Stories

The inhumanity of some of the *Ann Lee's* stories may be forced the more into prominence by their fair technique. The scene-setting is surer than in *Encounters*; dialogue is lively and has shape, and action (always my problem) seems under control. These pieces have more texture, body, substantiality, than their predecessors. There is less indecision: the critics, by perceiving what sort of writer I ought to be, had done much to help me direct my powers. I was, with now more deliberation, still concerned with the possibilities of atmosphere. One must recall that in the first half of the 1920s, the period in which my first books were written, the idea and potentials of "atmosphere" were accounted new. I had not heard of the thing till I read my notices. In trying to find words for the hazy queerness some places and a number of persons had for me, I was bona fide; I cannot accuse myself of being prey to a literary vogue. By now, much that came fresh to me has been (not by me) exploited and overused. There sets in a mistrust of what could be fuzziness. I still, however, think it would be a pity if a young person's liking for the imponderables (which, after all, are his own discoveries) were spoilt for him, or too much guarded against. One is most honest when one is most surprised; it is one's first perceptions that first surprise one.

There is a prettiness in the *Ann Lee's* stories—prettiness of hats in a shop, of a parrot on a flowing chestnut-tree, of the Contessina's juvenile muslins against a glittering lake-scene, of broken Roman brick walls—"*so solid yet with such a silver-pink bloom of impermanence.*" That younger sister of beauty delighted me. I was, as to one particular, still where I was when I wrote *Encounters*—I liked scenes and inanimate objects better than people. My pen was ready enough, as the stories

Excerpted from *Afterthought* (London: Longman Greens, 1962), 91–94. Reprinted by permission of the Curtis Brown Group, Ltd., London, literary executors of Elizabeth Bowen's estate. This preface was first published in 1926.

show, to dwell upon scenes of guilt and misery; but it was essential that the locale be pleasing, or at any rate piquant or picturesque. I found writing, though harder and harder work, to be an outlet for my frivolity—and I cannot, today, think the stories the worse for that. Had I not enjoyed them, they would have remained unwritten.

The principal *Ann Lee's* stimulus was travel: in a sense, everything I experienced *was* travel. Now that I had really become a writer, I could look back painlessly at my own past—two childhood stories, "The Visitor" and "Charity" are, I think, the most sterling in the collection. I was by now not only a writer but married, a matron, the mistress of a house. The sensation of actually *living* anywhere, as apart from camping or visiting, was new to me. We were living in the English Midlands, outside Northampton; a flat but reposing view of garden allotments stretched away almost to the horizon, outside the window in which my table was—the nearest high point, neighbours said, was the Ural Mountains. A canal-side walk inspired "Human Habitation," and the sunny tossing chestnut-tree, waxy with blossom, at the corner of our road, set off "The Parrot." I otherwise drew on the distant, rather than nearer, scene. Some days I caught a train and went to London; I visited Ireland to see my father; every spring brought me two weeks in Italy; in late summer my husband and I travelled in France. Between journeys I worked, at the knee-hole table in the projecting window, with an uninterruptedness I might envy now.

The enjoyment of writing the *Ann Lee's* stories was in one way clouded: *should* I be writing a novel? One reviewer of *Encounters* used the phrase, "these novels in miniature"; and Mr Sidgwick was certain I had it in me. My difficulty, as I had the wits to realize, was that I could not at that time expand my vision outside the range of an incident or an hour. I could spotlight, but not illumine steadily. I could expose or surprise people, but I had little sense of their continuity: I had a flitting mind. My view, to be a view at all, had to be dramatic, and I could not see how interplay between persons could sustain itself throughout the whole of a book—might not my characters, herded too long together, begin to exhaust or bore one another? Or, still worse, exhaust or bore me? The requisite for a novel is slow combustion; and I liked flashes. This transitional difficulty, into the long-term view, is no doubt generic to writers who begin as short-storyists. Re-reading my stories, I used to wonder whether any of them *could* have been extended: I always decided, not. Yet I saw, if adherence to the short story were to be a matter of sheer timidity, inelasticity, or of stunted competence, there would be a danger of the short story's coming, one day, to deaden under my hand. I wanted not so much to write a novel as to be able to write one if I wanted.

I don't know whether the on-the-move mood in which I wrote them has left any mark of the *Ann Lee's* stories. Possibly it made for tenseness—livid, pre-thundery weather, as in "The Storm." Up against human unknowableness, I made that my subject—how many times? The stories are questions posed—some end with a shrug, others with an impatient or a dismissing sigh. The nameless, unexplained man in *Ann Lee's*—"*scudded across their patch of visibility. By putting out a hand they could have touched him. He went by them blindly; his breath sobbed and panted. It was by his breath they knew how terrible it had been—terrible. Passing them blindly, he stabbed his way on into the fog.*" The fate of the missing woman in "The Secession" is not hinted at: nor is the lateness of Willy in "Human Habitation" ever explained. The couple in the Tivoli villa in "The Storm"—where do they go next? Yet I cannot consider those trick endings; more, it seemed to me that from true predicament there *is* no way out.

Ann Lee's was, like *Encounters*, received favourably. I wonder how, as a new book, it would fare today? The short story has grown up since 1926. I am glad the *Ann Lee's* stories are in existence. They are the work of a living writer whom I know in a sense, but can never meet.

Preface to The Demon Lover

The stories in the collection entitled *The Demon Lover* were written in wartime London—between the spring of 1941 and the late autumn of 1944. They were written for the magazines or papers in which they originally appeared. During these last years, I did not always write a story when I was asked for one; but I did not write any story that I was not asked for. For at the same time I have been writing a novel; and sometimes I did not want to imperil its continuity. Does this suggest that these *Demon Lover* stories have been in any way forced or unwilling work?: If so, that is quite untrue. Actually, the stimulus of being asked for a story, and the compulsion created by having promised to write one were both good—I mean, they acted as releases. Each time I sat down to write a story I opened a door; and the pressure against the other side of that door must have been very great, for things—ideas, images, emotions—came through with force and rapidity, sometimes violence. I do not say that these stories wrote themselves—aesthetically or intellectually speaking, I found the writing of some of them very difficult—but I was never in a moment's doubt as to *what* I was to write. The stories had their own momentum, which I had to control. The acts in them had an authority which I could not question. Odd enough in their way—and now some seem very odd—they were flying particles of something enormous and inchoate that had been going on. They were sparks from experience—an experience not necessarily my own.

During the war I lived, both as a civilian and as a writer, with every pore open; I lived so many lives, and, still more, lived among the packed repercussions of so many thousands of other lives, all under stress, that I see now it would have been impossible to have been writing only one book. I want my novel, which deals with this same

From *The Mulberry Tree: Writings of Elizabeth Bowen*, ed. Hermione Lee (New York: Harcourt Brace Jovanovich, 1986), 94–99. Reprinted by permission of Harcourt Brace Jovanovich, Virago Press, and the Curtis Brown Group, Ltd., London, literary executors of Elizabeth Bowen's estate. This preface was first published in 1945.

time, to be enormously comprehensive. But a novel must have form; and, for the form's sake, one is always having to make relentless exclusions. Had it not been for my from-time-to-time promises to write stories, much that had been pressing against the door might have remained pressing against it in vain. I do not feel I "invented" anything I wrote. It seems to me that during the war the overcharged subconsciousnesses of everybody overflowed and merged. It is because the general subconsciousness saturates these stories that they have an authority nothing to do with me.

These are all wartime, none of them *war*, stories. There are no accounts of war action even as I knew it—for instance, air raids. Only one character—in "Mysterious Kôr"—is a soldier; and he only appears as a homeless wanderer round a city. These are, more, studies of climate, war-climate, and of the strange growths it raised. I see war (or should I say feel war?) more as a territory than as a page of history: of its impersonal active historic side I have, I find, not written. Arguably, writers are always slightly abnormal people: certainly, in so-called "normal" times my sense of the abnormal has been very acute. In war, this feeling of slight differentiation was suspended: I felt one with, and just like, everyone else. Sometimes I hardly knew where I stopped and somebody else began. The violent destruction of solid things, the explosion of the illusion that prestige, power and permanence attach to bulk and weight, left all of us, equally, heady and disembodied. Walls went down; and we felt, if not knew, each other. We all lived in a state of lucid abnormality.

Till the proofs came, I had not re-read my stories since they were, singly, written. When I read them straight through as a collection, I was most struck by what they have in common. This integrates them and gives them a cumulative and collective meaning that no one, taken singly, has by itself. *The Demon Lover* is an organic whole: not merely a collection, but somehow—for better or worse—a book. Also, the order in which the stories stand—an order come at, I may say, casually— seems itself to have a meaning, or to add a meaning, I did not foresee. We begin with a hostess who has not learned how with grace to open her own front door; we end with a pair of lovers with no place in which to sleep in each other's arms. In the first story, a well-to-do house in a polite square gives the impression of having been organically dislocated by shock; in the last, a pure abstract empty timeless city rises out of a little girl's troubled mind. Through the stories—in the order in which they are here placed—I find a rising tide of hallucination. The stories are not placed in the time-order in which they were first written—though, by chance, "In the Square," placed first here *is* the first in the book I wrote, in a hot, raid-less patch of 1941 summer, just after Germany had invaded Russia.

The hallucinations in the stories are not a peril; nor are the stories studies of mental peril. The hallucinations are an unconscious, instinctive, saving resort on the part or the characters: life, mechanized by the controls of wartime, and emotionally torn and impoverished by changes, had to complete itself in *some* way. It is a fact that in Britain, and especially in London, in wartime many people had strange deep intense dreams. "Whatever else I forget about the war," a friend said to me, "I hope I may never forget my own dreams, or some of the other dreams I have been told. We have never dreamed like this before; and I suppose we shall never dream like this again." Dreams by night, and the fantasies—these often childishly innocent—with which formerly matter-of-fact people consoled themselves by day were compensations. Apart from them, I do not think that the *desiccation*, by war, of our day-to-day lives can be enough stressed. The outsize World War news was stupefying: headlines and broadcasts came down and down on us in hammerlike chops, with great impact but, oddly, little reverberation. The simple way to put it was: "One cannot take things in." What was happening was out of all proportion to our faculties for knowing, thinking and checking up. The circumstances under which ordinary British people lived were preposterous—so preposterous that, in a dull way, they simplified themselves. And all the time we knew that compared with those on the Continent we in Britain could not be said to suffer. Foreign faces about the London streets had personal pain and impersonal history sealed up behind the eyes. All this pressure drove egotism underground, or made it whiten like grass under a stone. And self-expression in small ways stopped—the small ways had been so very small that we had not realized how much they amounted to. Planning fun, going places, choosing and buying things, dressing yourself up, and so on. All that stopped. You used to know what you were like from the things you liked, and chose. Now there was not what you liked, and you did not choose. Any little remaining choices and pleasures shot into new proportion and new value: people paid big money for little bunches of flowers.

Literature of the Resistance has been steadily coming in from France. I wonder whether in a sense all wartime writing is not resistance writing? Personal life here, too, put up its own resistance to the annihilation that was threatening—war. Everyone here, as is known, read more: and what was sought in books—old books, new books— was the communicative touch of personal life. To survive, not only physically but spiritually, was essential. People whose homes had been blown up went to infinite lengths to assemble bits of themselves— broken ornaments, odd shoes, torn scraps of the curtains that had hung in a room—from the wreckage. In the same way, they assembled and checked themselves from stories and poems, from their memories, from one another's talk. Outwardly, we accepted that at this time individual destiny became an obsession in every heart. You cannot depersonalize persons. Every writer during this time was aware of the personal cry of the individual. And he was aware of the passionate attachment of men and women to every object or image or place or love or fragment of memory with which his or her destiny seemed to be identified, and by which the destiny seemed to be assured.

The search for indestructible landmarks in a destructible world led many down strange paths. The attachment to these when they had been found produced small worlds-within-worlds of hallucination—in most cases, saving hallucination. Writers followed the paths they saw or felt people treading, and depicted those little dear saving illusory worlds. I have done both in *The Demon Lover* stories.

You may say that these resistance-fantasies are in themselves frightening. I can only say that one counteracts fear by fear, stress by stress. In "The Happy Autumn Fields," one finds a woman projected from flying-bombed London, with its day-and-night eeriness, into the key emotional crisis of a Victorian girlhood. In "Ivy Gripped the Steps," a man in the early '40s peers through the rusted fortifications and down the dusty empty perspectives of a seaside town at the Edwardian episode that has crippled his faculty for love. In "The Inherited Clock," a girl is led to find the key to her own neurosis inside a timepiece. The past, in all these cases, discharges its load of feeling into the anaesthetized and bewildered present. It is the "I" that is sought—and retrieved at the cost of no little pain. And the ghosts—definite in "Green Holly," questionable (for are they subjective purely?) in "Pink May," "The Cheery Soul" and "The Demon Lover"—what part do they play? They are the certainties. The bodiless foolish wanton, the puritan other presence, the tipsy cook with her religion of English fare, the ruthless young soldier lover unheard of since 1916: hostile or not, they rally, they fill the vacuum for the uncertain "I."

I am sorry that my stories do not contain more "straight" pictures of

134

the wartime scene. Such pictures could have been interesting: they *are* interesting in much of the brilliant reportage that exists. I know that, in these stories, the backgrounds, and sometimes the circumstances, are only present by inference. Allow for the intensely subjective mood into which most of the characters have been cast. Remember that these impulsive movements of fantasy are by-products of the non-impulsive major routine of war. These are between-time stories—mostly reactions from, or intermissions between, major events. They show a levelled-down time, when a bomb on your house was as inexpedient but not more abnormal than a cold in your head. There was an element of chanciness and savageness about everything—even, the arrival at a country house for Christmas. The claustrophobia of not being able to move about freely and without having to give account of yourself—not, for instance, being able to visit a popular seaside resort, within seventy miles of London, between 1940 and 1944—appears in many: notably, in "Ivy Gripped the Steps." The ghostly social pattern of London life—or, say, the conventional pattern one does not easily break, and is loath to break because it is "I"-saving—appears in the vacant politeness of "In the Square," and in the inebriate night-club conversation, and in "Careless Talk." These are ways in which some of us did go on—after all, we had to go on *some* way. And the worthless little speaker in "Pink May" found the war made a moratorium for her married conscience. Yes, only a few were heroic purely: and see how I have not drawn the heroic ones! But everyone was pathetic—more than they knew. Owing, though, to the thunder of those inordinate years, we were shaken out of the grip of our pathos.

In wartime, even in Britain, much has been germinating. *What*, I do not know—who does, yet, know?—but I felt the germination; and feel it, here and there, in these stories now that I read them through. These are received impressions of happening things; impressions that stored themselves up and acquired force without being analysed or considered. These, as wartime stories, are at least contemporary—twenty, forty, sixty years hence they may be found interesting as documents, even if they are found negligible as art. This discontinuous writing, nominally "inventive," is the only diary I have kept. Transformed into images in the stories, there *may* be important psychological facts: if so, I did not realize their importance. Walking in the darkness of the nights of six years (darkness which transformed a capital city into a network of inscrutable canyons) one developed new bare alert senses, with their own savage warnings and notations. And by day one was always making one's own new maps of a landscape always convulsed by some new change. Through it all, one probably picked up more than can be answered for. I cannot answer for much that is in these stories, except to say that I know they are all true—true to the general life that was in me at the time. Taking singly, they are disjected snapshops—snapshots taken from close up, too close up, in the middle of the *mêlée* of a battle. You cannot *render*, you can only embrace—if it means embracing to suffocation-point—something vast that is happening right on top of you. Painters have painted, and photographers who were artists have photographed, the tottering lace-like architecture of ruins, dark mass-movements of people, and the untimely brilliance of flaming skies. I cannot paint or photograph like this—I have isolated, I have made for the particular, spot-lighting faces or cutting out gestures that are not even the faces or gestures of great sufferers. This is how I am, how I feel, whether in war or peacetime; and only as I am and feel can I write. As I said at the start, though I criticize these stories now, afterwards, intellectually, I cannot criticize their content. They are the particular. But through the particular, in wartime, I felt the high-voltage current of the general pass.

From the Preface to
The Second Ghost Book

Why ghosts should today be ubiquitous is another matter. Tradition connects them with scenes of violence—are we now to take it that any and every place is, has been or may be a scene of violence? Our interpretation of violence is wider than once it was; we are aware that the blow physically struck is but one means by which man injures man, that cruelty may be worst in its mental part, that the emotions have their own scale of torment, that the most deep-going outrages may be psychological. We fear that which hath power to hurt the soul. Inflictions and endurances, exactions, injustices, infidelities—do not these wreak their havoc, burn in their histories, leave their mark? *Who* knows what has gone on, anywhere? May not obsessions stay in the air which knew them, as a corpse stays nailed down under a floor? . . .

Fiction is the ideal pacing ground for the ghost—"apparitions," when they occur in real life, are apt to seem to lack meaning, or lack wholeness. About a ghost one longs to be told more—and of that, research often falls short: that, the imagination must supply. Yet ghost stories are not easy to write—least easy now, for they involve more than they did. We present here, in *The Second Ghost Book,* a series of adventures and experiments: each, it may be claimed, in its own way carries the stamp of other-reality. In our seeing of ghosts, each of us has exposed our susceptibilities, which are partly personal, partly those of our time. We are twentieth-century haunters of the haunted. The subject, at any rate, goes far back.

Excerpted from *Afterthought* (London: Longmans Green, 1962), 102–4. Reprinted by permission of the Curtis Brown Group, Ltd., London, literary executor of Elizabeth Bowen's estate.

"The Short Story in England"

The development of the short story in England has been interesting to watch. As an art form, it is still fairly new—roughly, the child of the twentieth century. Before 1900, short stories—and often, great ones— had indeed been written; but there was, I believe, a tendency to regard these as by-products, chance overflows from the brimming imaginations of novelists. Fine short stories, while they might delight the public, were not yet of technical interest to the critic. Kipling—the main body of whose prose work was in this form—*was* Kipling: unique, unquestioned, with a place of his own.

The freshness and force of his style, the variety of his subjects, his wide knowledge of men and countries, his equal command of the comic and tragic muse—it was those that struck contemporary readers. They did not pause to examine *how* the stories were told. And Kipling the artist tended to be obscured by Kipling the national institution. Only lately—only, that is to say, since the awakening of artistic interest in the short story form—has there been what one might call a delayed-action appreciation of Kipling's technique. Now, we see him as not only our first but also as one of our greatest artists in that particular line.

Yes, we took Kipling for granted. Ironically, perhaps, English interest in the short story was to wait to receive its impetus from abroad. Late nineteenth-century Europe had given birth to two outstanding short story writers—French Guy de Maupassant, Russian Anton Tchehov. The Maupassant stories, with their strong Gallic flavour, appealed to only a special public in England: none the less, their reputation spread. As with Kipling, the Maupassant stories' subjects were, at the time, more striking than was their concealed art. The impact of Tchehov on us was very different: no sooner were his stories translated into English than he began to be felt as an influence. Why? Because the

From *Britain Today* 109 (May 1945): 11–16. Reprinted by permission of the Curtis Brown Group, Ltd., London, literary executors of the estate of Elizabeth Bowen.

Tchehov stories deal more with mood than with action. To us in England that was something quite new; and it opened infinite possibilities. Mood (though it may be mood of a different kind) is, I think, as strong a factor with the English as with the Russians; the idea of expressing it was fascinating, and the suitability of the short story, for this purpose, soon came to be seen.

The short story promised to do in prose what had, so far, only been done in poetry. Isolating some perhaps quite small happening, it emphasized its significance by giving it emotional colour.

The first, and brilliant, exponent of Tchehov technique in England was Katherine Mansfield—be it clear that she added to her discipleship a genius altogether her own. The work of that young New Zealand woman, settled in England, appeared at a time that could not have been more propitious—the years following the first World War. A swing-back to reflectiveness, a revulsion against action, violence, and any form of systematized energy is, I imagine, characteristic of any post-war period. Individual feelings reassert themselves. Like small spring flowers, personal loves, pleasures, and fancies appear again, after the harsh, repressive winter of war.

Katherine Mansfield's tragically early death left her not lost to us as an inspiration. Throughout the 1920's, and into the 1930's, her imitators, inevitably, were many. What was better, quite independent talents found themselves encouraged, by her achievement, in their own belief in the short story. A. E. Coppard and H. E. Bates, with their lyrical but at the same time virile tales of the English country-side, showed that the English "atmospheric" short story need not stay, only, in the feminine sphere. Another woman short-storyist, Ethel Colburn Mayne—who had, I believe, been writing prior to Katherine Mansfield—began to come into greater prominence; though never quite the prominence she deserved.

William Plomer, before he was twenty, published his first collection, *I Speak of Africa.* Plomer (who has now much other work to his name) is, I think, still the English short-storyist whose development has been most continuous and most steady: he is now in his prime as a writer, and should be watched. For, more and more, as in the decades between the two World Wars the short story has become a literary cult, one has had to distinguish between the mere good technician (the writer, one might say, for writing's sake) and the man or woman of first-class imagination, who has something wholly original to say.

High in this class comes D. H. Lawrence; whose short stories are unweighted by any of the redundancies that may slow down his novels. All the vision, the fire, the gentleness, and the sheer observation of which Lawrence was capable come out, pure, in his stories. He was writing during the 1914–18 war; and the stories in the *England My England* and *The Ladybird* collections seem to me to have captured, as truly as anything in our literature, the psychological atmosphere of that time. And his post-war stories were to show no decline. Arguably (and I could support the argument) Lawrence is our finest short story writer. He is certainly in the rank of the first six. With him I should place Kipling, Somerset Maugham, Aldous Huxley, William Plomer and Katherine Mansfield. But here, I fear, I risk being controversial. Walter de la Mare's position is indefinable: he belongs more than half, always, in the poetic province. And James Joyce, Frank O'Connor, Liam O'Flaherty, and Seán O'Faoláin, as Irishmen, are outside my present scope.

As the short story has gained in literary prestige, "over-literariness" has become a danger with it. Of this danger, Somerset Maugham—perhaps because of what one might call his, in the good sense, man of the world qualities—has steered clear. And Aldous Huxley, in whom the aesthetic exuberance of the 1920's found high expression, steered clear too—perhaps by sheer mental vigour. But, alas, several writers who showed promise later "bogged down" in over-ambiguities. Their contempt for plot went too far. The Tchehov influence, as I have tried to show, had at the beginning been excellent. But soon a reaction against it must set in.

This reaction showed itself as the 1930's advanced. The tenseness and seriousness of that decade, in which England could not ignore the troubles of Europe or the storm clouds darkening her own horizon, began to reflect itself in our short stories—as they did in our drama and poetry. Social consciousness succeeded to aesthetic susceptibility. The general feeling that we must begin to act brought action back into prominence in our stories. Charming descriptive passages yielded place to quick-moving dialogue; and characters, instead of being poetically generalized, had to be clear-cut, perhaps prosaic, identifiable by the reader as types in everyday life. I say, "had to be." The art of the short story showed itself truly to *be* art in that it felt compulsions from the outside world. And also, in that, like a magic mirror, it was already reflecting what was to come. Spareness, energy, a respect for the fighting spirit (rather than for the luxurious sensibilities) of man, and a tendency to question the social order—all these appeared in the more representative stories written for some years prior to 1939.

Who were writers who showed this immediately pre-war trend? Arthur Calder-Marshall, Leslie Halward, James Hanley, G. F. Green are names that came most immediately to my mind. Hanely's sea stories have, it is true, a horrific, fantasmagoric quality that entitles them to a place apart. Arthur Calder-Marshall is, in the main, a novelist: his short stories are not many, but are first rate. Several isolated fine pieces—often, for instance, about the war in Spain—came from writers whose output remained small. The short-storyists of the 1930's were fired by their subjects, and less concerned with technique for its own sake. Or perhaps one should say, they strove to avoid showing that technique *had* been used. They were influenced, if at all, by the Americans—principally Hemingway. It may well have been Hemingway who, already admired here in the 1920's, first threw the slow motion, Tchehov-style story into discredit.

An alternative type of story was, it is true, still produced throughout the 1930's. Stylish, memorable in theme and highly imaginative in treatment, such stories were most often written by poets. The ever distinguished work of Osbert and of Sacheverell Sitwell shows, for instance, little deflection by world events—though, be it said, Osbert Sitwell's *Defeat* has embodied the whole of the tragedy of 1940 France. Peter Quennell, Dylan Thomas, and Stephen Spender (whose collection *The Burning Cactus* is to be recommended) also made experiments in this form.

Curiously enough—or is it so curious?—the actual outbreak of the long-dreaded war has sent the English short story soaring, with a new kind of hardy exuberance, into realms of humour, satire, fantasy, and caprice. Artistic release could not but follow the long tension. I do not say that tragedy and duress have not, also, imprinted themselves in our war-time stories. Nor do I mean that the short story has contributed, in any *unworthy* sense, to "escape" literature. No—but is it fair to say that true art never underlines the obvious? In peace-time, our short story artist had for subject those uneasy currents beneath the apparently placid surface. In war-time, the surface being itself uneasy, he plumbs through to, and renders, unchanging and stable things—home feeling, human affection, old places, childhood memories, and even what one might call those interior fairy tales (sometimes, perhaps, ridiculous; often touching) on which men and women sustain themselves and keep their identities throughout the cataclysm of world war.

The Horizon Book of Short Stories offers a fair cross section of short stories written since 1940—and, I think, bears out my generalizations. These stories, selected by Cyril Connolly, have all appeared in *Horizon*, from month to month. Very important, since war began, have been the number of periodicals or book-form publications ready to welcome, and make known, new short story writers. Besides *Horizon*, I instance *The Cornhill, Life and Letters, English Story, Penguin New Writing, New Writing and Daylight, Orion* and *The Windmill*. Seldom, in England, can the literary scene have been more propitious for fresh talent. But alas, ironically, few of the young are free to write—or to write much. The Forces, or exacting strenuous war work outside the Forces, have claimed them. Under the circumstances, it is amazing how many MSS. (these travelling, often, from the ends of the earth) *have* reached the London editors. It has been striking, also, how much imagination *has* been able to add to experiences that might, one would have thought, exceed it. I instance the N.F.S. firemen stories of William Sansom; also *The Last Inspection*—which, left us by Alun Lewis, shows what a tragic loss this young Welshman's death in India has been to the art of the short story.

I have said how those two collections of D. H. Lawrence's captured the time-spirit of the 1914–18 war. It would still appear to me that the short story is the ideal *prose* medium for war-time creative writing. For one thing, the discontinuities of life in war-time make such life a difficult subject for the novelist. For the novelist, perspective, and also a term of time in which to relate one experience to another, are essential—I suggest that we should not expect any *comprehensive* war novel until five, even ten years after hostilities cease. The short storyist is in a better position. First, he shares—or should share—to an extent the faculties of the poet: he can render the great significance of a small event. He can register the emotional colour of a moment. He gains rather than loses by being close up to what is immediately happening. He can take, for the theme of his story, a face glimpsed in the street, an unexplained incident, a snatch of talk overhead in a bus or train.

War-time London—blitzed, cosmopolitan, electric with expectation—now teems, I feel, with untold but tellable stories; glitters with scenes that cry aloud for the pen. So must our other cities, our ports and sea-coast, our factory settlements, our mobilized countryside. Already, the first of the harvest is coming in: I foresee a record crop of short stories immediately after the war. Of all the arts being practised in England now, none, I think, respond more quickly to impetus than does the art of the short story.

From "The Forgotten Art of Living"

There could be no end to idealizing the past: in vain we call up its darker side—the inhibitions, the banishments, the snobberies, the consuming grievances—in vain we recall that, as Proust said, art with its sublime trickery is at work in memory. Idealization apart, it remains a fact that, for people, life—the living of days—did once maintain a balance and hold in itself a charm. There was not only gusto, there was discrimination. . . . [F]amiliarity was a merit; objects seem to have taken on a peculiar virtue from having been often or even always seen. . . .

. . . [I]t must be for the illusion that we hope to rifle the past. The sickly dominance of nostalgia in our talk, writing and reading becomes accounted for. We cannot hear enough, apparently, about childhoods— provided these are set anything more than forty years back— . . . the trivialities of yesterday have become our literature. . . . Up from those pages flows illusory light; magic exhales from their banality.

Excerpted from *Good Living*, ed. A. G. Weidenfeld (London: Contact Publishing, 1948), xvii, xviii. Reprinted by permission of the Curtis Brown Group, Ltd., London, literary executors of the estate of Elizabeth Bowen.

From "Sources of Influence"

In studying the development of an artist, the factor of influences upon him must, I imagine, always be taken into account. Analysis of influence, its general force and its particular workings, devolves in the main on the critic and art-historian: this field is held to require specialized knowledge and aesthetic discernment possessed by few. By the rest of us painting, sculpture, music, architecture may be enjoyed without being historically comprehended: we react, that is to say, to the masterpiece without thought as to what may have been its complex origin. Where it is a matter of colour, form used plastically, or pure sound, we are inclined to leave the genesis of the work of art to the trained mind. But where the medium is language, all is different—words are the general property; they link with *our* experience, so the creative use of them comes within our critical scope. The writer is less at a distance than other artists; one does not require to be a specialist to study him. His evolution, the processes of his formation, lie open to any reader who cares enough—in this case, where influence is at work it almost always can be suspected, if not detected. The writer is amongst us; in number writers multiply every day; in our epoch writing, of all the arts, evokes most social interest and most human concern. With regard, then, to writers let us consider influence. . . .

Susceptibility, it should be understood, plays a great part in the make-up of the creative writer. He is susceptible to environment, to experience, and, in the same way and not less, to styles and energies in already existing art. From all three sources he is attracting influences; all of which will leave their mark on his work. It is the third, the aesthetic-literary, which is most easily recognized by the reader; and for which the writer is most often called to account, and indeed reproached. Style—the actual choice and rhythm of words—most often carries an influence, and most clearly shows it. But with style, vision

Excerpted from *Afterthought* (London: Longmans Green, 1962), 205–9. Reprinted by permission of the Curtis Brown Group, Ltd., London, literary executors of Elizabeth Bowens Estate

145

and outlook are interknit: did not Flaubert call style "a manner of seeing"? As we all know, a strongly directed film or a striking collection of pictures by one artist can so invade the receptive eye that, coming out of the cinema or the gallery, one continues for hours after to see life in terms of So-and-So's films or So-and-So's painting. A creative manner of seeing is infectious—small wonder that writers at the tentative stage find it hard to shake off the magic effect of a master's vision. And this may be true not only of visual but of moral angle. In fiction one senses the power, these days, of affective novelists such as Henry James, Faulkner, and Mauriac (unalike to each other as these may be). . . .

The influence of environment is the most lasting; and except in the case of "regional" writers, operates deepest down. Sometimes, the force of environment may be felt by a writer's conscious, sharp reaction against it. Admittedly, it is the atmosphere of the scenes of youth which is most often decisive—though it has happened that, some way on into life, a writer has stumbled upon a place, perhaps an entire country, which he in some way recognizes, which seems to claim him, and which offers a hitherto lacking inspiration to his art. In that case, there is a sort of psychological adoption: a new phase of freshness of feeling, equivalent to a second childhood, sets in. But the majority are haunted by the shadowy, half-remembered landscape of early days: impressions and feelings formed there and then underly language, dictate choices of imagery. In writing, what is poetically spontaneous, what is most inimitably individual, has this source—the writer carries about in him an inner environment which is constant; though which also, as time goes on, tends to become more and more subjective.

One must remember that the inner environment has been always, to a degree, selected: as we now know, there is an element of choice, however apparently involuntary, in memory. The writer is influenced by what he retains; and still more, perhaps, by the very fact that he has retained it—and the picture, by continuous dwelling upon, may be so much intensified as to become changed. Thus, though to an extent the environment creates the writer, he also plays a part in creating it— his art, by demanding this kind of sustenance, has reached back past the bounds of actual memory into a phantasmagoric hinterland quite its own.

Experience as an influence needs least comment: this is taken for granted—perhaps too much so. There is a tendency to think that the direct transcription of experience (into novel or poem) and the *action* of experience are synonymous. True action of experience on the creative powers is erratic, indirect and slow—also, in so far as writers do make use of their individual experience as persons, they almost invariably transform it. The experience which really influences art does not consist in drama or incidents; it is a sort of emotional accumulation, or, at its best, a slowly acquired deep-down knowledge. Experience is the reaction to what happens, not the happening itself—and in that sense experience is, like environment, to a degree selected. The meaning which is extracted from occurrences varies, and varies in its importance, according to the writer's choice as to feeling: he allows some things to "take" with him more than others. The catastrophic disaster, the sudden primitive joy, are, of course, irresistible: they improve themselves. These leave behind in the writer what he has most in common with humanity: it is by its power to co-ordinate what is major with what is small in life that the soundness of his art is to be tested.

Is it true that the writers of our day are too much subject to influence, from whatever source? Do they lack the resilience, the independent hardiness of their predecessors? Literary influence (the first) seems harder now to throw off than once it was: it has been said that we have too many disciples, too few masters. If this be so, it may be found that, as a generation, we writers are in a transitional, learning stage: the task of expression appears a vast one—the old simplicities of the world are gone; the artist is hard-pressed by what is happening round him. Our century, as it takes its frantic course, seems barely habitable by humans: we have to learn to survive while we learn to write. And *to* write, we must draw on every resource; to express, we need a widened vocabulary—not only as to words, as to ideas. The apprentice stage, given modern necessities, cannot be a long one: some of us there may be who will not outlive it. But at least we are keeping going a continuity: we may serve to link the past with the future masters.

From Bowen's Court

Life in these house-islands has a frame of its own. Character is printed on every hour, as on the houses and demesne features themselves. With buildings, as with faces, there are moments when the forceful mystery of the inner being appears. This may be a matter of mood or light. Come on round the last turn of its avenue, or unexpectedly seen down a stretch of lawn, any one of these houses—with its rows of dark windows set in the light facade against dark trees—has the startling, meaning and abstract clearness of a house in a print, a house in which something important occurred once, and seems, from all evidence, to be occurring still. . . .

. . . What runs on most through a family living in one place is a continuous, semi-physical dream. Above this dream-level successive lives show their tips, their little conscious formations of will and thought. With the end of each generation, the lives that submerged here were absorbed again. With each death, the air of the place had thickened: it had been added to. The dead do not need to visit Bowen's Court rooms—as I said, we had no ghosts in that house—because they already permeated them. Their extinct senses were present in lights and forms. The land outside Bowen's Court windows left prints on my ancestors' eyes that looked out: perhaps their eyes left, also, prints on the scene? If so, those prints were part of the scene to me.

The Bowens' relation to history was an unconscious one. I can only suggest a compulsion they did not know of by a series of breaks, contrasts and juxtapositions—in short, by interleaving the family story with passages from the history of Ireland. My family, though notably "unhistoric," had their part in a drama outside themselves. Their assertions, their compliances, their refusals as men and women went,

Excerpted from chapter 1 and the afterword to *Bowen's Court* (New York: Ecco Press, 1979), 20, 451, 452–59. Reprinted by permission of the Curtis Brown Group, Ltd., London, literary executors of the estate of Elizabeth Bowen. Originally published in 1942.

year by year, generation by generation, to give history direction, as well as colour and stuff. Each of the family, in their different manners, were more than their time's products; they were its agents.

I may seem to have made use of history to illustrate the Bowens rather than the Bowens to illustrate history. Inevitably, I have stressed such outside events as may make the Bowen story, since the coming to Ireland, more comprehensible and significant. But I have tried not to wrest from their larger contexts events relevant to the moral plan of this book.

In my re-writing of history, a considerable naivety may appear. In the course of my reading for *Bowen's Court*, I have learnt a good deal that I did not know. I am, evidently, not a historian, and it seemed to me more honest to leave my reactions to history their first freshness, rather than to attempt to evaluate. Conclusions have been suggested rather than drawn. I cannot tell to how many of my readers the past— this particular past of Anglo-Ireland—will be as new as much of it was to me, or to how many it is familiar already. My transcripts of history have, at least, been drawn from sources beyond reproach: I have relied upon no authority who did not place fact above passion or interest. The stretches of the past I have had to cover have been, on the whole, painful: my family got their position and drew their power from a situation that shows an inherent wrong. In the grip of that situation, England and Ireland each turned to the other a closed, harsh, distorted face—a face that, in each case, their lovers would hardly know. With the Treaty, with which I virtually close my book, a new hopeful phase started: I believe in its promise. But we cannot afford to have ghosts on this clearing scene. I wish not to drag up the past but to help lay it. A past that Ireland still too much dwells on is still by England not enough recognized. But also, acts of good will, and good intentions that did or did not miscarry, have not been allowed by Ireland to stand to the English score. . . . For my part, it has been necessary for me to embed my family story in at least some account of the growth of "the Protestant nation," and of the events that marked stages or declines in this growth. I have done my best to make the account fair.

I began to write *Bowen's Court* in the early summer of 1939. The first two chapters were, thus, completed before the outbreak of World War II. When, for instance, I wrote about ruins in County Cork there were as yet few ruins in England other than those preserved in fences and lawns. I do not know how much, after that September of 1939, the colour of my narration may have altered. The values with which I set out—my own values—did, at least to my own feeling, remain constant: they were accentuated rather than changed by war. The war-time urgency of the present, its relentless daily challenge, seemed to communicate itself to one's view of the past, until, to the most private act or decision, there attached one's sense of its part in some campaign. Those days, either everything mattered or nothing mattered. The past—private just as much as historic—seemed to me, therefore, to matter more than ever: it acquired meaning; it lost false mystery. In the savage and austere light of a burning world, details leaped out with significance. Nothing that ever happened, nothing that was ever even willed, planned or envisaged, could seem irrelevant. War is not an accident: it is an outcome. One cannot look back too far to ask, of what?

Inevitably, the ideas and emotions that were present in my initial plan of this book were challenged and sharpened by the succeeding war years in which the writing went on. I was writing (as though it were everlasting) about a home during a time when all homes were threatened and hundreds of thousands of them were being wiped out. I was taking the attachment of people to places as being generic to human life, at a time when the attachment was to be dreaded as a possible source of too much pain. During a time when individual destinies, the hopes and fears of the living, had to count for so little, I pursued through what might seem their tenuousness and their futility the hopes and fears of long-ago dead. I was writing about self-centred people while all faces looked outward upon the world. But all that— that disparity or contrast between the time I was writing in and my subject—only so acted upon my subject as to make it, for me, the more important. I tried to make it *my* means to approach truth.

Possibly, the judgements of war-time affected my view of my family? These unhistoric figures are made historic by the fact that, as I show, they once lived. So, I examine them as we now re-examine historic figures. I have stressed as dominant in the Bowens factors I saw as dominant in the world I wrote in—for instance, subjection to fantasy and infatuation with the idea of power. While I was studying fantasy in the Bowens, we saw how it had impassioned race after race. Fantasy is toxic: the private cruelty and the world war both have their start in the heated brain. Showing fantasy, in one form or another, does its unhappy work in the lives of my ancestors. I was conscious at almost every moment of nightmarish big analogies everywhere. Also, the idea of the idea of power governed my analysis of the Bowens and of the means *they* took—these being, in some cases, emotional—to enforce themselves on their world. I showed, if only in the family sphere, people's conflicting wishes for domination. That few Bowens looked beyond Bowen's Court makes the place a fair microcosm, a representative if miniature theatre. Sketching in the society of which the Bowens were part, and the operations behind that society, I extended the conflict by one ring more: again, its isolation, what might be called its outlandishness, makes Anglo-Irish society microcosmic. For these people—my family and their associates—the idea of power was mostly vested in property (property having been acquired by use or misuse of power in the first place). One may say that while property lasted the dangerous power-idea stayed, like a sword in its scabbard, fairly safely at rest. At least, property gave my people and people like them the means to exercise power in a direct, concrete and therefore limited way. I have shown how their natures shifted direction—or the nature of the *débordement* that occurred—when property could not longer be guaranteed. Without putting up any plea for property—unnecessary, for it is unlikely to be abolished—I submit that the power-loving temperament is more dangerous when it either prefers or is forced to operate in what is materially a void. We have everything to dread from the dispossessed. In the area of ideas we see more menacing dominations than the landlord exercised over land. The outsize will is not necessarily an evil: it is a phenomenon. It must have its outsize outlet, its big task. If the right scope is not offered it, it must seize the wrong. We should be able to harness this driving force. Not the will itself but its wastefulness is the dangerous thing.

Yes, the preoccupations of war time may have caused me to see Bowens in a peculiar or too much intensified light. Some of their characteristics, here, may be overdrawn. They were in most ways, I take it, fairly ordinary Anglo-Irish country gentry. I have done my best to come at, then to transmit to paper, a detached picture of them. In the main, I do not feel that they require defence—you, on the other hand, may consider them indefensible. Having obtained their position through an injustice, they enjoyed that position through privilege. But, while they wasted no breath in deprecating an injustice it would not have been to their interest to set right, they did not abuse their privilege—on the whole. They honoured, if they did not justify, their own class, its traditions, its rule of life. If they formed a too-grand idea of themselves, they did at least exert themselves to live up to this: even vanity involves one kind of discipline. If their difficulties were of their own making, they combatted these with an energy I must praise. They found no facile solutions; they were not guilt of cant. Isolation, egotism and, on the whole, lack of culture made in them for an independence one has to notice because it becomes, in these days, rare. Independence was the first quality of a class now, I am told, becoming extinct. I recognize that a class, like a breed of animals, *is* due to lapse or become extinct should it fail to adapt itself to changing conditions—climate alters, the feeding-grounds disappear. The gentry, as a class, may or may not prove able to make adaptations; that is one of the many things we must wait to see. To my mind, they are tougher than they appear. To live as though living gave them no trouble has been the first imperative of their make-up: to do this has taken a virtuosity into which courage enters more than has been allowed. In the last issue, they have lived at their own expense.

Bowen's Court, in that December of 1941 in which this book was finished, still stood in its particular island of quietness, in the south of an island country not at war. Only the wireless in the library conducted the world's urgency to the place. Wave after wave of war news broke upon the quiet air of the room and, in the daytime when the windows were open, passed out on to the sunny or overcast lawns. Here was a negative calm—or at least, the absence of any immediate physical threat. Yet, at the body of this house threats did strike—and in a sense they were never gone from the air. The air here had absorbed, in its very stillness, apprehensions general to mankind. It was always with some qualification—most often with that of an almost undue joy—that one beheld, at Bowen's Court, the picture of peace. Looking, for instance, across the country from the steps in the evening, one thought: "*Can* pain and danger exist?" But one did think that. Why? The scene was a crystal in which, while on was looking, a shadow formed.

Yes, there was the picture of peace—in the house, in the country round. Like all pictures, it did not quite correspond with any reality. Or, you might have called the country a magic mirror, reflecting something that could not really exist. That illusion—peace at its most ecstatic—I held to, to sustain me throughout war. I suppose that everyone, fighting or just enduring, carried within him one private image, one peaceful scene. Mine was Bowen's Court. War made me that image out of a house built of anxious history.

And so great and calming was the authority of the light and quiet round Bowen's Court that it survived war-time. And it did more than that, it survived the house. It remains with me now that the house has gone.

The house, having played its part, has come to an end. It will not, after all, celebrate its two hundredth birthday—of that, it has fallen short by some thirteen years. The shallow hollow of land, under the mountains, on which Bowen's Court stood is again empty. Not one hewn stone left on another on the fresh-growing grass. Green covers all traces of the foundations. Today, so far as the eye can see, there might never have been a house there.

One cannot say that the space is empty. More, it is as it was—with no house there. How did this come to be?

It was not foreseen. Early in 1952, upon my husband's retirement from work, he and I left London, to live at Bowen's Court. This was the life we had always promised ourselves. We brought back with us furniture which, originally Bowen's Court's, had been absent long— first in Dublin, afterwards in England: travelled tables and chairs were reunited with those which had never known anything but County Cork. The house, after its many stretches of patient emptiness, of re- turns only to be followed by departures, looked like, now, entering upon a new phase of habitation—full and continuous habitation, such as it had been built for. It made us welcome. This homecoming was like no holiday visit. In spite of the cold of a bitter January, all promised well. We had the spring of that year, and the early summer. But then one night, that August, Alan Cameron died in his sleep.

I, remaining at Bowen's Court, tried to carry on the place, and the life which went with it there, alone. Already I could envisage no other home. I should, I thought, be able to maintain the place somehow. Had not others done so before me? But I was unable to.

For seven years I tried to do what was impossible. I was loth to realise how impossible it was. Costs rose: I had not enough money, and I had to face the fact that there never would be enough. Anxiety, the more deep for being repressed, increasingly slowed down my power to write, and it was upon my earnings, and those only, that Bowen's Court had by now come to depend. (Does not the economic back-history of the Bowens, as shown in this book, the quarrels, the lost law-suits, the father-and-son conflicts, the spasms of *folie de grandeur*, account for that?) Matters reached a crisis. By 1959 it had become inevitable that I should sell Bowen's Court.

Part 2

The buyer was a County Cork man, a neighbour. He already was farming tracts of land, and had the means wherewith to develop mine, and horses to put in the stables. It cheered me also to think that his handsome children would soon be running about the rooms—for it was, I believe, his honest intention, when first he bought the place from me, to inhabit the house. But in the end he did not find that practicable, and who is to blame him? He thought at one time, I understand, of compromising by taking off the top storey (I am glad he did not). Finally, he decided that there was nothing for it but to demolish the house entirely. So that was done.

It was clean end. Bowen's Court never lived to be a ruin.

Loss has not been entire. When I think of Bowen's Court, there it is. And when others who knew it think of it, there it is, also. You will understand that I am more than ever glad that I wrote this book, and that I am grateful to Alfred and Blanche Knopf, who, having inspired the book in the first place, now are bringing it back into print again. Knowing, as you now do, that the house is not longer there, you may wonder why I have left my opening chapter, the room-to-room description of Bowen's Court, in the present tense. I can only say that *I* saw no reason to transpose it into the past. There is a sort of perpetuity about livingness, and it is part of the character of Bowen's Court to be, in sometimes its silent way, very much alive.

Part 3

THE CRITICS

Introduction

The critical attention Bowen's short fiction has received takes its cue from readings of her novels. Although critics may observe how the stories and novels differ in form and technique, in both cases she is read as a social critic, a psychological realist, and a dramatist of moral truth. Combining or separating these categories in their interpretations, most critics point to the influence of Bowen's Anglo-Irish origins. Sometimes this influence is seen as literary; occasionally readers point to parallels between the fiction and Bowen's life.

As noted earlier, however, interest in Bowen's historical and political concerns has been limited.[1] In fact, many critics abstract romantic or metaphysical themes from the role her cultural heritage plays in her work. In one instance John Hildebidle provides a mythic perspective on Bowen's Anglo-Irish roots. Referring to *Bowen's Court*, he argues that her childhood near Spenser's doomed Kilcoman Castle produced her stories of questers whose journeys lead to "places of magic, even of enchantment" in her work.[2] In another example Judith Bates sees "the heritage of horror indissociable from Ireland's past" in Bowen's "metaphysical horror of modern man before his ultimate fate."[3] This tendency to universalize—mythopoietically or metaphysically—the import of Bowen's widely varied short fiction is present in all the critical approaches to her work, perhaps lending it a wide appeal but also diffusing the power of her specific concerns.

Formalist Approaches

Discussions of Bowen's short stories often trace the literary heritage of her technique and style. A. C. Partridge, for example, points out the "Irishness" of Bowen's "subjective spirit" but argues that her emphasis on "vision over feeling" makes her more indebted to Henry James than to the Irish "formulaic oral practice."[4] George Brandon Saul, on the other hand, claims Bowen's stories have an "essentially un-Irish quality and character," the proof of which, he argues, is that "she is not of purely Irish ancestry."[5] He traces her lyrical descriptions of the

Irish landscape to D. H. Lawrence and her "indirect approach" to Katherine Mansfield (Saul, 59). Bates sees Bowen's dual heritage as responsible for the "partially detached viewpoint" for which her stories are noted (Bates, 81).

Formalists distinguish Bowen's short story method from her novels by first pointing out the way in which the short story limits the writer's scope and perspective and then describing the heightened effects of a more economical method. Jocelyn Brooke has observed Bowen's "lyrical intensity" as a distinguishing mark of her short story technique.[6] Partridge notes that while short fiction necessitates fewer events and a less complex plot, it encourages experiment with causality and structure. Bowen, he concludes, combines compression with an evocative, impressionistic method. Many of her stories are sketches without being anecdotal, for she successfully engenders a subjective technique with which to portray human relationships. In this way she can be both ironic and satiric, juxtaposing the language of the narrator with that of the characters.

Bowen's impressionism is seen to leave much to the reader's imagination. She renders elusive yet overdetermined possibilities for interpretation in heavily weighted images, such as the many gardens that appear in her stories, or in abrupt breaks in time and point of view, as in "The Happy Autumn Fields" and "The Demon Lover." In response to the former story critics are still debating whether Mary is dreaming or Bowen is creating "dual realities" or "saving hallucinations."[7] In the case of "The Demon Lover" Douglas Hughes argues that because the narrative point of view is restricted to that of Mrs. Drover and the image of her damaged house can be seen as "an objective correlative of Mrs. Drover's psychological state," we can read her character as psychotic.[8] Daniel Fraustino, on the other hand, finds evidence in the breaks and imagery that the terrorized woman is saving herself from a sadistic lover.[9]

Bates discusses Bowen's impressionism and ambiguity as resulting from techniques developed in her horror stories: images that intensify what is generally taken as "natural," such as the roses in "Look at All Those Roses"; the use of "animism," wherein such elements as moisture and light assume monstrous energy and drive; and characters' states of "dream-like intuition," which see horror in the ordinary (Bates, 84, 85, 87). Through oblique allusions—such as connecting red roses and blood by reference to damson jam in "Look at All Those Roses"—Bowen suggests an atmosphere of horror. Brooke notes that despite details of "places, moments, objects, and times of year," the sources of this horror cannot be identified for certain (Brooke, 12). But as Bates also shows, this atmospheric effect serves the more disturbing end of heightening the ambiguous horror produced by Bowen's psychological realism.

Bowen's Psychological Realism

Many critics see Bowen's formal elements as serving her psychological realism. In his analysis of "Mysterious Kôr" John Bayley notes how its "brusqueness . . . enhances the feeling of depth, of sympathy, experience realized," that it is "the single image . . . of an abandoned city . . . which compels Pepita."[10] He goes on to explain: "As the circumstances of war parody the changes and chances of life itself, so the 'finality' which Pepita craves glances at the nature of such a story itself. The story ends on its necessary note of finality but the situation it has brought into being continues to live in our consciousness. The two ends join, like the sleeping and waking life of the characters, a combination which produces the story's quite remarkable effect of close intimacy" (Bayley, 174–75).

Allen Austin notes that "it is on the matter of psychology that Miss Bowen's stories differ most from her longer fiction."[11] His survey of those he considers her best stories is thus called "A Divine Comedy" because they relate to Bowen's "pervasive concern with individual fulfillment" (Austin, 95). Austin elucidates his method as follows: "The Hell stories portray people entrapped in destructive or stagnating circumstances, capacities, or attitudes; the Purgatory inhabitants are those who, though likewise possessed of dehumanizing views or pursuing an unexamined life, are confronted with situations or characters which may 'save' them; Heaven encompasses the most explicitly irrational individuals—those who are employing 'divine' ways of maintaining their identity in the face of threatening circumstances" (Austin, 95).

Austin, like others, recognizes Bowen's comedy, but instead of seeing it as bringing relief or perspective to her social critique, he finds that her "detached, stoical humor" reinforces a "chilling effect" on her characters' odyssey into psychological depths (Austin, 95). Like many, Austin attributes Bowen's humor to Anglo-Irish origins. Mary Jarrett, for example, locates the source of Bowen's unsettling perspective on the collision of different realities in the writer's "Anglo-Irish ambivalence to all things English, a blend of impatience and evasiveness, a reluctance to be pinned down to a relationship."[12] According to this view, Bowen's characters create their own imprisoning psychological realities, but these realities are no more valid than others. In a psychological framework Bowen's ghosts are "the conscious or unconscious fiction of one of the characters," but they are taken seriously even as their existence is questioned (Jarrett, 74).

According to Fraustino, what makes Bowen's stories particularly unsettling to readers is that she presents sufficient evidence on either side to create a "thrilling suspense [that] seems almost to depend on the reader's own sense of dislocation, on the interruption of logical cause and effect" (486). In his view psychological interpretation appeals to readers as a way of ameliorating the story's disturbing effects, but its ambiguities and ambivalences warn us that such a reading may be interpolation rather than textually valid.

Bowen's Social Comedy

Several critics claim Bowen's psychological realism is integral to her social critique. In this way her Irish background is viewed as part of a literary heritage that combines elements of English and Irish social comedy. Thus Frank Tuohy sees "Her Table Spread" as "sum[ming] up a period of history . . . like James Joyce's 'The Dead,'" but only as it resonates "with peculiarly Irish experience" derived from Irish literary themes and strongly influenced by Jane Austen's social comedy,[13] Walter Allen's description of Bowen as a "writer of social comedy, the heir both to Jane Austen and Henry James," coincides with Victoria Glendinning's appraisal of Bowen as a writer of "modern comedies of manners" who connects with Virginia Woolf, Iris Murdoch, and Muriel Spark.[14]

Even in her melancholy ghost stories, in her tales of terror, and in her stories in which characters experience various states of hallucination or heightened or disturbed states of consciousness, Bowen is read as a social critic. Margaret Church connects Bowen to the socially conscious works of Iris Murdoch and Mary Lavin, "aware of the social scene and social responsibility."[15] From this perspective, "the unreality" in "The Demon Lover" or "The Happy Autumn Fields" is seen as hallucination resulting from the forces of war "calculated to destroy social organization and coherence" (Church, 158). Church and others place Bowen's combination of social critique, comedy. and elegy within the Irish literary tradition, which alternates between "joy and pain, sweetness and sorrow, . . . the melancholic undertone, the warning rumble in the distance, the laughter at the edge of the grave."[16] The effect of this synthesis in Bowen's work as it melds with the English realist tradition produces a gentle critique that contains no "bitterness" (Dunleavy, 72).

In pointing to the social contexts of Bowen's psychological concerns, George Kearns connects the values growing out of her dual identity to the fates she imagined for her characters:

> Character, for Bowen, is not uniqueness of personality, but a tangle of habit, situation, manners and class. There are codes everywhere, stable and unstable, and people are supposed to know by breeding, intuition, or luck, how to read them. Yet the intricacies of code never quite accommodate their lives, are always violated; something has gone just a bit wrong, not only within each story, but within the larger structure of the relatively comfortable classes of England and Anglo-Ireland. The money that supports those rooms and houses also comes in relative degrees of stability; what one was bred to, what one somehow expected, isn't always there.[17]

Bowen as a Moral Realist

The social and ideological contexts Kearns identifies in Bowen's work form the basis of James M. Haule's analysis of her work as a moral realist. His interpretation of "Mysterious Kôr" considers the changing "moral dilemma of women" in English society.[18] He analyzes these changes in three stages: the Victorians' assessment of "the battle for power" in middle-class life; the Edwardians' escape from "the spiritual and moral degeneration of a 'feminine' English society"; and the confrontation with World War II's threat to the life of the imagination (Haule, 213–14). Acknowledging Bowen's concern with the "English psychological scene," Haule links the social condition of women in her fiction with their personal frustrations and disenchantments (Haule, 214). Because he considers women's social and psychological experience apart from men's, Haule's portrait of Bowen's artistry is more complex than separate categories would permit. Presenting Pepita's imaginative struggle as a function of the "moral 'deficiency'" of her society grounds the story in Bowen's historical and ideological concerns. In this way the writer is seen as allying herself not only with discrete literary traditions but with a complex of ideological and political attitudes.

Some Implications of the Critical Approaches

Haule's multifaceted argument, shaped by his view of Bowen as a moralist, accords with the perspectives of critics like Partridge, who sees Bowen "emulating the French and Russian believers in universality" (Partridge, 171). With a universal approach, the different historical and cultural settings of "The Disinherited" and "Mysterious Kôr" are seen as the same "grim and uncompromising reality" whose "moral truths" are linked to the Victorian world of Rider Haggard (Haule, 211, 208). Although Haule's readings are closely argued from individual texts, they abstract themes in such a way as to make them fuse into a single pattern of meaning. This pattern conforms to Terry Eagleton's definition of the norm, which he ascribes to "the whole ideology of middle-class liberalism" and which has prevailed among literary theorists and critics until very recently.[19] Growing out of "The Great Tradition" of F. R. Leavis, this ideology, according to Eagleton, prescribes "the unique value of the individual and the creative realm of the interpersonal" (Eagleton, 42). It does so, however, by taking for granted a uniformly held definition of "individual," the result of which produces an idea of "spontaneous-creative life which grew more stridently abstract the more it insisted on the concrete" (Eagleton, 43).

The more abstract moral definitions become, the more difficult it is to recognize and validate individual variations based on experiences Kearns calls the "tangle of habit, situation, manner and class" (300). Thus despite Haule's sympathy for "the loss of a woman's power to feel," Pepita's vision is not valued as a "spontaneous-creative life"; rather, it is criticized as being a "vague presage of the evil inherent in the power of the imagination" (Haule, 214, 213). In equally universal terms Haule condemns Davina in "The Disinherited" as "corrupted" by the very "feebleness" and "deficiency" she has "the urge to overcome" and, in the final analysis, sees her as "amoral" (Haule, 209, 208). If a critic's moral abstraction can reduce character to a thumbnail moral judgment, it is no wonder that Edward Mitchell's assessment of Pepita and the female characters in "The Dancing Mistress" coincides with Haule's: Both see the women as resorting "to mental aberrations and destruction either real or symbolic," and Haule would concur with Mitchell's labeling "the essence of ["The Dancing Mistress"] . . . Perversion."[20]

Like other critics with an interest in moral realism, Haule posits a "reality" that remains so abstract it discredits his sympathy for the plight of Bowen's female characters. Despite his recognition that Bowen saw Rider Haggard's *She* as an imaginative antidote to women's diminished lives in middle-class English society, Haule finds that "the image of the female capable of a power beyond moral control" is morally untenable (Haule, 206).[21] This judgment arises out of the moral parameters of the critic who sees the writer as a moral realist, for the definition of moral realism implies a universally held value system to which critics see themselves and writers subscribing equally.

For these critics, Bowen's stories are about universal conflicts: innocence versus experience or, as Mitchell classifies her themes, "the antithesis between external fact and internal reality, between the objective condition and the projection of an internal world where feeling alone reigns" (Mitchell, 41). This approach takes Bowen's figure of "the giant battened down" and interprets it as the romantic imagination that must be reconciled to a social norm of disenchantment and compromise. Based on the tradition of comedies of manners, this norm implies an acceptance of a constant, transhistorical set of values. Regardless of social or historical change, these values assume what Cora Kaplan describes as "the possibility of a unified self and an integrated consciousness that can transcend material circumstance [and] is represented as the fulfillment of desire, the happy closure at the end of the story."[22] In such fashion Hildebidle interprets "Human Habitation" as being about an abstract, transcendent journey of discovery: "To arrive is to . . . have moved toward, but never quite reach a desired but usually ill-defined goal. But to arrive in a 'habitation' is to intrude; with a violence demonstrated not by any of the characters . . . but by the language of battle and near-rape. . . . To depart is to be launched . . . into uncertainty, to return from a temporary 'here' into a prevailing 'nowhere'" (Hildebidle, 91).

This analysis describes a moral and emotional journey in which no person is identified as coming and going. Because of its level of abstraction, "the language of battle and near-rape" remains undefined; we literally do not know who is doing battle with whom or why. We are asked to consider the story's central image—"a young woman, who watches and waits"—as though her presence and consciousness are integrated, in Kaplan's terms, with a vision that transcends material circumstances (Kaplan, 91). In this critical approach the young woman is as disembodied as the ghost that personifies the critic's sense of "an emotional and psychic 'presence'" (Kaplan, 91).

Critical approaches that distinguish Bowen's work within the English literary tradition explore her metaphorical constructs and images within the material circumstances of her cultural heritage. These approaches result in analyses of her characters rather than judgments. In her review of *The Collected Stories* Leslie Bayern uses the image of the high wall surrounding the garden at Bowen's Court as "a paradigm of how a people constructed an artificial world in the midst of, yet oblivious to, the larger world, and it is also what many characters in Elizabeth Bowen's stories do."[23] Bayern's use of this paradigm gives her access to the historical and political circumstances shaping the writer's creative consciousness and thus encourages the critic to share "the sympathy which Elizabeth Bowen herself gives to her characters" (Bayern, 23). Using "Mysterious Kôr" as our now-familiar point of reference, we can see how this method alters the previous views of Pepita.

Bayern extends her paradigm of the wall to show how Bowen's stories dramatize a universal sense of imaginative limits, "the larger world of sympathy and grief, death and love," and efforts to "reach across those walls, from inside or outside, and use imagination to join together the garden and the world" (Bayern, 23). When she discusses the individual story, however, this critic demystifies the allusion to the garden by locating it in a particular historical moment. Moreover, by avoiding the push to identify conflict in character or plot, Bayern discovers a more complex and ambivalent combination: "Though Pepita is herself building a garden in which to escape, it is a generous one. It is born of love and despair—love from Arthur who comprehends Pepita's need for Kor, and despair with a world where there is war and no room for lovers to be alone together. Pepita is escaping a world of destruction in order to find a world where creation can happen" (Bayern, 24). Julia Briggs's discussion of Bowen's ghost stories demonstrates the value of this approach. Briggs shows how "the strange juxtaposition of the everyday and the bizarre" need not represent a conflict or lead to reconciliation in order to achieve "a delicate sense of balance."[24] Expressing "all those ambivalences so characteristic of the ghost story," this juxtaposition renders the psychological and social conditions of wartime "in terms of a modern spiritual crisis" (Briggs, 181).

Although Bayern's work of criticism is also a review of Bowen's stories, it does not simply provide a thematic overview and assessment; it relates themes to elements of form and style. Bayern shows how "Bowen's stories are meticulously crafted. Every object contributes to the mood and theme. Houses become characters; places reflect the mood of the people. . . . Seasons, time of day, and contrasts between past and present all add to the completeness of the stories" (Bayern, 24). This integration of social criticism, metaphysical concerns, historical and political perspectives, and form enables criticism to recognize that "Bowen treats [her characters] both ironically . . . and with understanding" (Bayern, 24). This approach recognizes not only Bowen's legacies from Henry James, Jane Austen, and others but the way in which she is distinct from them. We are thus able to explore how she learned from her literary predecessors, revising their concerns and methods to suit her own vision of her own time and cultural identifications.

The reviews of Bowen's collected stories by William Trevor and Eudora Welty contain insights and observations that address many of the individual approaches of her critics. Most significantly, Trevor and Welty provide "a truer perception of [the] nature" of Bowen's art by seeing it "in very close affinity with its time and place."[25] Trevor and Welty place Bowen's formal and thematic concerns within a dual context they understand as both short story writers and critics. They view her lyricism and sense of mystery, along with her psychological, social, and moral concerns, as working in tandem with "the Irish mood" and "English connexion" that gave her "an angle which suggests a stranger on the edge of a circle of friends . . . an outsider's view."[26] In short, they see the cultural character of the writer and her craft as intertwined and indissoluble.

Celebrated short story writers themselves, Trevor and Welty bear witness to the necessary if unsettling influence of a writer's own time and place, as well as his or her history. Thus they see Bowen "belong[ing] in so many ways to the past" while being "one of the first practitioners within the new, modern movement" (Trevor, 131). Their reviews bear out Bowen's subtle and masterful negotiations between her evocation of a haunting, seemingly timeless atmosphere and her "awareness of place, of *where she was*, . . . her close touch with the passage, the pulse, of time" (Welty, 22).

165

Notes

1. Hermione Lee discusses Bowen's political philosophy in *Elizabeth Bowen: An Estimation* (London and Totowa, N.J.: Vision and Barnes and Noble, 1981).

2. John Hildebidle, *Five Irish Writers: The Errand of Keeping Alive* (Cambridge, Mass.: Harvard University Press, 1989), 91; hereafter cited in the text as Hildebidle.

3. Judith Bates, "Undertones of Horror in Elizabeth Bowen's 'Look at All Those Roses' and 'The Cat Jumps,'" *Journal of the Short Story in English* 8 (Spring 1987): 81, 89; hereafter cited in the text as Bates.

4. A. C. Partridge, "Language and Identity in the Shorter Fiction of Elizabeth Bowen," in *Irish Writers and Society at Large*, ed. Masaru Sekine (New York: Barnes & Noble, 1985), 171; hereafter cited in the text as Partridge.

5. George Brandon Saul, "The Short Stories of Elizabeth Bowen," *Arizona Quarterly* 21 (Spring 1965): 53–54; hereafter cited in the text as Saul.

6. Jocelyn Brooke, *Elizabeth Bowen* (London: British Council, 1952), 12; hereafter cited in the text as Brooke.

7. Brad Hooper, "Elizabeth Bowen's 'The Happy Autumn Fields': A Dream or *Not?*" *Studies in Short Fiction* 21 (Spring 1984): 153; hereafter cited in the text as Hooper.

8. Douglas Hughes, "Cracks in the Psyche: Elizabeth Bowen's 'The Demon Lover,'" *Studies in Short Fiction* 10 (1973): 412; hereafter cited in the text as Hughes.

9. Daniel Fraustino, "Elizabeth Bowen's 'The Demon Lover': Psychosis or Seduction?" *Studies in Short Fiction* 17 (Fall 1980): 486–87; hereafter cited in the text as Fraustino.

10. John Bayley, *The Short Story: Henry James to Elizabeth Bowen* (New York: St. Martin's Press, 1988), 174, 171; hereafter cited in the text as Bayley.

11. Allen Austin, *Elizabeth Bowen* (New York: Twayne, 1971), 94; hereafter cited in the text as Austin.

12. Mary Jarrett, "Ambiguous Ghosts: The Short Stories of Elizabeth Bowen," *Journal of the Short Story in English* 8 (Spring 1987): 71; hereafter cited in the text as Jarrett.

13. Frank Tuohy, "Five Fierce Ladies," in *Irish Writers and Society at Large*, 204; hereafter cited in the text as Tuohy.

14. Walter Allen, *The Short Story in English* (New York: Oxford University Press, 1981), 257. Victoria Glendinning, *Elizabeth Bowen: A Biography* (New York: Knopf, 1977), xv. See also her introduction to *Elizabeth Bowen's Irish Stories* (Dublin: Poolbeg Press, 1978).

15. Margaret Church, "Social Consciousness in the Works of Elizabeth Bowen, Iris Murdoch, and Mary Lavin," *College Literature* 7 (1980): 158; hereafter cited in the text as Church.

16. Janet Egleson Dunleavy "The Subtle Satire of Elizabeth Bowen and Mary Lavin," *Tulsa Studies in Women's Literature* 2 (Spring 1983): 158; hereafter cited in the text as Dunleavy.

17. George Kearns, "Fiction Chronicle," *Hudson Review* 34 (Summer 1981): 300; hereafter cited in the text as Kearns.

18. James M. Haule, "*She* and the Moral Dilemma of Elizabeth Bowen," *Colby Library Quarterly* 22 (December 1986): 213; hereafter cited in text.

19. Terry Eagleton discusses the development and changes in ideology in literary theory and criticism in England and the United States in *Literary Theory: An Introduction* (Minneapolis: University of Minnesota Press, 1983), 39; hereafter cited in text.

20. Edward Mitchell, "Themes in Elizabeth Bowen's Short Stories," *Critique* 8 (Spring–Summer 1966): 44, 43; hereafter cited in text.

21. In my study of Bowen's novels (*Elizabeth Bowen* [London:Macmillan, 1990]) I show the influence of *She* to be consistent with Bowen's revision of traditional plots for women.

22. Cora Kaplan, "Pandora's Box: Subjectivity, Class, and Sexuality in Socialist Feminist Criticism," in *Making a Difference: Feminist Literary Criticism*, ed. Gayle Greene and Coppella Kahn (New York: Methuen, 1985), 152; hereafter cited in the text as Kaplan. See also Nancy K. Miller ("Emphasis Added: Plots and Plausibilities in Women's Fiction," in *Feminist Criticism: Essays on Women, Literature, and Theory,* ed. Elaine Showalter [New York: Pantheon, 1985], 339–60) for a discussion of men's and women's conflicting ideas about verisimilitude as well as the negative reception of women's fictional plots.

23. Leslie Bayern, "Scaling the Garden Wall: *The Collected Stories of Elizabeth Bowen*," *Alternative Review of Literature and Politics* 1 (September 1981): 23; hereafter cited in the text as Bayern.

24. Julie Briggs, *Night Visitors: The Rise and Fall of the English Ghost Story* (London: Faber, 1977), 181; hereafter cited in the text as Briggs.

25. Eudora Welty, "Seventy-nine Stories to Read Again," the *New York Times Book Review*, 8 February 1981, 22; hereafter cited in the text as Welty.

26. William Trevor, "Between Holyhead and Dun Laoghaire," *Times Literary Supplement*, 6 February 1981, 132; hereafter cited in the text as Trevor.

William Trevor

There are echoes of mystery in many of Elizabeth Bowen's stories, like reverberations after an explosion that has not itself been heard. It was part of her subtlety that she dealt so often and so confidently in such shadows, in the ghosts that lurk beneath mundane reality, and in the inaccessible. One of her best stories, "The Happy Autumn Fields," begins:

> The family walking party, though it comprised so many, did not deploy or straggle over the stubble but kept in a procession of threes and twos. Papa, who carried his Alpine stick, led, flanked by Constance and little Arthur. Robert and Cousin Theodore, locked in studious talk, had Emily attached but not quite abreast. Next came Digby and Lucius, taking, to left and right, imaginary aim at rooks. Henrietta and Sarah brought up the rear.

This family idyll is cruelly shattered because time has somehow become muddled. The scene changes to London in the blitz, to a dangerously rickety house in which a girl is obsessed by the family who walked so long ago through the autumn fields and then rested in their drawing room:

> They were back. Now the sun was setting behind the trees, but its rays passed dazzling between the branches into the beautiful warm red room. The tips of the ferns in the jardinière curled gold, and Sarah, standing by the jardinière, pinched at a leaf of scented geranium. The carpet had a great centre wreath of pomegranates, on which no tables or chairs stood, and its whole circle was between herself and the others.
>
> No fire was lit yet, but where they were grouped there was a hearth. Henrietta sat on a low stool, resting her elbow above her

"Between Holyhead and Dun Laoghaire" (review of *The Collected Stories of Elizabeth Bowen*), *Times Literary Supplement*, 6 February 1981, 131. © 1981 by Times Newspapers, Ltd. Reprinted by permission.

head on the arm of Mamma's chair, looking away intently as though into a fire, idle. Mamma embroidered, her needle slowed down by her thoughts. . . .

What are these people to the girl in the bombed house, or she to them? In fact, it doesn't matter. It is enough that the story is charged with the connection between past and present. As the walls tumble down around her, the girl weeps over the intensity of emotion that possessed a happy family and made it what it was. In despair at the emptiness of her own time, she cries:

> How are we to live without natures? We only know inconvenience now, not sorrow. Everything pulverizes so easily because it is rot-dry; one can only wonder that it makes so much noise. The source, the sap must have dried up, or the pulse must have stopped, before you and I were conceived. So much has flowed through people; so little flows through us. All we can do is imitate love or sorrow. . . .

There are echoes of another kind in Elizabeth Bowen's stories, pattering through even the most English of them. These are the tell-tale hints of the Irish mood she shared with Maria Edgeworth, Sheridan Le Fanu, John Banim at his best, the Somerville and Ross of *The Real Charlotte*. The family of "The Happy Autumn Fields" is not an English but an Irish one; the landscape not that of Suffolk or Hampshire but of County Cork. It is typical of the woman she was that nowhere in the story does Elizabeth Bowen say so. In her Anglo-Irish way she assumed all that must surely be obvious.

She was born in Dublin in 1899 and died seventy-four years later, to be buried in the small Protestant churchyard of Farahy, County Cork. Her lifetime spanned the most momentous decades of Ireland's history and saw the demise of the Anglo-Irish tradition to which she and her family belonged. There is no such thing today as an Anglo-Irish novelist, playwright, poet or painter, although the term continues to be rather quaintly misused on this side of the Irish Sea.

The Bowens had come to Ireland with Cromwell. They built the famous Bowen's Court near Mitchelstown, resisted an attack of the United Irishmen in the rising of 1798, and at the time of the Famine displayed such charity that it has never since been forgotten in the neighbourhood. Their world, its pillars those of the Protestant Ascendancy and the English connexion, produced an idiosyncratic culture and a way of life that was wholly different from its apparent equivalent in England. Endlessly bewildering to the outsider, bubbling with eccentricity and often at odds with itself, it marvelled at the antics of the natives who lay outside its pale, or scolded them for being silly. Before it withered away it had whipped the country into such obedient shape that when the moment came its scions were able to provide thousands of docile Irishmen to rally round the flag in England's squabble with the Kaiser.

Elizabeth Bowen was very much part of all that. She passionately loved Bowen's Court, the landscape of County Cork and the people among whom she asked to be buried. But she was educated in England, became a vehement supporter of Churchill's cause, wrote more about the English and England than about the Irish and Ireland, and pointed out that "the Anglo-Irish were really only at home in mid-crossing between Holyhead and Dun Laoghaire."

Nationality matters in novels and short stories only when it makes itself felt, and Elizabeth Bowen now belongs less to Ireland than to literature. But any assessment of her work, especially of her stories, cannot quite escape the lost world into which, as a person, she was born at just the wrong time. As a writer, she took part of her strength from that predicament.

Like many Irish writers, she found the short story a natural form and wrote most naturally when bound by its conventions. "The short story is a young child," she declared, "a child of this century." She was right, but I believe she would also have agreed that this particular child thrived so well in Ireland because it came of a family of old hands and delighted in its defiance of them.

The Victorian novel had raised its head at a time when Ireland wasn't ready for it. Disaffected, repressed, stricken with poverty, suffering from the conflicts of the two languages, the Irish had neither the leisure nor the energy to perform at such length, nor was there in Ireland a nicely stratified society off which the more rambling literary form might feed. Instead, the storytellers of the villages and the countryside continued to maintain their position in the prevailing confusion, and their influence has been considerable. Even today the Irish have a tendency to talk and argue in anecdotes—but more to the point, perhaps, is the fact that story-telling of one kind or another was still very much alive when Chekhov decided to turn the form inside out. It was this continuing vigour that made the small revolution he begun so relevant and so exciting in Ireland, enticing the Irish imagination for generations to come. Elizabeth Bowen, who belonged in so many ways to the past, was one of the first practitioners within the new, modern movement.

There are seventy-nine stories in this volume, with an excellent introduction by Angus Wilson. He puts it succinctly and with accuracy when he writes: " . . . the instinctive artist is there at the very heart of her work and gives a strength, a fierceness and a depth to her elaborations, her delight in words, her determination that life seen will only survive on the page when it has met the strictest demands of form and elegance." No story here is unworthy of inclusion; a couple perhaps are on the way to becoming classics. Stories such as "A Day in the Dark," "Tears, Idle Tears" and "The Happy Autumn Fields" are so coolly evocative that they have acquired in their relatively short lives a timeless hallmark. "The Demon Lover" has—technically—a flawlessness that no novel can ever have.

Elizabeth Bowen possessed the short-story writer's darting curiosity, and an imagination that could become lighter and more volatile than the novelist's. She wrote as hungrily about one subject as the next, finding her stories in the supernatural, in sexuality and love and friendship, in lives wasted, time wasted, in houses, families, dreams, nightmares, fantasies, happiness. Nothing could be more different from the over-ripe suppuration of "Her Table Spread" than the calmness turned to panic in "The Cat Jumps." The claustrophobia of "Breakfast" is a far cry from the sad imprisonments of "The Tommy Crans" or the wartime chatter of "Careless Talk." The single common obsession is a concern for the truth about the human condition.

Her own statement that she was inspired by the unfamiliar is borne out in story after story. She came to know England well, but always wrote about the English from an angle which suggests a stranger on the edge of a circle of friends. London, which features so much in her writing, was observed with the eye of a fascinated visitor:

> Full moonlight drenched the city and searched it; there was not a niche left to stand in. The effect was remorseless: London looked like the moon's capital—shallow, cratered, extinct. It was late, but not yet midnight; now the buses had stopped the polished roads and streets in this region sent for minutes together a ghostly unbroken reflection up. The soaring new flats and the crouching old shops and

houses looked equally brittle under the moon, which blazed in windows which looked its way.

The value of this outsider's view was something she strongly sensed: having established her role as that of a traveller forever on the way either to Holyhead or Dun Laoghaire, she stuck to it rigorously. It is no accident that she wrote so many stories before deciding to set some in the Ireland of her childhood. The familiar had to be blurred by the perspective of time and seen afresh:

> Along Dublin bay, on a sunny July morning, the public gardens along the Dalkey tramline look bright as a series of parasols. Chalk-blue sea appears at the ends of the roads of villas turning downhill—but these are still the suburb, not the seaside. In the distance, floating across the bay, buildings glitter out of the heat-haze on the neck of Howth, and Howth Head looks higher, veiled.

Naturally, some of these stories are less successful than others. A few are slight, several somewhat flat, others tinged with obscurity. The effort of achieving an effect often shows, so that a story—or part of one—seems breathless and overwritten. I don't agree with Angus Wilson that Elizabeth Bowen did not have an ear for the speech patterns of those outside her own class; but I do think that more than occasionally, when searching for the common touch, she failed to find it and caused a certain amount of damage by trying. (The common touch has nothing to do with class distinctions: it's the ability to appeal to limited sensibilities in the aristocracy as much as in the working class.)

A story I have already mentioned, "The Cat Jumps," is one of her most renowned but it seems to me to suffer rather badly in this kind of way. It tells of a house in which a murder has been committed and which is later bought by a no-nonsense couple who refuse to be affected by the shadow of drama. A weekend party is marvellously observed: awful people full of Kraft-Ebbing and Forel who patronize the bad taste of the murdered Mrs Bentley, "her little dog's memorial tablet, with a quotation on it from *Indian Love Lyrics*." A few of Mrs Bentley's fingers were found, at the time, in the dining-room; while the remainder of her hand turned up in the library. The bath in which she was finally laid to rest is still in place, "square and opulent, with its surround of nacreous tiles." The atmosphere, the interplay of the previous owners and the present ones, the vitality that appears to have possessed the house but no longer does, is brilliantly and wittily conveyed. The story gets nicely going but then, close to the end, there is a sudden disastrous change of mood; like a fog, disbelief descends.

But even Elizabeth Bowen's failures have interest enough to fascinate. She did not "develop" or improve (few short-story writers do) but she did set her own standards and must in the end be judged by them. She was well aware that the short story is the art of the glimpse, that in craftily withholding information it tells as little as it dares. She likened what she called the "short storyist" to the poet, since both must be able to "render the significance of the small event." With style and affection she celebrated that exercise herself: the creation of something memorable out of practically nothing, the glimpsing of the gold beneath the dross.

Eudora Welty

It is not unusual for a period of neglect to follow upon a good writer's death. Elizabeth Bowen, the Anglo-Irish author of nine distinguished novels, six collections of superb short stories and five other books of criticism, memoirs and other nonfiction, died in 1973. Certainly she will command a perpetuity of readers, many of whom have followed and loved her work for 50 years. But her books have not been easy to come by since her death. For this one feels she would have been sorry; her turn of mind was always toward the young, especially the writers to come, and she would have particularly liked her books to take their chances with them. And in their behalf, it could be asked: What writer now coming after her could fail to be nourished by her work, exhilarated by her example? She wrote with originality, bounty, vigor, style, beauty up to the last. Her old publisher and friend Alfred Knopf does

"Seventy-nine Stories to Read Again" (review of *The Collected Stories of Elizabeth Bowen*), *New York Times Book Review*, 8 February 1981, 22. Reprinted by permission of the *New York Times*.

an important service for Elizabeth Bowen's readers everywhere in bringing out this present volume of *Collected Stories*. Angus Wilson provides it with an appreciative introduction, generous with personal feeling, valuable for its knowledge of her life and the changing times in which she wrote. He is well situated to give a critical perspective from which to view her work today.

The appearance of all 79 stories in one volume makes several new pleasures possible. The famous stories we know in their own right are seen here in the context of their original book editions. To see anew these bright stars set among their own constellations, to read again "Mysterious Kôr" in company with "Summer Night," "The Happy Autumn Fields," "Ivy Gripped the Steps" and "The Demon Lover" is to experience in its full force that concentration of imaginative power which was hers.

We can gain, too, a truer perception of its nature. Her work was in very close affinity with its time and place, as we know. She recalled, in a preface to her "Early Stories" when they were republished 25 years later, that her story "Daffodils" "overflowed from uncontainable pleasure in the streets of St. Albans on one March afternoon." The lyric impulse was instinctive with her.

In "Her Table Spread," we're at a dinner party in a remote Irish castle overlooking an estuary on a rainy night; in the estuary is the rare sight of a visiting English destroyer. The heiress Miss Cuffe, 24 but "detained in childhood," is "constantly preoccupied with attempts at gravity, as though holding down her skirts in a high wind." And now the destroyer will possibly land, and the officers, uninvited as they are, might still quite naturally call upon the castle. They are momently expected by Miss Cuffe. There is irrepressible excitement, rocketing hilarity at the dinner party. Candles blaze in the windows, there are wet peonies on the table, through the windows can be seen the racing lantern—Miss Cuffe is out there waving signals—and now the piano is playing: the visiting English concert pianist—this was to have been the occasion to allow *him* to meet the heiress—has been asked for a Viennese waltz. At moments notes can be heard through the gates of sympathetic conversation. A whole welcoming world is being made out of that wet, lonely, amorous Irish night.

They are all asleep at the end, even the bat in the boathouse; while the rain goes on falling on the castle, and below in the estuary the destroyer, still keeping to itself, is steaming its way slowly out to sea.

As it ends the story can be seen to be perfect, and the perfection lies in the telling—the delicacy, the humor, above all the understand-ing that has enveloped but never intruded upon it, never once pricked the lovely, free-floating balloon.

Elizabeth Bowen's awareness of place, of *where she was*, seemed to approach the seismic; it was equaled only by her close touch with the passage, the pulse, of time. (Not only what o'clock it was; She used to say, "I am the same age as our century," a fact she enjoyed.) There was a clock in every story and novel she ever wrote; those not in running order were there to give cause for alarm. Time and place were what she *found* here. Her characters she invented, in consequence.

The lyric impulse itself, which goes loose in the world, is anywhere and everywhere; any lucky human being may be its instrument. Eliz-abeth Bowen, however, was—and was from the start—a highly con-scious artist. Being alive as she was in a world of change affected her passionately. The nature and workings of human emotions magnetized her imagination; with all her artist mind she set forth to comprehend, and thus capture, human motives—men's, women's and children's. Time and place that she was so aware of, sensitive to, conveyed to her: situation. Human consciousness meant urgency: drama. Her art was turned full range upon a subject: human relationships.

Writing did not take for Elizabeth Bowen the direction or the form of "self-expression." From the first, she wrote with enthrallment in the act of writing itself. The imaginative power to envision a scene—acute perception, instinctive psychological insight, in an intensified form—was her gift. It became the greatest gift of an artist who was profoundly happy to give the rest of her life to fathoming it.

The passage of time has deactivated "The Needle-case." There are no longer "fallen women," so designated, whose doom it was to earn their living by sewing dresses for other women in other women's houses, poor souls, taking their meals upstairs from a tray. The story dates, and is only mentioned because it constitutes the exception in the 79. The others don't date and will not; their subjects are major.

"The Disinherited" is one of a number of Bowen stories of the dis-locations arising from social and psychological disturbance. Davina, young, rebellious, without money, living off an aunt and cadging money from the baleful chauffeur, leads a life of mortification and un-certainty. "Had she had sphere, space, ease of mind, she might have been generous, active, and even noble." She and the young wife of a university professor from the raw new housing development, unlikely friends, team together for an evening, borrowing money from the rude chauffeur, driving through the uncertain autumn night under the strain of lost maps, changed plans, undelivered messages, toward a supposed party. Stood up at the first rendezvous, the two women eventually blunder into the right but unfamiliar house, which is not prepared for their coming:

Lying on the settee at an angle to the fire, "an enormous, congested old lady slept with her feet apart, letting out stertorous breaths. Her wool coatee was pinned over the heaving ledge of her bust with a paste brooch in the form of a sailing-ship, and at each breath this winked out a knowing ray. Her hands, chapped and knouty, lay in the trough of her lap. Half under her skirts a black pair of kitchen bellows lay on the marble firekerb. There was not much more furniture in the room.

"'That is Mrs. Bennington, who takes care of me. She's so nice,'" says Oliver, their host.

This story of a long and misspent evening, in which everything is at cross purposes, miscarries, is misdirected, and every intention seems as lost to the world and as in the way as old Mrs. Bennington, is a turning kaleidoscope of shifting, fragmented lives. The startling moment when Prothero, the chauffeur, comes into view seated before the table in his quarters and writing a letter gives us the interlocking piece. Nothing so far has come up in the story as true, as straightforward and brutally lined out, as plain and simple and never to be changed or subject to change, as Prothero's letter addressed to a woman named Anita, which is the full account of how and why he murdered her. At the end of his long day he writes the letter and then burns it in the stove; he writes in every night and burns it. "So his night succeeded each other." What interlocks the fragments is the cause of their being— it is the bursting power of despair.

Prothero's letter is an example of the extraordinary tour de force of which Elizabeth Bowen was capable. Her imaginative power to envision a scene is almost hallucinatory here; it makes one feel that she might have put herself within the spell of its compulsion. I think it is a fact that she knew out of her experience how close great concentration could come to the hallucinatory state. That a story *has* a life of its own she would be the first to grant.

How closely she brings "The Disinherited" home to us today! She published it first in 1934.

Her sensuous wisdom was sure and firm; she knew to its last reverberation what she saw, heard, touched, knew what the world wore in its flesh and the clothing it would put on, how near the world came, how close it stood; in every dramatic scene it is beside us at every moment. We see again how pervasive this knowledge was through her stories.

And firmly at home in the world, Elizabeth Bowen was the better prepared to appreciate that it had an edge. For her, terra firma implies the edge of a cliff; suspense arises from the borderlines of experience and can be traced along that nerve. Her supernatural stories gave her further ways to explore experience to its excruciating limits, through daydream, fantasy, hallucination, obsession—and enabled her to write as she did about World War II.

In the unsurpassable "Mysterious Kôr," her most extraordinary story of those she wrote out of her life in wartime London, the exalted, white, silent, deserted other city of Kôr occupies the same territory as bombed-out London through the agency of the full moon at its extreme intensity. In "The Happy Autumn Fields" a direct hit in an air raid has opened a woman's house and displaced the present as she lies on her bed; it lets in instead a walking party of her family of 50 years ago on a momentous day in bright fall in a different country; young twin sisters, her ancestors, cement their lives together with a pledge of love promised to be undying. The bomb victim transfers her life.

Of all the stories, it is "Summer Night" that I return to. Not only Emma, bidding her husband good night, driving stockingless through the Irish evening to an assignation with her lover; not only her little daughter Vivie at home, jumping frenzied up and down on her bed like a savage with snakes chalked all over her; but all the characters in "Summer Night" might be in nothing but their skins, exposed to the night.

Aunt Fran, wrapping the savage in an eiderdown, instructs her to kneel and say her prayers. Then in her own room, "the room of a person tolerated," the woman makes her outcry at last: "It's never me, never me, never me! . . . I'm never told, never told, never told. I get the one answer, 'nothing.'" "There are no more children: the children are born knowing," thinks the despairing women. "And to wrap the burning child up did not put out the fire. You cannot look at the sky without seeing the shadow, the men destroying each other. What is the matter tonight—is there a battle? This is a threatened night." (And war is indeed raging, of course, across the water.)

Emma arrives at her lover Robinson's house; she must wait—he has callers; they see her car. There is Justin, the tormented abstainer from life, starved for talk, who will find no other way out of his urgency than by writing a letter after he gets home to tell Robinson, who is never likely to read it, "The extremity to which we are each driven must be the warrant for what we do and say." (It had been a mistake, of course, to ask him before leaving that unpremeditated question, "What is love like?") Robinson is a solid, ordinary, coarse-grained, incurious man. Justin's sister Queenie know this. Her deafness is not a barrier to her awareness of what goes on between people in a room. The night has carried her back to her girlhood, to the chaste kiss of her one and only love. The serene, unhearing, aging lady at the story's end is drifting to sleep on her pillow: "This was the night she knew she would find again."

This unforgettable story, the most remarkable of a group of longer ones, is an example of the sheer force of the Bowen imagination. What other writer could have *propelled* the whole of "Summer Night" from its rushing headlong start to its softly subsiding conclusion, like a parachute let down to earth gently folding in its petals? The turmoil of all these passionate drives, private energies that in their own directions touch yet never can merge or become one together, is yet all magical; their passions become part of the night sky and part of the world in wartime.

All carries its momentum; this is the truth that seems to emerge. Time is *passing*. Places are *changing*. This is what speed is. There is suspense everywhere, all the time: we are living in its element, racing to keep up with being alive. And in the end there is no rest or help for anything but what lies in the acceptance of love.

That the collection richly reconfirms the extraordinary contribution Elizabeth Bowen has made to English letters alleviates the pain one feels at their neglect since her death. Their vitality is their triumph. Read them again. You may even, like me, discover that there is one you have never read before, though I thought I knew her work. "A Day in the Dark," her last story, is the last one in the book. It is a growing girl's story of the accidental way in which one learns the name of the deepening feeling that one has come to live with. An old lady tauntingly remarks to her, "Oh, I'm sure you're a great companion to him." What she has felt for her uncle is love. "There was not a danger till she spoke." Like many another of these stories, it is its own kind of masterpiece.

Chronology

1899 Elizabeth Bowen born 7 June to Florence Colley Bowen and Henry Cole Bowen at Herbert Place, Dublin.

1907 Moves to England with her mother.

1912 Florence Bowen dies. Elizabeth moves to Harpenden in Hertfordshire, England, to live with an aunt.

1914 Enrolls in Downe House School in Kent.

1919 Begins first of two terms at school of art in London.

1923 First collection of short stories, *Encounters*, published. Marries Alan Cameron.

1925 Moves to Old Headington, Oxford.

1927 *Ann Lee's* published.

1928 First novel, *The Hotel*, published.

1929 *The Last September* published. *Joining Charles and Other Stories* published.

1930 Henry Bowen dies, and Elizabeth inherits Bowen's Court. Reviews and essays begin to be published in such periodicals as *Tatler* and *New Statesman*.

1931 *Friends and Relations* published.

1932 *To the North* published.

1934 *The Cat Jumps and Other Stories* published.

1935 *The House in Paris* published. Moves to London when her husband is appointed to the BBC.

1937 Appointed to the Irish Academy of Letters.

1938 *Death of the Heart* published.

1940 Joins Ministry of Information to study Irish attitudes about World War II. Serves as air-raid warden in London.

1941 *Look at All Those Roses and Other Stories* published.

1942 *Seven Winters, Bowen's Court*, and *English Novelists* published.

1944 Bowen's townhouse in Regent's Park bombed.

1945 *The Demon Lover and Other Stories* published.

1946 Bowen's only play, *Castle Anna*, produced at Lyric Theater, Hammersmith. Begins broadcastng for the BBC.

1948 Receives Companion of the British Empire.

1949 *The Heat of the Day* published. Receives honorary doctorate from Trinity College, Dublin.

1950 *Collected Impressions* published.

1951 *The Shelbourne Hotel* published. Moves to Bowen's Court with her husband.

1952 Alan Cameron dies.

1955 *A World of Love* published. Becomes writer-in-residence at the American Academy in Rome.

1956 Begins series of creative artist appointments in American colleges: Bryn Mawr, Princeton, University of Wisconsin. Receives honorary doctorate from Oxford University.

1959 Sells Bowen's Court.

1960 Bowen's Court torn down by the farmer who bought it. *A Time in Rome* published.

1962 *Afterthought* published.

1964 *The Little Girls* published.

1965 Moves to villa in Hythe, Kent. *A Day in the Dark and Other Stories* published.

1969 *Eva Trout* published.

1970 *The Good Tiger* published.

1973 Dies on 22 February.

1974 *Pictures and Conversations* published.

Selected Bibliography

Primary Works

The Collected Stories of Elizabeth Bowen. Introduction by Angus Wilson. New
York: Knopf, 1981. First Stories: "Breakfast," "Daffodils," "The Re-
turn," "The Confidante," "Requiescat," "All Saints," "The New House,"
"Lunch," "The Lover," "Mrs Windermere," "The Shadowy Third,"
"The Evil That Men Do—," "Sunday Evening," "Coming Home." The
Twenties: "Ann Lee's," "The Parrot," "The Visitor," "The Contessina,"
"Human Habitation," "The Secession," "Making Arrangements," "The
Storm," "Charity," "The Back Drawing-Room," "Recent Photograph,"
"Joining Charles," "The Jungle," "Shores: An International Episode,"
"The Dancing-Mistress," "Aunt Tatty," "Dead Mabelle," "The Working
Party," "Foothold," "The Cassowary," "Telling," "Mrs. Moysey." The
Thirties: "The Tommy Crans," "The Good Girl," "The Cat Jumps,"
"The Last Night in the Old Home," "The Disinherited," "Maria," "Her
Table Spread," "The Little Girl's Room," "Firelight in the Flat," "The
Man of the Family," "The Needlecase," "The Apple Tree," "Reduced,"
"Tears, Idle Tears," "A Walk in the Woods," "A Love Story," "Look at
All Those Roses," "Attractive Modern Homes," "The Easter Egg Party,"
"Love," "No. 16," "A Queer Heart," "The Girl with the Stoop." The
War Years: "Unwelcome Idea," "Oh, Madam . . . ," " Summer Night,"
"In the Square," "Sunday Afternoon," "The Inherited Clock," "The
Cheery Soul," "Songs My Father Sang Me," "The Demon Lover,"
"Careless Talk," "The Happy Autumn Fields," "Ivy Gripped the Steps,"
"Pink May," "Green Holly," "Mysterious Kôr," "The Dolt's Tale." Post-
war Stories: "I Hear You Say So," "Gone Away," "Hand in Glove," "A
Day in the Dark."

Uncollected Short Fiction

"Brigands." In *The Silver Ship*, edited by Cynthia Asquith, 183–200. London
    and New York: Putman, 1932.
"Candles in the Window." *Woman's Day*, December 1958, 32, 81–83.
"The Claimant." In *The Third Ghost Book*, edited by Cynthia Asquith, 9–17.
    London: James Barrie, 1955.
"Comfort and Joy." *Modern Reading* 11–12 (1945):10–16.
"Emergency in the Gothic Wing." *Tatler*, 18 November 1953, 18–19, 52.

"Flavia." In *Mr. Fothergill's Plot*, 33–36. New York: Oxford University Press, 1931.
"The Good Earl." In *Diversion*, edited by H. W. Chapman, 133–146. London: Collins, 1946.
"Happiness." *Woman's Day*, December 1959, 58, 122–24.
"I Died of Love." In *Choice: Some New Stories and Prose*, edited by William Sansom, 129–37. London: Progress Publishers, 1946.
"Just Imagine." In *Best British Short Stories*, edited by Edward J. O'Brien, 82–93. London: Jonathan Cape, 1927.
"Pink Bisquit." *Eve*, 22 November 1928, 34–35, 76, 78, 80.
"Salon des Dames." *Weekly Westminster Gazzette*, 7 April 1923, 16–17.
"So Much Depends." *Woman's Day*, September 1951, 72, 149–50.

Novels

The Death of the Heart. London: Victor Gollancz, 1938. New York: Knopf, 1939. Harmondsworth: Penguin, 1986.
Eva Trout, or Changing Scenes. New York: Knopf, 1968. London: Jonathan Cape, 1968. Harmondsworth: Penguin, 1986.
Friends and Relations. London: Constable, 1931. New York: Dial Press, 1931. Harmondsworth: Penguin, 1985.
The Heat of the Day. New York: Knopf, 1949. London: Jonathan Cape, 1949. Harmondsworth: Penguin, 1986.
The Hotel. London: Constable, 1927. New York: Dial Press, 1928.
The House In Paris. London: Victor Gollancz, 1935. New York: Knopf, 1936. Harmondworth: Penguin, 1986.
The Last September. London: Constable, 1929. New York: Dial Press, 1929. Harmondsworth: Penguin, 1985.
The Little Girls. New York: Knopf, 1964. London: Jonathan Cape, 1964. Harmondsworth: Penguin 1985.
To the North. London: Victor Gollancz, 1932. New York: Knopf, 1933. Harmondsworth: Penguin, 1985.
A World of Love. New York: Knopf, 1955. London: Jonathan Cape, 1955.

Nonfiction

Afterthought: Pieces about Writing. London: Longmans Green, 1962.
Anthony Trollope: A New Judgment. London: Oxford University Press, 1946.
"The Art of Reserve or the Art of Respecting Boundaries." *Vogue*, 1 April 1952, 116–17.
Bowen's Court. London: Longmans Green, 1942. New York: Knopf, 1942. New York: Ecco Press, 1979.
Collected Impressions. London: Longmans Green, 1950. New York: Knopf, 1950.

English Novelists. London: William Collins, 1942.

"The Experience of Writing." Notes to a lecture delivered at Wellesley College, 20 March 1950. Henry W. and Albert A. Berg Collection, New York Public Library.

"The Forgotten Art of Living." In *Good Living,* edited by A. G. Weidenfeld, 17–28. London: Contact, 1948.

The Mulberry Tree. Edited by Hermione Lee. New York: Harcourt Brace Jovanovich, 1986.

Pictures and Conversations. New York: Knopf, 1975.

Seven Winters. Dublin: Cuala Press, 1942.

The Shelbourne Hotel. New York: Knopf, 1951. London: George C. Harrap, 1951.

"The Short Story in England." *Britain Today,* May 1945, 11–16.

A Time in Rome. New York: Knopf, 1960. London: Longmans Green, 1960.

Secondary Works

Allen, Walter. *The Short Story in English.* New York: Oxford University Press, 1981.

Armstrong, Nancy. "The Rise of the Domestic Woman," in *The Ideology of Conduct,* ed. Nancy Armstrong and Leonard Tennenhouse, 96–141. New York: Methuen, 1987.

Atkins, John. *Six Novelists Look at Society: An Inquiry into the Social Views of Elizabeth Bowen, L. P. Hartley, Rosamund Lehmann, Christopher Isherwood, Nancy Mitford, C. P. Snow.* London: John Calder, 1977.

Auerbach, Nina. *Woman and the Demon. Life of a Victorian.* Cambridge, Mass.: Harvard University Press, 1982.

Austin, Allen. *Elizabeth Bowen.* New York: Twayne, 1971.

Bates, Judith. "Undertones of Horror in Elizabeth Bowen's 'Look at All Those Roses' and 'The Cat Jumps.'" *Journal of the Short Story in English* 8 (Spring 1987):81–91.

Bayern, Leslie. "Scaling the Garden Wall: *'The Collected Stories of Elizabeth Bowen.'*" *Alternative Review of Literature and Politics* 1 (September 1981): 23–24.

Bayley, John. *The Short Story: Henry James to Elizabeth Bowen.* New York: St. Martin's Press, 1988.

Blodgett, Harriet. *Patterns of Reality: Elizabeth Bowen's Novels.* The Hague: Mouton, 1975.

Briggs, Julia. *Night Visitors: The Rise and Fall of the English Ghost Story.* London: Faber, 1977.

Brooke, Jocelyn. *Elizabeth Bowen.* London: British Council, 1952.

Brooks, Peter. *Reading for the Plot: Design and Intention in Narrative.* New York: Vintage, 1985.

Chessman, Harriet. "Women and Language in the Fiction of Elizabeth Bowen." *Twentieth Century Literature* 29 (Spring 1983):69–85.

Chodorow, Nancy. *The Reproduction of Mothering: Psychoanalysis and the Sociology of Gender.* Berkeley: University of California Press, 1978.

Church, Margaret. "Social Consciousness in Elizabeth Bowen, Iris Murdoch, and Mary Lavin." *College Literature* 7 (1980):158–63.

Craig, Patricia. *Elizabeth Bowen.* Harmondsworth: Penguin, 1986.

Davenport, Gary. "Elizabeth Bowen and the Big House." *Southern Humanities Review* 9 (Winter 1974):27–34.

Dunleavy, Janet. "The Subtle Satire of Elizabeth Bowen and Mary Lavin. *Tulsa Studies in Women's Literature* 2 (Spring 1983):69–82.

Eagleton, Terry. *Literary Theory: An Introduction.* Minneapolis: University of Minnesota Press, 1983.

Edwards, Lee R. *Psyche as Hero: Female Heroism and Fictional Form.* Middletown, Conn.: Wesleyan University Press, 1984.

Figes, Eva. *Sex and Subterfuge: Women Writers to 1950.* New York: Persea, 1982.

Flax, Jane. "The Conflict between Nurturance and Autonomy in Mother-Daughter Relationships and within Feminism." *Feminist Studies* 4 (June 1978): 171–91.

Flora, Joseph M., ed. *The English Short Story, 1880–1945.* Boston: Twayne Publishers, 1985.

Fraustino, Daniel. "Elizabeth Bowen's 'The Demon Lover': Psychosis or Seduction?" *Studies in Short Fiction* 17 (Fall 1980):483–87.

Friedman, Ellen G. "'Utterly Other Discourse': The Anticanon of Experimental Women Writers from Dorothy Richardson to Christine Brooke-Rose." *Modern Fiction Studies* 34 (Autumn 1985):353–70.

Gilbert, Sandra, and Susan Gubar. *No Man's Land: The Place of the Woman Writer in the Twentieth Century.* Vol. 1, *The War of the Words.* Vol. 2, *Sexchanges.* New Haven, Conn.: Yale University Press, 1988, 1989.

Gill, Richard. *Happy Rural Seat.* New Haven, Conn.: Yale University Press, 1972.

Gindin, James. "Ethical Structures in John Galsworthy, Elizabeth Bowen, and Iris Murdoch." In *Forms of Modern British Fiction,* edited by Alan W. Driedman, 15–41. Austin: University of Texas Press, 1975.

Glendinning, Victoria. *Elizabeth Bowen: A Biography.* New York: Knopf, 1978.

———. Introduction to *Elizabeth Bowen's Irish Stories.* Dublin: Poolbeg Press, 1978.

Greene, Gayle. "Feminist Fiction and the Uses of Memory." *Signs: Journal of Women in Culture and Society* 16 (Winter 1991):290–321.

Greene, George. "Elizabeth Bowen: Imagination as Therapy." *Perspective* 14 (Spring 1965):42–52.

Hall, James W. *The Lunatic Giant in the Drawing Room.* Bloomington: Indiana University Press, 1968.

Hanson, Clare. "The Free Story." In *Elizabeth Bowen: Modern Critical Views*, edited by Harold Bloom, 139–51. New York: Chelsea House, 1987.

Hardwick, Elizabeth. "Elizabeth Bowen's Fiction." *Partisan Review* 16 (1949):114–21.

Harkness, Bruce. "The Fiction of Elizabeth Bowen." *English Journal* 44 (December 1955):499–506.

Haule, James M. "*She* and the Moral Dilemma of Elizabeth Bowen." *Colby Library Quarterly* 22 (December 1986):205–14.

Heath, William. *Elizabeth Bowen*. Madison: University of Wisconsin Press, 1961.

Hildebidle, John. *Five Irish Writers: The Errand of Keeping Alive*. Cambridge. Mass.: Harvard University Press, 1989.

Hirsch, Marianne. *The Mother-Daughter Plot: Narrative, Psychoanalysis, Feminism*. Bloomington: Indiana University Press, 1989.

Hooper, Brad. "Elizabeth Bowen's 'The Happy Autumn Fields': A Dream or Not?" Studies in *Short Fiction* 21 (Spring 1984):151–53.

Hughes, Douglas. "Cracks in the Psyche: Elizabeth Bowen's 'The Demon Lover.'" *Studies in Short Fiction* 10 (1973):410–13.

Jarrett, Mary. "Ambiguous Ghosts: The Short Stories of Elizabeth Bowen." *Journal of the Short Story in English* 8 (Spring 1987):71–79.

Juhasz, Susan. "Texts to Grow On: Reading Women's Romance Fiction." *Tulsa Studies in Women's Literature* 7 (Fall 1988):231–59.

Kaplan, Cora. "Pandora's Box: Subjectivity, Class, and Sexuality in Socialist Feminist Criticism." In *Making a Difference: Feminist Literary Criticism*, edited by Gayle Greene and Coppelia Kahn, 146–76. New York: Methuen, 1985.

Kearns, George. "Fiction Chronicle." *Hudson Review* 34 (Summer 1981): 300.

Kenney, Edwin J. *Elizabeth Bowen*. Irish Writers Series. Lewisburg, Pa.: Bucknell University Press, 1974.

Kershner, R. B. "Bowen's Oneiric *House in Paris*." *Texas Studies in Language and Literature* 28 (Winter 1986):407–23.

Lassner, Phyllis. *Elizabeth Bowen*. London: Macmillan, 1990.

Lee, Hermione. *Elizabeth Bowen: An Estimation*. London and Totowa, N.J.: Vision and Barnes & Noble, 1981.

Lohafer, Susan, and Jo Ellen Clarey, eds. *Short Story Theory at a Crossroads*. Baton Rouge: Louisiana State University Press, 1989.

Lowenthal, David. *The Past Is a Foreign Country*. Cambridge: Cambridge University Press, 1985.

McCormack, W. J. "Mask and Mood." *New Statesman* 103 (3 February 1981):19 20.

Medoff, Jeslyn. "'There Is No Elsewhere': Elizabeth Bowen's Perceptions of War." *Modern Fiction Studies* 30 (Spring 1984):73–81.

Meredith, David W. "Authorial Detachment in Elizabeth Bowen's 'Ann Lee's.'" *Massachusetts Studies in English* 8, no. 2 (1982):9–20.

Michie, Helena. "Not One of the Family: The Repression of the Other Woman in Feminist Theory." In *Discontented Discourses: Feminism/Textual Intervention/Psychoanalysis*, edited by Maureen Barr and Richard Feldstein, 15–28. Urbana: University of Illinois Press, 1989.

Miles, Rosalind. *The Female Form: Women Writers and the Conquest of the Novel.* London and New York: Routledge & Kegan Paul, 1987.

Miller, Nancy K. "Emphasis Added: Plots and Plausibilities in Women's Fiction." In *Feminist Criticism: Essays on Women, Literature, and Theory*, edited by Elaine Showalter, 339–60. New York: Pantheon, 1985.

Mitchell, Edward. "Themes in Elizabeth Bowen's Short Stories." *Critique* 8 (Spring–Summer 1966):50.

Moss, Howard. "Interior Children." *New Yorker*, 5 February 1979, 121–28.

O'Connor, Frank. *The Lonely Voice: A Study of the Short Story.* Cleveland: World Publishing, 1963.

O'Faolain, Sean. "A Reading and Remembrance of Elizabeth Bowen." *London Review of Books*, 4–17 March 1982, 15, 17.

———*Short Stories: A Study in Pleasure.* London: Collins, 1948.

———*The Vanishing Hero: Studies in the Novelists of the Twenties.* Boston: Little, Brown, 1957.

Partridge, A. C. "Language and Identity in the Shorter Fiction of Elizabeth Bowen." In *Irish Writers and Society at Large*, edited by Masaru Sekine, 169–79. New York: Barnes and Noble, 1985.

Quinn, Antoinette. "Elizabeth Bowen's Irish Stories—1939–1945." In *Studies in Anglo-Irish Literature*, edited by Heinz Kozok, 314–21. Bonn: Bouvier, 1982.

Saule, George Brandon. "The Short Stories of Elizabeth Bowen." *Arizona Quarterly* 21 (Spring 1965):53–59.

Sayers, Janet. *Sexual Contradictions: Psychology, Psychoanalysis, and Feminism.* London: Tavistock, 1986.

Sellery, J'nan M., and William O. Harris. *Elizabeth Bowen: A Bibliography.* Austin: Humanities Research Center, University of Texas, 1981.

Smith-Rosenberg, Carol. "The Female World of Love and Ritual: Relations between Women in Nineteenth-Century America." *Signs: Journal of Women in Culture and Society* 1 (Autumn 1975):1–30.

Tuohy, Frank. "Five Fierce Ladies." In *Irish Writers and Society at Large*, edited by Masaru Sekine, 199–206. New York: Barnes and Noble, 1985.

Trevor, William. "Between Holyhead and Dun Laoghaire." *Times Literary Supplement*, 6 February 1981, 131.

Vannatta, Dennis., ed. *The English Short Story: 1945–1980.* Boston: Twayne Publishers, 1985.

Welty, Eudora. "Seventy-nine Stories to Read Again." *New York Times Book Review*, 8 February 1981, 22.

Yaeger, Patricia. *Honey-Mad Women: Emancipatory Strategies in Women's Writing.* New York: Columbia University Press, 1988.

Index

Index

The Author

Phyllis Lassner received her Ph.D. from Wayne State University and teaches women's studies and composition at the University of Michigan. She has published a critical study of Elizabeth Bowen's novels and a study of Rose Macaulay's *Dangerous Ages* and Karin Michaelis's *The Dangerous Age.* Her essays on Marilynne Robinson and Jayne Ann Phillips are included in *Mother Puzzles: Daughters and Mothers in Contemporary American Literature* and *American Women Writing Fiction.* Her work on British women writers of World War II appears in the special peace/war issue of *Mosaic,* and a recent essay in the journal *Rhetoric Review* combines her interests in feminist and composition studies.

The Editor

Gordon Weaver earned his Ph.D. in English and creative writing at the University of Denver, and is currently professor of English at Oklahoma State University. He is the author of several novels, including *Count a Lonely Cadence, Give Him a Stone, Circling Byzantium*, and most recently *The Eight Corners of the World*. His short stories are collected in *The Entombed Man of Thule, Such Waltzing Was Not Easy, Getting Serious, Morality Play*, and *A World Quite Round*. Recognition of his fiction includes the St. Lawrence Award for Fiction (1973), two National Endowment for the Arts fellowships (1974 and 1989), and the O. Henry First Prize (1979). He edited *The American Short Story, 1945–1980: A Critical History* and is currently editor of the *Cimarron Review*. Married and the father of three daughters, he lives in Stillwater, Oklahoma.